POLITICS AND GOVERNMENT IN THE VISEGRAD COUNTRIES

Also by John Fitzmaurice

AUSTRIAN POLITICS AND SOCIETY TODAY

THE BALTIC: A Regional Future

First published in Great Britain 1998 by
MACMILLAN PRESS LTD
Houndmills, Basingstoke, Hampshire RG21 6XS and London
Companies and representatives throughout the world

A catalogue record for this book is available from the British Library.

ISBN 0–333–65964–3

First published in the United States of America 1998 by
ST. MARTIN'S PRESS, INC.,
Scholarly and Reference Division,
175 Fifth Avenue, New York, N.Y. 10010

ISBN 0–312–21561–4

Library of Congress Cataloging-in-Publication Data
Fitzmaurice, John.
Politics and government in the Visegrad countries : Poland,
Hungary, the Czech Republic and Slovakia / John Fitzmaurice.
p. cm.
Includes bibliographical references (p.   ) and index.
ISBN 0–312–21561–4 (cloth)
1. Europe, Central—Politics and government—1989–   2. Post
-communism—Europe, Central.   I. Title.
JN96.A58F57   1998
320.943'09'049—dc21   98-17297
                                                                                CIP

This book is printed on paper suitable for recycling and made from fully managed and
sustained forest sources.

9   8   7   6   5   4   3   2   1
06   05   04   03   02   01   00   99   98

Printed and bound in Great Britain by
Antony Rowe Ltd, Chippenham, Wiltshire

Politics and Government in the Visegrad Countries

Poland, Hungary, the Czech Republic and Slovakia

John Fitzmaurice

For GP

Contents

Acknowledgements

This book is the result of almost ten years of active interest and research in the history and politics of central Europe. A very large number of people in the four countries have given their active encouragement to this project and have assisted the author with his research during numerous visits to the region over several years, by giving often extended interviews and information.

They are too numerous all to be mentioned individually. Some made a particularly important contribution to my understanding of the complex realities of the region and I would like to thank them individually. In Hungary, I was graciously received by President Göncz. I also interviewed Mr Kovacs, now Foreign Minister, Mr Orban, Chairman of the FIDESZ (Young Civic Democrats), and Mr Balint Magyar, Alliance of Free Democrats (SDS) Coalition negotiator. In the Czech Republic, I would like to single out Mr Spacik, Spokesman for President Havel, Mr Milos Zeman, Chair of the Social Democratic Party (CSSD) and now Speaker of the National Assembly, Mr Jiri Dienstbier, former Foreign Minister, and Mr Kalvoda, Chairman of the Civic Democratic Alliance (ODA). In Slovakia, I met Mr Kucan, Foreign Minister in 1994, Mr Hrasko, Democratic Left Environment Minister in 1994 and Mr Hofbauer [Movement for a Democratic Slovakia (HZDS)], Minister of Public Works in the second Meciar Cabinet. In Poland, I met Mr Kwasniewski, then only leader of the SdRP (Reform Communists), Mr Tadeusz Mazowiecki, Poland's first non-communist Prime Minister after 1989, Mr Leszek Balcerowicz, the 'Big Bang' Finance Minister, Mr Saryuz-Wolski, Minister for European Integration, Mr Martin Swieciki, Mayor of Warsaw, and Mr Garlicki, Judge in the Constitutional Court.

I owe a very considerable debt of gratitude to those who have helped me with the organisation of interviews and meetings on the spot. In Hungary, my friend and guide in Hungarian affairs Mr Tamas Kende of the ELTE University in Budapest often did the impossible in arranging meetings. In Bratislava, Mrs Kovacova of the Foreign Ministery was always helpful. In the Czech Republic, I should like in particular to thank Mrs Navarova, Head of the International Department of the ČSSD. In Poland, Minister Saryuz-Wolski took a personal interest in my project, and his staff in Warsaw and Mrs Hazyk of the Polish Mission to the European Union (EU) in Brussels were of assistance above and beyond the call of duty in organising my programme. I thank them all for their kind-ness and commitment. I hope that the result does justice to their efforts.

As something of a technological luddite, I have for the first time taken the plunge and done the word-processing of this book myself. That would have been entirely impossible without the ever-efficient, patient and willing help of my colleague and friend Gerda Postelmans, who was always able to put me on the right track. I would like to express my sin-cere thanks to her for that, and for her supportive friendship and interest in the project.

This book has been something of a labour of love. It expresses my love of this region and its peoples and is a modest contribution to rediscovering them. All errors of fact and especially of interpretation are naturally my own.

JOHN FITZMAURICE

List of Abbreviations

ASW	Association of Slovak Workers (Workers Party)
AWS	Solidarnosc Electoral Alliance
BBWR	Non-Party Reform Block
CC	Constitutional Committee
CDU	Christian Democratic Union
CEI	Central European Initiative
CIS	Commonwealth of Independent States
CMUS	Czech and Moravian Centre Union
COMECON	Council for Mutual Economic Assistance
COMINFORM	Communist Information Bureau
CSCE	Conference on Security and Cooperation in Europe
CSKOS	Czech Confederation of Trade Unions
CSL	Czech People's Party
CSMADOK	Czechoslovak Hungarian Cultural Association
CSSD	Czech Social Democrats
CSU	Christian Social Union
DDR	German Democratic Republic
DPP	Democratic People's Party
DU	Democratic Union
DUS	Democratic Union of Slovakia
EBRD	European Bank for Reconstruction and Development
ECE	Economic Commission for Europe
EDU	European Democratic Union
EFTA	European Free Trade Area
EU	European Union
EUCD	European Union of Christian Democrats
FDP	Free Democratic Party (Germany)
FIDESZ	Civic Democrats/Young Democrats
FKGP	Independent Smallholders Party
FPÖ	Freedom Party (Austria)
HZDS	Movement for an Independent Slovakia
ICFTI	International Confederation of Free Trade Unions
IMF	International Monetary Fund
KDH	Christian Democratic Movement (Slovakia)
KDNP	Christian Democratic Party (Hungary)
KDS	Christian Democratic Party (Czech)

KDU	Christian Democratic Union
KLD	Liberal Democrat Congress (Poland)
KOR	Committee for Workers Defence
KPN	Confederation for an Independent Poland
KSC	Communist Party of Czechoslovakia
KSCM	Communist Party of Bohemia and Moravia
LB	Left Block
LSNS	Liberal and National Socialist Party
LSU	Liberal and Social Union
MDF	Hungarian Democratic Forum
MIEP	Hungarian Truth and Light Party
MKDM	Hungarian Christian Democratic Movement (Slovakia)
MSZMP	Hungarian Socialist Workers Party
MSZOSZ	Hungarian Socialist Trade Union Organisation
MSZP	Hungarian Socialist Party
NACC	North Atlantic Cooperation Council
NATO	North Atlantic Treaty Organisation
NGO	Non-Governmental Organisation
NS	National Socialist
ODA	Civic Democratic Alliance
ODS	Civic Democratic Party
OF	Civic Forum
OPZZ	Organisation of Polish Trade Unions
ÖVP	Austrian People's Party
PAX	Peace (Polish Catholic Organisation)
PC	Centre Party
PES	Party of European Socialists
PfP	Partnership for Peace
PHARE	EU Aid Programme for Central Europe
PL	Peasant Accord
PPS	Polish Socialist Party
PSL	Polish People's Party (Peasant Party)
PZPR	United Polish Workers Party
ROP	Movement for the Reconstruction of Poland
RSC	Czech Republican Party
SD	Free Democrats
SDL	Party of the Democratic Left
SdRP	Social Democracy of the Republic of Poland
SDS	Alliance of Free Democrats
SDSS	Social Democratic Party of Slovakia
SI	Socialist International

SLD	Party of the Democratic Left (Slovakia)
SMCS	Single Member Constituencies
SNS	Slovak National Party
SPD	Social Democratic Part of Germany
SPÖ	Social Democratic Party of Austria
SZOT	Socialist Confederation of Trade Unions
UP	Union of Labour
UPR	Union of Realist Politics
UW	Union of Freedom
VdSKGP	Federation of German Socio-Cultural Societies in Poland
ZchN	National Christian Union
ZRS	Association of Slovak Workers

Introduction

The four countries of the Visegrad Group that are the subject of this book – Poland, Hungary, the Czech Republic and Slovakia – will soon be full members of the European Union. The Copenhagen European Council of June 1993 declared for the first time that they were in principle eligible for membership, provided that they met certain additional conditions relating to respect for pluralist democratic principles, human rights and development of a market economy. This opened the way to conversion of their associated status into full membership within a reasonably short period of time. The Essen European Council (December 1994) went a step further and set in train a more proactive strategy of preparation for membership. The long-standing calls by political leaders in the region such as Presidents Havel and Walesa and Prime Ministers Antall and Horn of Hungary for full membership by the end of the millennium now look much less utopian than they did when first uttered in 1990 and 1991. This target will, like most in the European Union, slip, but it now looks within the realms of real possibility.

We can therefore expect to welcome the first central European members into the Union within a mere five to ten years. In the meantime, the EU's relations with them will intensify across the board. They form a vital part of western security, as a buffer zone between the EU core and less stable Russia and former Soviet Republics. The security and stability of this central European area is of vital concern to US in Western Europe. Their internal development, both in the political and economic spheres, is of concern to EU countries because it forms part of the preconditions of membership laid down in Copenhagen that the EU will have to evaluate in due course. Increasingly, the enlargement process is coming to be recognised as a joint venture between the EU and the central Europeans, in which both have a stake and a responsibility. This means that mutual cooperation in a common strategy is required to ensure the necessary convergence and adaptation on both sides. Thus, their process of transition is a matter of concern to the West.

Before 1989, Western Europeans saw central Europe as it were through a glass darkly. It was a region shrouded in cold war mystery and mystique. These were, in the indifferent words of Minister Neville Chamberlain at the time of Munich in 1938, 'far away countries of which we know little'. Indeed, as late as 1988, COMECON and the EU did not recognise each other. Now, at long last, these countries that long formed an integral part of European culture and history, are realising their return to Europe and a positive normalisation.

They will constitute together a significant force within the enlarged EU and NATO, bringing new sensitivities, cultures and issues to the table. Collectively, they will represent an additional 70 million citizens and an important new market. Poland alone, with 40 million inhabitants is larger than Spain, one of the EU's 'big five'. It will therefore be important to include these central European states in studies of comparative politics in the EU. It will be important to know how their political systems work, what makes them tick, what problems and issues they will bring to the EU's decision-making process and how they will interact with the other EU members. That is the purpose of this book. It seeks to provide an accessible comparative and thematic guide to the political systems of the four countries. It will set the basic data for each country in a comparative regional framework and against the background of the problems of transition from communism. In seeking to treat these countries as normal western democracies like any others, albeit with their own history and specific problems, the book aims to make a modest contribution to their return to Europe, which is their earnest desire.

1 A Modern History of the Region

The modern history of the three, and now since 1993, four, states of the Visegrad Group, Poland, Hungary, the Czech Republic and Slovakia, that constitute the northern tier of the central European corridor begins after the Balkan Wars of 1912–13 and the First World War. Before then, the whole corridor from the Baltic to the Black Sea and the Adriatic was ruled by four increasingly ramshackle multinational empires. To the south in the Balkans, the Ottoman Empire had retained significant European territories as far north as Macedonia until the Balkan Wars. Greece, Serbia, Romania, Montenegro and Bulgaria had already emerged from Ottoman rule as independent states in the course of the nineteenth century. Austrian, Russian and Ottoman interests met and clashed in the region, and indeed it was here, in Sarajevo, that the First World War was kindled. The Austro-Hungarian dual monarchy lay astride the centre of the corridor from Vienna to Lvov and the Russian border, covering some dozen nationalities in an increasingly uneasy and volatile equilibrium. It included the Czech lands which belonged to the Austrian half of the Empire. The semi-autonomous Hungarian Kingdom that formed the other half of the dual monarchy included not only modern post-Trianon Hungary, but also modern Slovakia, Croatia, the Serb Voivodina and Transylvania that has been Romanian since 1920. To the north, the German Empire included northern and western Poland, which had been acquired through the three eighteenth-century partitions of Poland and extended to Königsberg in East Prussia. To the north and east lay the Russian Empire, including Finland, the Baltic States and eastern Poland, including Warsaw, enjoying various though limited degrees of autonomy within the Tsarist Empire. The First World war set a time-bomb ticking within each of these Empires. None had resolved the issue of increasing nationalist pressures nor of democratic reform that was closely linked to the nationalities question. All expected a short war that would restore their prestige and shore up the status quo. None could stand the long war with which they were actually faced.

The centrifugal forces of internal nationalism only gathered critical momentum in the last phase of the war. The Revolutions in Russia were a decisive catalyst in direct and indirect ways. Before then, the various nationalities had largely remained loyal to 'their' respective Empires,

1

even the slavs of Austro-Hungary and Germany, though this was a severe dilemma for them. For the western allies, Tsarist Russia's internal policies were an embarrassment, but she was a vital ally, forcing Germany to fight on two fronts. Indeed, though the Russian Offensive of the summer of 1914 ended in defeat at Tannenberg, it was a key factor in enabling France to ride out the German tidal wave in that summer. Later, in the Second World War, vast Russian manpower reserves and the luxury of space and winter tied down significant German and Austrian forces all through the war. On the other hand, the Russian alliance made it impossible to pursue an active democratic policy of support for the Slav nationalities within the Empires of the two Central Powers, as no doctrine of self-determination would be accepted by the Tsar. Hence, until 1917, allied policy towards the increasingly restive nationalities and the future of these multi-national Empires remained vague and no more general statement of war aims was issued. Even when, under American pressure, an initial statement came to be issued, it significantly still refrained from proposing the dismemberment or even the democratisation of these two Central Powers' Empires, limiting itself to traditional territorial, economic and military demands on them.

The almost simultaneous collapse of the Russian Empire and the entry of the United States into the war in the spring of 1917 significantly altered the situation. The way was open for a radical new policy and this was also now opportune. For a short time, there was actually a coincidence of interests between allied realpolitiker such as Clemenceau, Orlando and Lloyd-George and the idealist President Wilson. French geopolitical strategists were beginning to contemplate a longer-term situation without Russia as the eastern pillar of French policy of encirclement of Germany. A new central European alliance system was needed to replace Russia. This could only be found in newly created or resurrected states from the debris of the old Central Powers. They would be beholden to France, and together Poland, Czechoslovakia, Romania and the new South Slav Kingdom might compensate for the loss of Russia and constitute a new alliance system. France was thus easily persuaded to support exiled nationalist claims for statehood that the Russian alliance had impeded. These new positions could easily fit into the Wilsonian rhetoric of self-determination.

THE SETTLEMENT

In many ways, the Versailles settlement, though perhaps the only settlement possible at that time and under the given circumstances, was in fact the worst of all possible worlds. On the one hand, it appeared too draconian and even vengeful to gain any voluntary acceptance by Germany or other losers such as Hungary. On the other hand, its mechanisms for both enforcement and peaceful revision were inadequate and defective. Above all, it failed to mobilise the United States in favour of the League of Nations, the chosen instrument of collective security and enforcement, designed by the American President Woodrow Wilson himself. It also dangerously excluded and isolated the new Soviet Union. It penalised Germany severely, but could not hope to eliminate German power as a long-term threat to France. It could not therefore build confidence between the principal enemies of the Great War, France and Germany. It sought to underpin the territorial and political settlement that it established with the objective moral principle of self-determination enshrined in Wilson's Fourteen Points. In his vision, such a moral settlement based on national states would in itself banish conflict. However, on the ground, these high principles were never a clear guide to action and could not be consistently and equitably applied, even if the will to do so had existed, which it often did not. Firstly, the principle of self-determination was only half-heartedly espoused by the Leaders of the European allied powers and was in any case directly contradicted by several secret treaties concluded during the earlier part of the war with minor allies such as Italy, Serbia and Romania. Secondly, and even more seriously, in Central Europe, minorities were not neatly territorially packaged in areas adjacent to their ethnically sister nations. They actually lived in haphazard and isolated pockets, as islands in Slav seas. Thus, Hungarians lived inside Romania, separated from Hungary proper. Germans lived everywhere in the Czech lands and on the Polish coast. The Dalmatian coast was an ethnic patchwork. Why indeed could the rump of Austria, indisputably of German language, not join the German Reich, as it sought to do? Why should the Sudeten German areas not join Austria or Germany, as ethnic considerations would require ?

The outcome, inevitably, was a patchy, inadequate and messy application of the principle, that was in any case often overridden by strategic considerations. As a result, it was perceived as victors' justice and failed to gain acceptance. Worse, the multi-national Empires, whose vocation and indeed raison d'être was to be multi-ethnic, were replaced by a series of weaker supposedly ethnic nation states that in fact remained multi-national, but with one dominant ethnic group that identified itself with the state, creating exclusion, rather than inclusion. This was to prove an unstable recipe for disaster.

As John Maynard Keynes was to point out in his famous and polemical *The Economic Consequences of the Peace* (1926), the peacemakers mostly ignored the economic issues and in many cases aggravated already difficult economic situations by their decisions. Massive reparations were imposed on Germany that could never be met, but which contributed to the hyperinflation and then mass unemployment that made the rise of Hitler possible. In central Europe, the broad economic spaces created by the three multi-national Empires were fragmented and were replaced by competitive protectionism and autarchy. The industrial regions of Bohemia were cut off from their Austrian and Hungarian markets. This autarchy and protectionism fatally went hand in hand with political nationalism and state-building.

In the area that we are dealing with, three new states arose out of the debris of the Great War. The Austro-Hungarian dual monarchy was dismembered completely and ceased to exist. It contributed territory to all the successor states in the region. Since the settlement of 1867, it had become two Kingdoms linked by the person of the Emperor and certain minimum joint competences and institutions in foreign affairs, defence, trade and finance. After 1920, the two Kingdoms were separated and territories were redistributed between them and both lost to neighbouring victor allied powers. The pre-1914 Hungarian Kingdom had been in itself a multi-ethnic state. It now lost two-thirds of its territory, including Transylvania and the Banat to Romania; The Voivodina, Croatia and parts of Dalmatia to the new south Slav Kingdom of Serbs, Croats and Slovenes (Yugoslavia after 1929); Upper Hungary (Slovakia) to the new Czechoslovak Republic and Burgenland (except Sopron) to Austria. Austria lost the Czech lands to the new Czechoslovakia; Galicia and Ruthenia to Poland; South Tirol to Italy and its part of Dalmatia to Yugoslavia. Both were reduced to their ethnic hard-core, though Germans and Hungarians were lost to neighbouring states. Austria was specifically forbidden to join with Germany, as its Parliament had initially proposed to do in 1918. In remained a small and vulnerable alpine Republic until the Anschluss with the Third Reich in March 1938.

As required by Wilson's Fourteen Points, the Polish state was resurrected and achieved access to the Baltic sea, though it did not gain Danzig, which became a Free City under the League of Nations. German East Prussia was therefore cut off from the rest of the Reich. Soviet attempts to invade Poland and establish a Red Republic at least in the eastern areas failed by 1920 and the eastern border was fixed far to the east, taking in large non-Polish, white Russian areas. This frontier was always contested by the USSR. In the west, the ethnic Polish area of

Teschen was eventually awarded to Czechoslovakia, as part of a French policy of favouritism towards that ally and Poland did not gain all of coal-rich Silesia. Poland occupied Vilnius (Vilno in Polish), the capital of the new Lithuanian state, which was forced to move its capital to Kaunas. Poland was thus resurrected in something close to her eighteenth-century historic pre-partition borders.

The problem of Czechoslovakia was quite different. Whilst it did have some medieval and pre-modern basis, it had never existed as a state in that form. It was a new concept, born of considerations of ethnic nationalism and strategic concerns. Before 1918, the future components of the new Czechoslovak state had developed quite separately in their respective Kingdoms of the Empire, with no contact between them on the ground and no senses of common identity. The idea of a Czechoslovak nation developed among nationalist exiles abroad, in the United States and in France, such as the future Presidents Tomas Masaryk and Edvard Benes, the Slovak Stefanik. They realised that a purely Czech nation would barely counterbalance the Germans who would need, for strategic territorial reasons, to be included within its borders. Nor would a Czech state be strong enough on its own to defend its independence in the region. For the Slovaks, joining their Czech cousins, though perhaps not ideal, was the only realistic way of escaping the Magyarising tutelage of the Hungarians. It was therefore above all a marriage of Slav sentiment and reason that from the beginning was beset with misunderstandings. For many Slovak nationalists such as Hozda and Tiso, there was contained in the founding pacts (the Pittsburgh and Philadelphia agreements between Czech and Slovak exiles) at the very least an implicit commitment to some form of Slovak autonomy, which could include a federal structure. This was never lived up to in the new state, and in any event, the allied powers and in particular France promoted the idea of a strong, centralised Czech-dominated state for strategic reasons.

INTERNATIONAL POLITICS IN THE REGION BETWEEN THE WARS

The first decade after the Great War saw an unnatural power vacuum in the region. Both Germany and the Soviet Union were simultaneously weak and introverted, unable to exercise a wider regional influence. Though traditional and future enemies and rivals for regional hegemony, both were now united as revisionist powers, seeking to overturn the Versailles settlement in the region. There were always temptations to cooperate despite their ideological and geopolitical differences which only grew after Hitler came to power in Germany in 1933. The Rapallo pact and later the Molotov–Ribbentrop pact, as well as the more secret cooperation between the Reichswehr and the Red Army in the 1920s, were dramatic reminders that this option existed and could be used and fuelled the ambiguity of international relations in this period.

The region was divided into revisionist and status quo powers. As well as Germany and the USSR, Italy, Austria, Hungary and Bulgaria belonged to the revisionist camp, which sought to undermine and ultimately revise the Versailles settlement, including its territorial provisions. Poland, the three Baltic Republics (Estonia, Latvia and Lithuania), Czechoslovakia, Romania, Yugoslavia and Greece were status quo powers, supporting the settlement. Indeed, several owed their very existence as states to the settlement. These status quo powers became the main allies of France in the region, providing an alternative to the lost Russian alliance as a means of containing Germany. Based on this common interest in containment of Germany and – fatal ambiguity – the USSR, France rapidly established a network of bilateral treaties with its central European allies: Poland (1921), Czechoslovakia (1924), Romania (1926). These early bilateral treaties led to a series of additional treaties between the states of the region themselves, promoted by France: the Czechoslovak–Yugoslav Defence Pact in 1920; the Yugoslavia–Romania Pact of 1921, aimed at Bulgaria; the Czech–Romanian Pact of 1921 directed against Hungarian revisionism. In 1922, two of the Baltic states (Estonia and Latvia), Finland and Poland concluded a Baltic Entente, aimed at containing a Soviet threat. It will be clearly seen that there were two fatal flaws in these arrangements. They were mainly only directed at lesser threats and, secondly, there was no alliance between Poland and Czechoslovakia who were the main allies of France in the region.

Attempts to transform these cross-cutting bilateral treaties into a wider multilateral alliance between France and all its central European status quo allies met with only very limited success, though the Little Entente Pact was concluded in 1933 between Yugoslavia, Czechoslovakia and Romania. Here again, Poland was conspicuous by its absence.

These efforts failed partly because animosity remained strong between the two key central European states, Poland and Czechoslovakia over Teschen and between Poland and Lithuania over the occupation of Vilnius. Significantly, Poland never joined the Little Entente. Nor could the various status quo powers, whose local interests often diverged, find a common threat perception: local revisionism from Hungary, Italy or

Bulgaria; resurgent Germany or communist expansionism from the USSR. Yet, as both Germany and the USSR revived after 1933, it became imperative to reach a lucid evaluation of relative threats and act accordingly by either seeking to enter the growing German political and economic sphere or by seeking an alliance with the USSR and the western powers. There was unfortunately no middle way, as this was a very difficult choice for many in the region. Poland, fatally, hesitated, concluding non-aggression pacts both with the Soviet Union (in 1932 and 1934) and with Germany (1934). In 1939, she fatally undermined the Anglo-French efforts to reach an alliance with the USSR against Germany, by refusing to consider any military cooperation with the Soviet Union and by taking part in the dismemberment of Czechoslovakia with Nazi Germany. As it was, only Czechoslovakia had been ready to form a serious alliance both with the west and with the USSR against Germany in 1938, but she had been abandoned by the western powers.

The situation was further muddied by the formation of 'revisionist' alliances and local Balkan pacts directed essentially against Soviet revisionism. Thus, Mussolini's Italy concluded pacts with Romania (aimed at the USSR over Bessarabia), with Albania (1926), Hungary (1927) and Austria in 1930. In 1934, Italy supported Austria against the first Nazi threat. By 1938, Italy had concluded that she needed an alliance with the strongest of all the revisionist powers, Germany. This led to the Axis Pact in 1938 and the abandonment of the earlier small revisionist pact between Italy, Austria and Hungary that had been against German interests. By 1938 all revisionism was subsumed on the back of Germany's dramatic revisionist successes and local claims depended effectively on German arbitration, as in the two Vienna Awards of territory to Hungary at the expense of Czechoslovakia and Romania.

Stalin drew the inevitable conclusion from Anschluss, Munich and the final dismemberment of Czechoslovakia in 1939. The eastern settlement was collapsing and its western promoters were failing to act to protect it. At best they seemed indifferent to German expansionism and the expense of their eastern European allies or too weak to prevent it. At worst, from the Soviet perspective, they at times seemed to see some moral justification to German revisionism and covertly seemed to prefer to accept German expansion to a Soviet alliance. The USSR was in danger of isolation and finding itself alone against a resurgent Germany. Seen against this background, the notorious Pact of 23 August 1939 between Hitler and Stalin seemed a logical and rational step. It established spheres of influence, divided their common enemy Poland a fourth time and made it possible for Hitler to risk war in the west, if that turned out to be the result of his aggression against Poland. The Pact raised the curtain on the Second World War.

In the immediate aftermath of the war, hard lessons were drawn from this dismal record. It was realised that divisions between states with objectively convergent interests had been fatal. It was also realised that the unnatural situation of a power vacuum that had been the erroneous basis of policies in the early inter-war period would never recur. After 1945, German hegemonic ambitions had been replaced by the USSR, which was self-evidently destined to be the dominant power in the region and was indeed recognised as such by all. At the same time, there was a strong disillusionment with the west, even among anti-communist Poles and Czechs. Indeed, Benes explicitly recognised this. It was concluded that the presence of minorities, especially German minorities, had fatally weakened the post-Versailles states. All these elements were to considerably colour post-1945 consciousness and conduct and do much to explain the relative ease with which communist regimes installed themselves throughout the region.

DOMESTIC POLITICAL DEVELOPMENTS BETWEEN THE WARS

The new states faced many pressing problems. The governments in Austria and Hungary had to win at least a minimum of acceptance for the draconian settlements imposed on them by the Treaties of St Germain (Austria) and Trianon (Hungary). This was an absolute necessity for the legitimacy of these new and much reduced states. This was particularly difficult in Hungary, where the settlement led to a short, but bloody Bolshevik intermezzo, ended by Romanian intervention. The new Czechoslovak and Polish states had to actually impose their borders on the ground against their Austrian, German, Hungarian and Soviet neighbours and against internal minorities who wanted to opt for another statehood. This they had to do essentially on their own, as the allies had few troops on the ground in the region. The spectre of the Bolshevik revolution also hung over the region. It led to short-lived communist republics in Hungary and Bavaria and attempted communist coups in Austria and a serious war between Poland and the USSR. The demobilisation of the former Imperial armies also caused economic and law and-order problems. The fragmentation of former large-scale imperial economic markets was also a serious problem. There was very real hardship and shortages in all the new states. There were also major conflicts about state-building: about the appropriate constitutional structures, electoral systems, form of government (presidential or parliamentary), centralisation or decentralisation, rights of minorities and agrarian reforms that were often linked with minority issues.

Despite the theoretical commitment to national states, most of the new states actually were very far from ethnically homogeneous and were from the outset beset with severe problems of dealing with minorities, which often rejected integration. Hungary, which had lost 67 per cent of it pre-war territory and 59 per cent of its pre-war population was as a result 90 per cent Hungarian and the most ethnically homogeneous state in the region. The most significant minority was the Germans (7 per cent). Czechoslovakia on the other hand, as constituted in 1920 (Bohemia, Moravia, Silesia, Teschen, Slovakia, Carpato-Ruthenia), remained very much the old "vielvölkerstaat' in miniature. Czechs were only 48.9 per cent, and with the Slovaks (15.4 per cent) the Slav element still only represented 64.3 per cent of the total population. The main minorities (1921) were Germans (22.9 per cent; almost 40 per cent in the Czech lands), with many local and regional majority positions; Hungarians (5.5 per cent overall and about 12 per cent in Slovakia, with majority positions along the Danube), Ruthenes (3.4 per cent) and Jews (2 per cent). In 1930 only 65.5 per cent of the population of Poland were ethnic Poles. The largest national minorities were Ukrainians/Ruthenes (17.8 per cent), Germans (4.1 per cent), and White Russians (3.4 per cent). Jews made up 7.5 per cent of the population.

POLAND

The strongman of Polish politics in the inter-war period was, until his death in 1935, Marshal Pilsudski, hero of the war of national independence against the Soviet Union in 1920. Indeed, until 1921, the new state did not have settled borders, though it did have some inherited political structures from the short-lived German-sponsored Polish Kingdom, though that had naturally only covered part of the territory of post Versailles Poland. A provisional constitution gave wide civil and military powers to Marshal Pilsudski, which was necessary in the early confused and dangerous period. He became Head of State and Commander of the Army. A coalition Government was then formed under the world famous pianist Paderewski, uniting the Socialist and National Democrat tendencies. A Constituent Assembly was also elected. Debate then raged about the form of government. The left – supporters of Pilsudski – wanted a strong presidency. The right and the peasant parties, whose key figure was Witos, on the other hand wanted a parliamentary system. The new constitution was a compromise. The president was to be elected by Parliament for seven years. He was accorded quite wide powers, but could only dissolve Parliament with the agreement of a three-quarters majority of the Senate (upper house). The bicameral Parliament was elected by proportional representation for five years. Pilsudski himself considered the presidency too weak and retired from the scene. His socialist successor was immediately assassinated and a compromise candidate, though one acceptable to Pilsudski, was then elected. A confused period then followed, with several weak governments falling in rapid succession. However, the electoral victory of Witos in 1926 provoked Pilsudski to return to active politics through a military coup, supported by the socialists, who still at that stage regarded Pilsudski as close to them. This proved to be a serious mistake.

Pilsudski did not become president himself, but pulled the strings from his position as Minister of War and Inspector General of the Army. The army was his power base and the main pillar of the new regime. The presidency was strengthened and the powers of Parliament reduced. A unitary party called 'Government Bloc' was established, similar to other authoritarian parties across the region that flourished during this period. The socialists belatedly realised their error and joined with the other democratic opposition parties in forming a common opposition platform in 1930. Pilsudski then dissolved parliament and by a combination of propaganda, manipulation and severe repression won a majority for the Government Bloc. Thereafter, the system became increasingly authoritarian and especially after Pilsudski's death (1935) less and less popular. It became in effect a military dictatorship and so remained until Poland's defeat in September 1939.

HUNGARY

After the short-lived Soviet Republic under Bela Kun and two comic-opera attempts by former Emperor Karl to regain at least his Hungarian throne, it was decided to formally retain the Monarchy, but to leave the throne deliberately vacant under a Regent as Head of State. Admiral Horthy was chosen as Regent. Until the 1930s, the system remained relatively democratic, though weighted towards conservatism.

The powers of the Regent were initially actually quite limited. Real day-to-day executive power was in the hands of the government that was responsible to the lower house of parliament, elected on a broad franchise, though except in Budapest voting was not secret until 1939. The more conservative, largely appointed Upper House did not initially have an absolute veto on legislation. There remained some restrictions on press freedom and freedom of assembly, and as almost everywhere in the region at the time, the Communist Party was prohibited, but not the Social Democrats, who were represented in Parliament right up to 1944. Over the inter-war period, the country was ruled by four shifting conservative alliances, whose main components were the same, but whose centre of gravity shifted constantly to the right, away from liberalism towards authoritarianism, after 1932.

After 1932, the powers of both the Upper House and the Regent over legislation were gradually reinforced. However, despite the ever stronger fascistoid tendencies within the ruling bloc, the parliamentary system and a limited degree of pluralism survived until 1944. Measures against Hungarian Jews for example remained mild for the region in spite of Hungary's participation in the war on the German side after 1941. Hungarian forces suffered severe losses at Stalingrad. As the Red Army neared Hungary's eastern border in the summer of 1944, Horthy made a botched attempt, via the western powers, to get out of the war or change sides as the Romanians managed to do. At this point, the country was occupied by the Germans and the local fascist Arrow Cross formed a short-lived overtly Nazi Government.

CZECHOSLOVAKIA

Czechoslovakia was, whatever its imperfections, the only central or eastern European state to come close to making democracy work during the inter-war period and indeed, left to itself, it might well have succeeded. By 1934, it was the only democracy in Europe south of Denmark and east of Switzerland. In fact, there were then only twelve democratic states in the whole continent. It was thus a democratic island in an authoritarian sea, which in itself made its position more difficult. Its most serious problem was that the dominant Czech ethnic group represented less than half the total population and was increasingly contested by three increasingly alienated and vocal minorities that cooperated among themselves and were even prepared to seek the support of outside powers against the Czechs. These were the Germans, Slovaks and Hungarians. By 1929, some real progress was being made in integrating the most important minority, the Sudeten Germans, into the state. Progress was being made in state-building. Until the world economic crisis hit this most industrialised part of eastern Europe, Czechoslovakia enjoyed a standard of living and social provision close to that of the Scandinavians of that time. The impact of the economic crisis was exacerbated by the rise to power of Adolf Hitler, who championed the cause of the Sudeten Germans. German support undermined non-nationalists among the Sudeten Germans and deprived them of all motivation to seek accommodation within the Czechoslovak state. The discomfiture of Prague then provoked the Slovaks and the Hungarians, with open German support, to up the ante, demanding ever more autonomy, which finally destroyed Czechoslovakia in 1938–9.

The key figures in Czechoslovak political life were the first and second presidents, Masaryk and Benes, who had led the independence struggle from exile. The President was elected by Parliament for seven years. He was a non-executive president, with limited legal powers, but very great prestige and moral authority at least in the case of the first two holders of the office. Real executive power was in the hands of the Prime Minister and Cabinet. There were two houses of Parliament: the National Assembly with 300 members and the Senate with 150 members, elected for five years by proportional representation, with a low threshold for representation. There were often nearly thirty parties in parliament and twelve cabinets held office during the First Republic. All were broad coalitions of five or six parties, making consensus difficult and often the lowest common denominator.

The party system was complex. It was in reality three different party systems: a Czech party system, a Sudeten German party system and a Slovak party system. There were also Polish and Hungarian minority parties. Within each party system, there was at least initially a normal right–left spectrum. For example, in the early years, the largest German party was the German Social Democratic party, that operated separately from the Czech Social Democrats. By the mid-1920s, the German and Slovak parties had accepted the state and took part in coalitions in Prague, but both ceased to do so in the atmosphere of nationalist polarisation that set in after the mid-1930s. The almost four million Sudeten Germans were emboldened by the support of almost 80 million Germans in the Reich. This threat led Slovak nationalists to harden their position and break off cooperation with Czech institutions and parties.

There were five main parties during the First Republic, covering the left, centre and democratic right, which governed the country in shifting coalitions, coopting other parties from time to time. From left to right, there were the Social democrats, the more moderate National Socialists (not Nazis), the Catholic Populist Party, the National Union and the Agrarian Party. The Communist Party, originally opposed to the state, turned in a steady 10 per cent of the vote. After Munich, it supported the state and stood with the democratic parties.

THE POST-WAR PERIOD:THE COMMUNIST INTERMEZZO

All three countries suffered severe losses and damage both from the Occupation and the liberation battles, though the scale was far greater in Poland and Hungary. Warsaw and Budapest were devastated. Warsaw was a pile of ruins with a population of only a few hundred in January 1945. Almost all of Czechoslovakia's Jews, an important part of her cultural mix, perished in the Holocaust. With the total defeat of Germany and her unconditional surrender and the liberation of central and eastern Europe up to the Elbe by the Red Army, it became clear that the region would fall within the Soviet geopolitical sphere of influence. Poland was, as it were, moved bodily westwards. She lost the areas east of the old Curzon line that were not ethnically Polish and received Gdansk on the coast, southern East Prussia (Masuria) and Pomeranian and Silesian areas east of the Oder–Neisse rivers, which became her western border with Germany. She also gave up Vilnius to the Soviet Republic of Lithuania. Hungary was of course an enemy state and therefore was subject to an allied Soviet-controlled Armistice Commission until the Peace Treaty was signed in Paris in 1947. She lost her territorial gains from the two Vienna Awards. The Munich Agreement was nullified and Czechoslovakia restored within her pre-1938 frontiers, though without the Carpato-Ukraine, which was ceded to the USSR. She made very minor gains on the south bank of the Danube, near Bratislava at the expense of Hungary, which were later to prove important in terms of controlling the Danube waters.

The German population in all three states was almost totally expelled in 1945 and 1946. Some 1.5 million Poles moved west from the areas beyond the Curzon line and were often resettled in the new western areas. About 100,000 Hungarians were expelled from Slovakia. Some 3.3 million Germans were expelled from Czechoslovakia; almost 4 million from Poland and 2.2 million from East Prussia, and 400,000 from Hungary. As a result, the central European states finally became ethnically homogeneous. This was a deliberate goal, especially in Czechoslovakia, where the expulsion took place despite there being no change in pre-war frontiers. It was a radical way of neutralising any internal trojan horse. This nationalist card was played by the local communist and non-communist authorities alike.

Defence of the expulsions became an unalterable part of the mythology of the regimes, especially in Czechoslovakia. In the 1980s a 'revisionism' on the whole issue and its wider domestic and international political implications got under way in Czech dissident and Chartist circles and continued after 1989, leading to controversial expressions of regret by President Havel. Apart from moral condemnation of these collective expulsions, often carried out in the most inhuman way, a wide range of other arguments were brought into the debate. The first tentative distancing from the mythology of the regime regarded the expulsions as a tragic necessity, then understandable if not justifiable in the anti-German atmosphere of the time. It was then argued that the expulsion and denial of the rule of law to those who, in the thesis of the Czechoslovak Government on the nullity of the Munich Agreement, remained, after all, Czechoslovak citizens, was profoundly illogical, and seriously undermined democracy, opening the way for the communist take-over and binding Czechoslovakia into an alliance with the USSR and creating an atmosphere in which later political terror and illegality could flourish. Some even argued that the non-communist parties made a serious miscalculation in supporting the expulsions, since the moderate elements in the German minority might later have constituted a stronger political base for them.

The processes by which the communist regimes became installed across the region were complex, gradual and uneven, owing much, but by no means everything, to the presence of the Red Army and the sense of belonging to the Soviet geopolitical sphere. The process was gradual, but by 1948 it was complete everywhere. As we have seen, there was little reason for nostalgia for the pre-war regimes. Even if the non-communist parties were not directly implicated in collaboration with the occupier, they were vulnerable to such charges. They were weak and in disarray, without any clear and credible political alternative to offer. They appeared defensive and reactive.

The communists on the other hand, though few in number were well organised, had clear goals and appeared dynamic and seemed to be the wave of the future, especially as they benefited from the prestige of the Red Army. They proposed a broad-based programme of reforms as part of a reconstruction strategy. These included land reform and measures against speculators that had wide popularity. They also took up the nationalist mantle, demanding tough measures against the German minorities and collaborators. That created a permanent state of political mobilisation that wrong-footed and then swept up the centre-right, which could only seek to moderate rather than change the direction of events.

Certainly, the communists possessed some major advantages, but also some not insignificant disadvantages. The support of the Red Army was not an unmixed blessing, especially in Poland. They were small and nowhere were they a mass party. Above all, as loyal instruments of Soviet policy, they had to avoid acting too blatantly and so provoking a reaction from the western allies that Stalin sought to avoid at that time. Soviet and hence local communist strategy was one of prudence and gradualism, at least until September 1947. This dictated a policy of the broad popular front, rather than a direct and immediate communist seizure of power. Thus, the communists did not seek to occupy the most high-profile ministries such as the Prime Minister or the Minister of Foreign Affairs, but rather those such as Interior, Security, Information, Agriculture (land reform) and Social Affairs that would maximise their capacity to destabilise their opponents and extend their network of patronage. They left Ministries such as Finance that would have to take unpopular decisions to other parties. This enabled them to undermine and destabilise other parties whilst formally cooperating with them as coalition partners.

Of course, this popular front strategy imposed a degree of gradualism on the communists that they might have otherwise avoided, but its advantages were definitely greater. It enabled the communists to run with the hare and ride with the hounds. They could both operate from within the government machine and agitate from outside it, as if they were in opposition. Most importantly, it prevented the numerically stronger non-communist parties from governing without them, as normal parliamentary practice would have allowed. In Hungary, the most extreme case, the Smallholders Party won 57 per cent of the vote in the 1945 election, but still felt obliged to govern with the communists and suicidally left them the Interior Ministry. Here, perhaps, Hungary's position as an ex-Axis state under allied tutelage played a role.

The Soviet Union was not just a puppet-master pulling the strings, as it were. Benes for example actively sought to exploit the Soviet alliance against Slovak nationalists, and Stalin obliged. There is now evidence that it was as much pressure from local communists as Stalin's diktat that led to the infamous decision to refuse Marshall Aid in July 1947. The local communists were far more afraid of possible western interference in their economic management and a lifeline to their non-communist parties than Moscow was.

It would also be difficult to demonstrate that there was, as many in the west thought during the early part of the cold war, any detailed master plan for imposing control on central and eastern Europe, though clearly it was a general goal to be achieved if possible. As the cold war set in and it became clear that no more could be obtained by stealth, but that the west had neither the will nor the means to roll back what had been achieved between 1944 and 1947, it was decided to accelerate the process and consolidate the Soviet sphere. Following a COMINFORM (Communist Information Bureau) Conference in Silesia in September 1947, it was decided to liquidate the remaining areas of genuine coalition and power-sharing in Czechoslovakia in particular and proceed with the division of Germany. Full party control was imposed across the region.

In Poland, the process had been rapid. Full communist control, albeit behind the facade of coalition, had already been achieved by the time of the delayed parliamentary elections in 1946. By the time of the second post-war election in Hungary, the Smallholders Party saw their support dwindle from 57 per cent to 17 per cent, as the party was undermined and sabotaged by the communists. By 1948, full party control had been imposed. In Prague, by February 1948, the non-communist parties realised that they would have to force a confrontation with the communists, which they duly did over political appointments in the police. However, their strategy was ill-prepared and amateurish. They failed to mobilise popular support and did not ensure the backing either of the armed forces or of President Benes. In the ensuing crisis, the non-communist ministers resigned, hoping to force the collapse of the Government and new elections, but they were not supported by the President and the communist Prime Minister simply replaced them. Communist control was complete in Czechoslovakia and thus in the whole region.

The next stage was for the revolution to eat its own children, as the saying goes. Stalin sought to impose total control and loyalty to the Soviet Union and to him personally on the leaderships of all the central and eastern European communist parties. First, all non-communist influence in these societies was eliminated and they were closed to the outside world. Then a series of Kafkaesque purges were set in motion. Those who had only just finished imposing communist control, often by the most ruthless police methods, now found themselves accused of treason, espionage, anti-party activity. Many were executed or imprisoned for long periods, often after torture. Those purged were the most independent-minded, those with some local power base. Often they had spent the war outside the Soviet Union in the west, in the underground at home or in France. Many had fought in the Spanish civil war. Many were Jews and the whole campaign had an odour of anti-semitism. These trials were grotesque. Lifelong communists confessed to having been 'agents of imperialism'. Total stalinist control was imposed, but the longer-term consequences were severe. It deprived the local communists of any residual legitimacy and roots in their local societies and made them appear what they had become, puppets and agents of soviet policy. When in the mid-1980s, under pressure from Gorbachev, the local communists were called upon to become independent political actors in their societies, it was too late. They were then unable to return to such a role, which they had briefly followed between 1944 and 1948.

The death of Stalin on 5 March 1953 did not lead to an immediate liberalisation in the region. Indeed, the satellite party leaderships had the greatest difficulty in interpreting the confused and tentative signals coming out of Moscow. There were some welcome signs of detente with the west. The Korean War was ended, the war in Indo-China was concluded, the Soviet bases in Finland were returned and the Austrian State Treaty was signed. Yet, domestically, this had little impact on the situation in central Europe, though there was some slackening in the purge trials and repression and some of the most Stalinist leaders left the scene.

The dramatic detonator of change came with Khrushchev's secret speech to the 20th Congress of the Communist Party of the Soviet Union (CPSU) in February 1956. It sent tremors throughout the whole Soviet bloc. Its impact was most dramatic in Poland and Hungary. Czechoslovakia remained calm and there were no changes in line or leadership.

In Poland and Hungary, the 20th Congress led radical and dramatic events. In Poland, demonstrations and strikes in industrial areas such as Poznan and in the Warsaw region, came close to provoking Soviet military intervention. However, the Soviet leadership was finally convinced that the situation could be safely controlled by bringing back the former purged General Secretary Gomoulka at the head of a reformist leadership. Gomoulka thus returned and calm returned, without the party having to make any serious or longer-term concessions. Indeed, the actual content of the reforms was quite modest. Private agriculture, cultural life and the Catholic Church all benefited from the slightly more liberal situation.

In Hungary, the signature of the Austrian State Treaty and the withdrawal of Soviet forces from Vienna and eastern Austria in October 1955 had a profound impact. It offered a real example of peaceful Soviet retreat from positions won at the end of the war, which was encouraging to Hungarian aspirations. In the face of rising and increasingly organised demands from society for change, which at first crystallised around demands for rehabilitation of the former party secretary Rajk and other purge victims, reinstatement of Imre Nagy and the retirement of some of the more Stalinist leaders, the party leadership was weak, divided and indecisive. The limited moves it made in the direction of change were too little and too late. By mid-October 1956, a revolutionary situation was developing in Budapest and several other towns as students issued a fourteen-point programme demanding the return to power of Imre Nagy, the only communist trusted by the people. After clashes, Nagy was recalled on 24 October. At first, his actions were timid and were accepted by the Soviet leadership. Under growing pressure from the mass movement that was sweeping through society and with an apparent green light from the Soviet side, the new leadership put itself boldly at the head of the reform movement. The measures it then proposed, involving free, multi-party elections and withdrawal from the Warsaw Pact, went further than either the Czech leadership in the Prague Spring in 1968 or Solidarnosc in 1989. Now, the Soviet leadership could not ignore these developments which would have led to chain reactions elsewhere. Intervention was swift and brutal. The Nagy government was crushed and replaced by a collaborationist government under Janos Kadar. Thousands were killed in street fighting; nearly 400 were executed and 22,000 imprisoned and 220,000 Hungarians went into exile abroad.

The long-term consequences were less negative and more paradoxical than at first appeared. It became clear to the opposition and actually to the party as well that there were unwritten limits which could not be crossed. It demonstrated that a direct 'counter-revolutionary' challenge, seeking to replace the communist system, could not hope to succeed without a change in the geopolitical situation. On the other hand, the party had to accept that it could only command the reluctant acquiescence of society, not its loyalty. Tellingly, Kadar redefined the leading role of the party in a much more modest fashion, which did not demand the hearts and minds of the people, saying 'Who is not against us is with us'. This inevitably led to a more open society, more rights to travel abroad and economic reform to legitimise the regime through its economic performance. The New Economic Mechanism, introducing some market elements and greater scope for small private business, was brought in 1968. At first, this approach of economic reform without political reform achieved a real degree of success, but by 1980 had run its course, as it reached the limit of what could be achieved without more radical structural reform and as the economic crisis set in, leading to inflation, slower growth and debt.

Czechoslovakia remained calm during the dramatic events of 1956 in Poland and Hungary, but it was here that the next phase in the long-term decline of communism took place during the Prague Spring in 1968. This time, it was Hungary that did not move and Hungarian forces even took part in the invasion that followed in August 1968 to suppress the reform movement. The Prague Spring was a different and less frontal approach than in Budapest in 1956. It was a process of reform, to be initiated and controlled by the party, from the top down, but in which popular support would play an important part, as civil society developed. The Prague Spring was, as with most events in Czechoslovak politics, intimately linked with the problem of Slovak nationalism that had been severely repressed in the post-war period. Alexander Dubcek was able to become First Secretary at the head of a broad reformist coalition in the party only because he was a Slovak and could build on his existing Slovak power base. The Prague Spring was almost Gorbachevian in its inspiration. It sought to reform the party and bring its closer engagement with society, so as to breathe new life into the system. Thus, the party's Action Programme for reform, adopted on 5 April 1968, and even the far more radical *Two Thousand Words Manifesto* issued by intellectuals, remained moderate. There were no proposals to introduce political pluralism, free elections to challenge the leading role of the party or to alter Czechoslovakia's foreign policy.

Even the limited programme of reform that was proposed was seen as a threat by the Soviet leadership and even more by the aging communist leaders in the other Warsaw Pact countries. Despite assurances from the Czechoslovak leadership during several bilateral and multi-lateral meetings during the spring and early summer that the situation would remain under party control and that the reform movement would actually strengthen the party, a military intervention was considered necessary and carried out on 21 August 1968 by Soviet and other Warsaw Pact armies.

Normalisation, as it was called, saw a long period of occupation, under a Government that was prepared to cooperate in the normalisation process. The leaders of the Prague Spring movement at all levels were gradually eased out of all positions of responsibility and deprived of any capacity to influence public opinion. There were no show trials along the lines of the 1940s. Dubček was only removed from office in April 1969, but 500,000 members were expelled from the party, mostly Czechs, and numerous dissidents were imprisoned over the years, again mostly Czechs. Slovakia retained its one gain from the Prague Spring, the formal federalisation of the country, a long-standing Slovak demand. A Slovak, Gustav Husak, was elected Federal President and General Secretary of the party. The massive expansion of the military–industrial complex, with great economic benefits was located in the more politically reliable Slovakia. The post-1968 dissident movement was mainly found among Prague intellectuals and in the Charter 77 after 1977 and had little impact in Slovakia.

Events in Poland and Hungary in 1956 and Czechoslovakia in 1968 showed that neither direct confrontation, nor a gradualist, controlled reform from the top down, under the broad aegis of the party could succeed. This was to lead to creative and radical new thinking and new strategies in opposition circles in all countries, based on the concept of civil society.

2 The Collapse of Communism

In Chapter 1 we looked at the process by which communist regimes in fact became relatively easily installed in the then three states of the Visegrad region. We also looked at different unsuccessful attempts to replace or reform these regimes, all of which would seem to point to the solidity of the communist system in central and eastern Europe. It is therefore legitimate to ask how such an apparently entrenched and monolithic system could collapse so suddenly and rapidly in 1989, with almost no resistance.

The most immediate explanation might be that the system had been eroded away from within and had become a facade with no substance.

When the vital prop of Soviet support was removed, the system had no adaptative capacity. A reform process based on the Gorbachevian strategy of Glasnost and Perestroika, using the party as its main instrument, could no longer work because the party was so isolated from society, so dependent on Soviet support that it was no longer capable of acting as an independent political force as it had no credibility with public opinion, which saw it as alien and increasingly irrelevant. Dissidents were more inclined to simply ignore the party than to try to confront it or change it. This was a dramatic change from the 1950s and 1960s.

Much of this evolution had been quiet and subterranean, a form of salami tactics in reverse. New thinking was evolved, simultaneously and in parallel in several countries, both by intellectuals and practical activists among the working class. If, as seemed axiomatic by 1970, the Communist party could be neither removed nor reformed, could it be, as it were, unplugged from society, isolated and ignored? Could new and wider 'party-free' space be created, whilst avoiding a direct challenge to the hegemony of the party in the political and foreign policy spheres? Could the party thereby be forced to evolve forms of power-sharing with a civil society that was independent of the party? These were the key questions of the 1970s and early 1980s. Communist parties were obliged to evolve and regroup after 1956 and 1968. They were obliged to make do with a much less totalitarian control of societies that were, whether they liked it or not, much more open to the outside world and which had demonstrated that they refused to do more than outwardly comply with the dictates of the party. The parties had to accept or at least tolerate a diminished sphere of control, which then made the idea of forms of power sharing less and less unthinkable and more and more necessary. The Communist party sought to shift the grounds of its legitimation from the ideological to the economic. Legitimation would now be based on the ability of the regime to deliver a better standard of living, which for much of the 1970s it proved able to do, at least in Czechoslovakia and Hungary.

With post-1989 hindsight, it is clear that these changes, seen initially as tactical shifts designed to ensure the survival of the party leaderships then in power, actually represented a far more dangerous slippery slope. First, economic success required greater openness, foreign capital and technology, which created potentially dangerous dependence and opened these hitherto closed economies to external economic forces such as recession and inflation. It was also dangerous for the party to seek to base its legitimation on objective, quantifiable yardsticks that could be verified and were open to international comparison. It was also dangerous for a supposedly overarching scientific ideology to admit a degree of relativity, which was inherent in any power sharing with civil society. The party was thereby itself admitting, as it were, of its own volition, that it was not omniscient. If that was so in some areas, then why should it not be so in others?

Another watershed development that fitted perfectly into this new pattern was the Helsinki Final Act concluded under the Conference on Security and Cooperation in Europe (CSCE) in 1975. Ironically, the idea of the CSCE originally came from Moscow and had aroused considerable suspicion in the west and among dissidents in central Europe. In its original form, as proposed by the USSR, it would simply have been a pan-European agreement to endorse and confirm the European territorial and political status quo that had emerged from the Second World War. This was accepted by the west, but only with the proviso that peaceful change in the status quo should explicitly not be ruled out. The price of this geopolitical agreement, imposed by the west, was the so-called 'third basket', dealing with humanitarian issues, that could also be seen as a first tentative implementation of two of the ten basic principles of the CSCE, that is 'Respect for human rights and fundamental freedoms, including freedom of thought, conscience, religion or conviction' and 'Equality of peoples and their right of self-determination'. More importantly, the west obtained agreement that there should be periodic review conferences which could monitor compliance. By the Vienna Follow-Up Conference in 1986, this very general language had been tightened to include an obligation to guarantee to everyone the right to know his rights. Governments were committed to publish and make accessible legislation and procedures relating to human rights and fundamental freedoms and to 'respect the right of their citizens to contribute actively, individually, or in association with others to the promotion and protection of human rights and fundamental freedoms'. Taken literally, these were far-ranging obligations that would have had a dramatic effect on political life in central European countries. However, their governments no doubt regarded them as simply formal obligations, a required price for other western concessions. They argued that in any case, human rights were respected by them and that these texts needed to be read with the general clause on 'non-intervention', making these matters purely internal. This view was not accepted by the west.

As a result, human rights in central Europe became a matter of international concern to the whole CSCE membership that was subject to ongoing external review. Internally, it now became possible, on the basis of the Helsinki Final Act and its follow-up documents, both to claim one's human rights and those of others and to campaign in favour of human rights, without crossing the line into open subversion and anti-state activity. This new issue-oriented, low-key, semi-legal approach fitted exactly the new doctrines of developing a civil society in an autonomous space not subject to control by the party.

The Helsinki process also opened up another crucial network. It opened the way for new alignments within each bloc and for informal contacts across traditional ideological barriers. Peace activists in the west worked with human rights activists in Poland or Czechoslovakia. There were valued contacts between dissidents in different central European countries.

Poland led the way in this new phase, both in terms of developing the new ideology of a civil society free of the party and in working out the practical means of turning these new ideas into reality. This also required forging new alliances. In 1968, the workers had not supported the intellectuals, and in the 1970 events on the coast, the intellectuals had not shown solidarity with the workers. The key breakthrough came in 1976, with the creation of the KOR (Workers Defence Committee) bringing together intellectuals, Church people and workers for the first time. It served to support victims of repression after the 1976 strike wave against price rises and to mobilise political support for the workers' movement. It was out of this alliance that the independent trade union Solidarnosc grew. Of course the election of a polish Pope in 1978 was a key catalytic factor.

After the August strikes in the Lenin Shipyard and other industrial enterprises along the coast and elsewhere, the party was forced to recognise

Solidarnosc, which with the support of the Church and its intellectual advisors became, under it leader Lech Walesa, a power in the land for almost eighteen months with ten million members. Afterwards, nothing could ever be the same again, even if on this occasion the attempt to create structures outside the party had not succeeded. Despite the imposition of martial law in December 1981 and a dark period of repression for Solidarnosc activists over the next seven years, the impact of Solidarnosc and indeed its offshoots were never lost completely and the longer-term consequences continued to be felt not only in Poland, but all over the region. It had been demonstrated that the party could no longer exert total control, that in certain favourable circumstances it could be forced to negotiate with society and reach a compromise with it.

Though Solidarnosc failed in the short term, the reverberations were felt all over central Europe. This gave new strength and encouragement to the movements for human rights that were building on the Helsinki process and moving into the ideological void left by the progressive withdrawal of the communist parties from the ideological high ground into technocratic management of forms of 'negative legitimation', based mainly on economic performance of at least a relative kind. This was a high-risk strategy, since if the then quite reasonable economic growth performance were to weaken, then the regime would be devoid of any legitimation.

The new anti-politics did not challenge the regime overtly, nor did it contest it directly in the economic field, leaving this, as it were, to events. It sought to develop a new moral dimension, based on wider and wider areas of party-free space in which an autonomous civil society could develop that might in time force the party into a more equal dialogue with society, as had briefly happened in Poland. The exponents of these ideas were writers and intellectuals, some of whom were later to play a key political role. Havel's idea of 'living in truth' and avoiding moral collaboration with the system was widely replicated in different forms throughout these writings. Its exponents were Lesak Kolakowski, Adam Michnik and Jacek Kuron in Poland. They were also active practitioners in Solidarnosc. In Hungary, György Konrad and Janos Kis were the main theoreticians of anti-politics. In Czechoslovakia its exponents were Jan Patocka, the first spokesman of Charter 77, and above all the playwright Vaclav Havel. These currents gave rise to Charter 77, the KOR, and were strongly represented first in the open Solidarnosc and then in its underground continuation after 1981 and the Hungarian dissident movement that linked up with the environmental activists of the Danube Circle in opposing the Gabčikovo/Nagymaros dam project. By the mid-1980s, with Perestroika, these new forces found themselves, at least in Poland and Hungary, in a paradoxical competition and dialectic with party reformers about the future of the system, between reform and overthrow.

Returning to Poland, in reality something of a stand-off had now resulted. Political normalisation did nothing to resolve the underlying economic problems and certainly did nothing to strengthen the capacity of the regime to undertake tough reforms. The party could stay in power, but could not resolve the real structural economic problems that had piled up. Nor, on the other hand, could it give way to those who might carry through reform. It was only with the worsening of the economic situation and the arrival of Gorbachev in power in the USSR in March 1985 that the regime came to contemplate breaking the infernal Polish circle.

New avenues now opened up. A first attempt at a new approach, but without dialogue with the opposition, came with the Referendum on 29 November 1987 on twin proposals of massive price rises, coupled with timid political reforms. Only 67 per cent voted and neither bill gained the necessary approval of 50 per cent of the voters. The Sejm enacted the bills anyway. This was the worst of all worlds. On 31 August 1988, the Government finally accepted that it would have to enter into dialogue with Lech Walesa and Solidarnosc. This then led on to the first Round Table in central Europe, between the government, Solidarnosc and the Church.

The Round Table produced a real breakthrough: semi-democratic elections that would breach the power monopoly of the party. A Senate was created with 100 members to be entirely freely elected, with veto powers. In the lower house (Sejm), under a complex arrangement, 35 per cent of the seats only were to be open to the opposition. The remaining 65 per cent were shared between the communists and their smaller allies. The Sejm could only overrule the Senate veto by a two-thirds majority. A new strong presidency, tailor-made for Mr Jaruzelski, was established. He was to be elected by an electoral college composed of both Houses of Parliament. At the time, this seemed a radical and extraordinary compromise by the regime. Solidarnosc controlled all the opposition nominations to both Houses. It won 99 Senate seats and all the of the open Sejm seats. Furthermore, the small allies of the communists (peasants and democrats) became more restless and created an unstable situation in the Sejm. Jaruzelski was elected President with difficulty and the communists had to go further than intended and concede a coalition Government, led by a Solidarnosc Premier, Tadeusz Mazowiecki. His government contained 13 Solidarnosc ministers, seven from the small parties and four communists. It won a vote of confidence by 378 votes to

4 with 41 abstentions. This Government held until after the collapse of communism elsewhere and by then seemed an anachronism. The pressures of governing, the outside events and the ambition of Lech Walesa soon split the broad church Solidarnosc into populist and intellectual wings. Walesa identified with the populists and campaigned against his own Solidarnosc government, pressing for faster reform. Jaruzelski was forced to step down and in the first direct popular election of the President, Walesa defeated both his Prime Minister and an unknown, rather shady businessman and became President in December 1990. A new government was formed, but the compromise Parliament remained until the end of 1991. A radical big-bang economic reform was pushed through and proved successful, though it created many real or imagined losers, which made it politically unpopular. A series of complex coalitions then held office, based on the various parties emerging from the collapse of Solidarnosc. The most long-lived of these under Hanna Suchoka saw through significant economic reforms, a limited constitutional reform (the so-called 'Little Constitution') and a reform of the electoral law, making the system less proportional and hence limiting fragmentation. This electoral reform enacted by a Sejm dominated by ex-Solidarnosc parties turned out to be something of an own goal. At the 1993 elections there was certainly a reduction in the number of parties represented in the Sejm, but most of the more rightist, Catholic ex-Solidarnosc parties failed to get over the hurdles introduced by the new electoral law. The post-communist SLD (Party of the Democratic Left) and the Peasant Party, PSL (Polish People's Party), were the only possible coalition partners. Then, in 1995, Lech Walesa was defeated in the presidential election by his post-communist rival, Aleksander Kwasniewski. The general election held on 21 September 1997 saw a victory for the Solidarity Electoral Alliance (AWS) that had been brought together around Solidarnosc, following the defeat of Lech Walesa, to redress the divisions of the right that had cost it so dear in 1993 and 1995. A coalition of AWS and UW (Union of Liberty) was then formed, with Jerzy Buzek (AWS) as Prime Minister.

Events in Hungary and Czechoslovakia were soon to surprise everybody and overtake Poland, which until now had led the pack. By the early 1980s, the first Hungarian reform model – prudent economic and cultural reform, without political reform – had run its course and had no more to offer. It was undermined by debt, recession, inflation and falling economic growth in the wake of the oil crisis and by gathering environmental protest against the Gabčikovo/Nagymaros dam project. As a result, even before Gorbachev, some party reformers were already beginning to think the unthinkable – some form of power sharing, giving a new legitimation to the system, enabling it to resolve the growing problems of society which required tough measures.

The first opening came in 1985 with the first multi-candidate (though not multi-party) elections. Twenty-five of the 77 independent candidates were elected. Voices began to be raised calling for the retirement of Party Secretary Janos Kadar and some form of power sharing, similar to what actually emerged in Poland in 1989. By 1987, the debate had spread inside the party apparatus itself, around figures such as Imre Pozsgay. Independent groups, though not yet officially parties were now legalised. By 1988, the main post-communist parties had emerged, with the centre-right populist MDF (Hungarian Democratic Forum), and the liberal FIDESZ (Young Democrats) and Alliance of Free Democrats (SDS).

At the 1988 Party congress, Kadar finally stepped down and was replaced by a balanced leadership, which could neither lead nor contain the coming reform process. The power struggle was on. Nationalism, in the form of support for ethnic Hungarians outside her Trianon borders and protest against Gabčikovo/Nagymaros, re-emerged and formed a powerful multi-headed battering-ram against the citadel of the regime, at first sharing a common interest with the party reformers.

Alongside the prudent, crabwise reform process desired by the Party, a chaotic acceleration of the process set in, fuelled by MDF victories at by-elections, and the opening of the iron curtain border to Austria. The pressure was now on the reformers. They needed to accelerate the process even more if they were to stay ahead of the opposition outside the Party. Reformers won control of the Party, which now split. The way was open to free elections.

The key question was how. The Party reformers wanted a strong presidency, elected directly by the people, so as to capitalise on their greater public recognition. The opposition, especially the liberals, wanted a parliamentary republic, with strong checks and balances built in. The opposition managed to block the reformers' scheme by winning a referendum. This opened the way to a Round Table, that agreed on a new constitutional and electoral system. Elections held in April and May 1990, in two rounds under a mixed plurality and PR system, greatly multiplied the effect in seats of a small plurality of votes. The MDF, operating now as a broad-based centre-right *Volkspartei*, came through and emerged as the largest party with 164 out of 386 seats. It was able to form a stable centre-right coalition with the Smallholder and Christian Democrats as junior partners, under Joszef Antall, controlling 229 of the 386 seats in parliament. In part, this rested on compromise with the opposition, whose votes were needed for many laws requiring a two-thirds majority. Arpad Gönscz, a Free Democrat leader, became President of the Republic. The government lasted its full four-year term, despite splits, mostly from the right, both in the MDF (Hungarian Democratic Forum) and the faction-ridden Smallholders Party.

The impact of the government's economic policy and its somewhat authoritarian style earned it rapid unpopularity. Long before the 1994 election, its defeat had become inevitable. The key question was who would then win. The largest opposition in 1990, the Free Democrats, were soon overtaken by FIDESZ, until that bubble burst. The post-communist Hungarian Socialist Party (MSZP) came from behind, running on a moderate domestic and foreign policy platform under the popular Gyula Horn and entered the campaign with poll ratings of over 30 per cent. It won an absolute majority of seats, but preferred to form a centre-left coalition with the Free Democrats (SDS).

Czechoslovakia remained quiescent during the whole pre-transition period in Hungary and Poland, under its post-Prague Spring conservative Slovak-dominated leadership. Such little dissidence as there was remained almost totally confined to Prague intellectual circles. For the first time since the founding of the Republic in 1918, the Slovaks seemed in favour. Otherwise, normalisation had only engendered alienation and passivity and not opposition. The regime was not seriously challenged, but then nor was it able to regain popular support. The situation was a stand-off.

However, as 1989 went on, there were small signs of greater opposition mobilisation, with demonstrations of growing size for the commemoration of the self-immolation of Jan Palach in January, of the Soviet invasion in August and of independence day on 28 October. The movement was amplified after the fall of the Berlin wall on 9 November. An official, authorised demonstration on 17 November commemorating the murder of a student by the Nazis in November 1939 was hijacked into an anti-regime demonstration and was heavily repressed by the police. Rumours, perhaps even manipulated by pro-Gorbachev elements in the security forces to discredit the conservative leadership, spread that a student had in fact been killed. This led to student strikes and demonstrations, that were soon joined by others. They then ballooned into short general strikes, demonstrations and mobilisation of the people not only in Prague, but also in Bratislava and Brno.

The Party moved to pre-empt the movement by a minimal response, with some minor policy changes and leadership changes, including the

General Secretary Jakes, who resigned. But this was by now too little and too late, as the opposition was in the process of finding an organised voice and leadership in the person of Vaclav Havel and the Občansky Forum (OF) or Civic Forum and its Slovak equivalent, People against Violence (VPN).

Very rapidly, the whole Politburo was forced to resign and with it the old hard-line government, and a new power-sharing government, including such opposition figures as Komarek and Dienstbier, was formed under the Slovak party reformer Marian Čalfa. The security service was dissolved, the iron curtain border was literally dismantled and the leading role of the party was removed from the constitution. Using obscure recall procedures, Alexander Dubček became a Deputy and then President of the National Assembly, and on 29 December Vaclav Havel was elected President of the Republic.

A Round Table then worked out the new electoral law, which was a variant on the old pre-war electoral law, proportional representation with a 5 per cent threshold. The election was held on 8–9 June 1990, with a 90 per cent turnout. OF and VPN won clear-cut victories, though with only 29.3 per cent in Slovakia, VPN did not win an absolute majority. For this reason, coalitions between OF/VPN and the Christian democrats were formed at both Republican (Czech and Slovak) and Federal levels, which also gave a more comfortable political base and the necessary two-thirds constitution building majority.

However, under the strain of the process of economic transition, constitution building and purging the old regime – issues which occurred everywhere – and the specifically Czechoslovak problem of Czech/Slovak relations and the future form of the state, OF and VPN split into feuding factions and then into parties. Thus, the first Parliament set to run for only two years actually solved none of these issues before the 1994 elections. Indeed, if anything Czech/Slovak relations had got worse and the problem of the future of the Czechoslovak state even more intractable.

Earlier negotiations had already revealed growing centrifugal tendencies between the two Republics. In the Czech Republic support was growing for radical economic reform under then Finance Minister Vaclav Klaus, whereas there was no support for such a radical course in Slovakia. The Slovaks were adopting increasingly nationalist positions and were preoccupied with the conflict with Hungary over the Gabčikovo/Nagymaros dam and with their own Hungarian minority. No compromise on reforming federalism had been able to be achieved.

The election confirmed these trends and two irreconcilable majorities emerged in the two Republics; the radical Klaus became Prime Minister in the Czech Republic, and Vladimir Mečiar, a Slovak nationalist and populist, became Premier in Slovakia. All that then remained was to arrange for the split-up of the country as peacefully as possible and this became an accomplished fact on 1 January 1993, when Slovakia and the Czech Republic became separate states. This outcome became inevitable and finally perhaps was preferred by Klaus, who did not want to slow down the Czech reform process, even though it was probably opposed by public opinion.

In the Czech Republic, Havel returned as President and Klaus remained as Prime Minister, leading a four-party centre-right coalition, dedicated to fast-track market reform. It remained in power up to the 1996 general election. At that election, the outgoing coalition became a minority government, missing an overall majority by two seats. However, it was able to continue, with a certain 'tolerance' from the opposition CSSD, the main victors in the election.

Within one year of the 1996 election, the Czech economy was hit by a severe crisis, with devaluation, bank failures, rising unemployment, a falling growth rate and drastic cuts in public expenditure. The Czech economy was no longer a model. Many of the problems of restructuring that had been deferred by the Klaus government now came home to roost. Prime Minister Klaus had to publicly confess the government's failure and eat a large dose of humble pie, which to put it mildly did not come easily to him. There were numerous ministerial reshuffles and criticism from within the coalition from the smaller KDS (Christian Democratic Party) and ODA (Civic Democratic Alliance) partners. ODA was also hit by a crisis of a quite different provenance, as its leader Jan Kalvoda was forced to resign for claiming bogus doctorak qualifications. This may seem almost comical to us, but in central Europe there is enormous respect and prestige attaching to academicians. The KDS kept hesitating whether to leave the coalition, but did not do so. The Government was also criticised by President Havel. However, since CSSD was not eager to come to the rescue of Mr Klaus, preferring to leave him, as Mr Zeman dramatically put it, 'to drink his own hemlock to the depths', there was no alternative government in the wings.

In line with a trend observable in crisis situations elsewhere in the region, President Havel ended the political crisis directly caused by the resignation of Vaclav Klaus from the Premiership, but much longer in gestation, by the appointment of Czech Central Bank Governor Josef Torovsky as his successor on 2 January 1998. This new government, composed of both pro- and anti-Klaus factions within ODS and the two other outgoing coalition parties (KDU-CSL and ODA), won a vote of confidence in Parliament. It stayed in office only until the Parliamentary elections on 19 June. As a result of the severe internal crisis in ODS, Finance Minister Ivan Philip, former leader of the small KDS party that merged with ODS in 1995, left ODS. At the same time, 30 of 68 ODS deputies (the anti-Klaus faction) formed a new party, the Union for Liberty, opening a new and more unstable period in Czech politics.

Slovak politics was much more stormy, under the charismatic, but highly controversial Mečiar. Splits and defections in his HZDS Party (Movement for Democratic Slovakia) brought about his downfall and replacement for a brief period in 1994 by broad anti-Mečiar coalition of both left and centre-right. It had hoped to continue after the September 1994 election, but Mečiar won enough support with two coalition nationalist-populist partners to return to power.

The Slovak government remained in office, though the coalition continued to be unstable. There were continuing serious conflicts between Mečiar's HZDS and the two smaller coalition partners, who came close to breaking the coalition both over privatisation policy, especially in the media, and over the representation of opposition parties in parliamentary committees, which they supported.

The vendetta against President Kovac continued, without any consensus emerging. The so-called 'Blue Coalition' of opposition parties, including the Hungarian parties, but excluding the SDL, collected signatures for a referendum for direct popular election of the President, as a way of breaking the impasse in Parliament, where neither Mečiar nor the opposition can muster the constitutionally required three-fifths majority to remove the President now or elect a successor in 1998. This referendum was supposed to be held at the same time as a referendum on NATO membership. First of all it was contested before the Constitutional Court by the government. It was declared legal by the Court and binding on Parliament, though the necessary amendment could not be directly enacted by referendum. This was yet another recipe for impasse. In any case the referendum was sabotaged by the Interior Minister. This led to both boycott and confusion. Only 9 per cent voted and both referenda were declared invalid. After both international and internal protests, including the resignation of the Foreign Minister, Mečiar has sought some limited dialogue with the opposition, mediated by President Kovac.

Both countries applied for EU membership in 1996.

3 Economy and Society

The four Visegrad states – Poland, the Czech Republic, Slovakia (until 1993 Czechoslovakia) and Hungary – form a compact area between Germany and Austria in the west and the states of the former USSR in the east. They are bounded by the Baltic in the north and the Danube river in the south. They are cut by the Sudeten and Carpathian mountain ranges, which divide Poland off from the other states. Poland is an extension of the North European plain and like the latter is drained by rivers that flow from south to north west – the Oder, the Vlatava and the Elbe, the Vistula and the Bug. The Danube is the great exception, flowing from its source eastward, turning through two 90-degree turns to end up in the Black Sea, forming the barrier and often the political frontier between central Europe and the Balkans. Hungary to the east of the Danube is also an open plain. The region is historically and culturally part of western Europe, but its eastern Marches now represents a vital strategic zone between Germany and the core of the European Union to the west and the Russian zone to the east.

The total population of the Visegrad region is just over 64 million, that is close to the size of Germany and equivalent to the other larger EU states. Poland on its own has a population of 38.8 million, larger than Spain. Poland is the largest state in central Europe, both in terms of its population and its land area. Perhaps surprisingly, the population density of the region is very even,with little variation from one state to the other, at between 113 and 122 inhabitants per square kilometre. The largest city in the region is Budapest, with 1.9 million inhabitants, in 1994, falling from over 2 million in 1980. It is followed by the other capitals, Warsaw with 1.6 million and Prague with 1.2 million. Bratislava, the capital of the newest state in the region, is much smaller with only 450,000 inhabitants. Poland has several large towns with over 300,000 inhabitants: Poznan (527,000) and Wroclaw (593,000) in the western industrial part of Poland; the Baltic port city of Gdansk (450,000) in the north, the former capital, Krakow (700,000) in the south and Lublin (320,000) in the east. In the Czech Republic, the second city is Brno, the Moravian capital, with 372,000 inhabitants, followed by Ostrava with 350,000 and the western industrial city of Plzn with 170,000 inhabitants. The second city of Slovakia is Kosiče in the east of the country with 240,000 inhabitants. In Hungary, the largest city in western Hungary is Györ with 130,000. In central Hungary, the main centres are on or near the Danube: Miskolc with 189,000 inhabitants, Szeged with 179,000 and Pecs with 172,000. The second largest city in Hungary is the Protestant centre of Debrecen over to the east, with 217,000 inhabitants. The balance of population in Hungary is 19.4 per cent in Budapest, 44.4 per cent in towns and 36.2 per cent in the countryside. In Poland, 61.2 per cent of the population lives in urban areas and 38.8 per cent in rural areas. From these figures, and the even population density figures, it can be seen that all these countries are in the process of rapid urbanisation.

The peoples of Poland, Slovakia and the Czech Republic are predominantly west Slavs, speaking west Slav languages and using the western alphabet. They are part of the western catholic tradition. On the other hand, the Hungarians are not a Slav people. They originated in central Asia. Hungarian is not an Indo-European language. It is part of the Finno-Ugrian family and as such is related only to Estonian and Finnish.

Before the Second World War, these states were all, despite the efforts of the peace-makers, unstable, multi-ethnic states. The dominance of the 'staatsvolk' was never secure enough to permit it to exercise relaxed tolerance towards its minorities. For Hungary, which lost almost two-thirds of its population and territory in the Trianon Treaty, the problem was less the existence of minorities within its borders, for these now become few, but rather the presence of ethnic Hungarians in all the neighbouring states just outside its borders. This and the associated irredentism was then, as now, a factor making for instability. For Poland and Czechoslovakia, the problem was the existence of minorities, especially German minorities, which could obtain the support and patronage of the powerful 'mother state'. This situation radically changed after the war, with the defeat of both Germany (and with it Austria) and Hungary and the expulsion of Germans and to a lesser extent Hungarians. The remaining minorities were thereafter obliged to keep a low profile. Now, the issue of internal minorities is objectively marginal, except perhaps in Slovakia, and was certainly kept marginal until 1989. In all four states, the 'staatsvolk' is now predominant. Even in Slovakia, it is 85.7 per cent of the whole population. Hungarians make up about 11 per cent, mainly living in the Danube valley, from just downstream of Bratislava to Estergom on the Danube Bend. Here Hungarians often represent the local majority. The only other significant minority is Romany/ Sinti (1.4 per cent). There are only 3,300 Jews in Slovakia. In Hungary, 96.6 per cent of the population is ethnic Hungarian and the only significant minority is German (1.6 per cent, but with no defined regional base). Hungary has the only sizeable Jewish Community in the region, with 80,000–100,000 people, mostly in Budapest. Ninety-eight per cent of the Polish population is ethnic Polish. The minorities are significant in absolute numbers, though small in percentage terms. These are Germans, in Silesia, and Ukrainians, White Russians and Lithuanians all near the eastern border of Poland. After the Holocaust and further exoduses after 1945, in 1956 and 1968, there now remain barely 5,000 Jews in Poland. With the expulsion of the Sudeten Germans from the Czech lands in 1945–6, there are no ethnic minorities remaining in the Czech Republic, except a small Slovak minority remaining after the split.

Whilst this book is not about the economies of the Visegrad states, an understanding of their respective economic situations, before and after the transition, is vital to understanding their present political development. Therefore, a very short summary of their economic situation, prospects, policy choices and current problems 'vaut le détour', as the famous Michelin guides put it. It is important to remember that the old regime itself had, in its last phase, made the economy its chosen battle-ground. This was especially true of the new breed of pragmatic party technocrats. They, and no one else, had opted for the economy as the yardstick by which they would be judged, fatally for them as it turned out. Initially, it seemed an easier option than regaining ideological support in an increasingly unideological age. For a time, it appeared that a capacity to deliver at least a degree of economic growth and a sense of increasing economic well-being might counter rising political and national aspirations. It proved a flawed, high-risk strategy. The communist planned economies could not hope to compete with the west. Indeed, the process of economic competition required the opening of these economies at least partially to the world economy, which eventually led to importing inflation, recession, rising energy costs and market pressures in the export-orientated sectors. The greater openness also afforded more basis for comparison with the west. The process became irreversible. The only possible response was to accelerate reform and hence open the economy even more to external pressures and influences. But, without structural and hence political reforms, the process of economic reform on its own soon reached its outer limits and proved an ineffective halfway house. The feel-good factor remained elusive.

This experience inevitably meant that the reform process after 1989 was also going to be judged on its ability to deliver economic prosperity or at least some real prospect of it. The transition therefore became, as we have seen, a twin-track, with parallel economic and political reform. Both tracks were necessary to the successful emergence of a functioning civil society that can underpin and broaden democracy. Increasingly, political debate is, as elsewhere, now taken up with divergences about economic management and the speed and direction of economic reform. Furthermore, economic transition is the key to unlocking EU membership, which forms a major policy objective in all four countries.

It should be noted that the three – later four – countries started from very different positions, both in 1945 and in 1989. Pre-war Czechoslovakia had been a fairly industrialised country, with a standard of living approaching that of its western neighbours, unlike Poland and Hungary. It also suffered the least material war damage to its economic infrastructure. During the communist period, there were significant variations in the economic policies of the three countries. For example, there was never any large-scale collectivisation of agriculture in Poland. Indeed, over 80 per cent of Polish farms had always remained in the private peasant sector, though subject to numerous centrally planned obligations and restrictions. Hungary had been engaged in forms of 'soft' market reforms since 1968. These were extended to the service sector in 1982. A significant private sector was also developing and the legal framework for a market economy was gradually put in place between 1985 and 1990, including removal of trade monopolies and a tax reform. Hungary therefore did not have the same need for a dramatic 'big-bang' economic reform. This was far from the case in Poland and Czechoslovakia. In Poland private employment outside agriculture remained under 10 per cent. A politically motivated industrial location policy after 1968 had led to the forced industrialisation of more politically reliable Slovakia and the creation of massive and uneconomic state enterprises, especially in the armaments sector in eastern Slovakia.

Let us now turn to look at the economic situation of the four countries today. The immediate aftermath of the fall of communism was a dramatic collapse of the old economic structures, and with it a fierce fall in production, GDP, and real wages and, except in the Czech Republic, a serious rise in unemployment. Now, all have returned to positive growth. Inflation remains above western levels, but has stabilised. Unemployment has now ceased to rise and has stabilised, though mostly at higher levels than in the west, except in the Czech Republic, where it has remained below 4 per cent.

THE CZECH REPUBLIC

Czechoslovakia, especially the Czech lands, was industrialised even before the First World War. Bohemia and Moravia were the industrial heartland of the Austro-Hungarian Empire, with large-scale mining and heavy industry. This firm base is now showing through to advantage, despite the fact that before 1989, Czechoslovakia was the most rigid of the communist planned economies. The Czech Republic is now well placed to assume an economic motor role in the region and achieve its early integration into the world economy. All the necessary legislation and economic institution-building is now in place, and a considerable amount of privatisation and decentralisation of economic decision-making has occurred. The reorientation of trade away from the former COMECON states towards the EU and OECD is well advanced. The Czech crown is stable and close to convertibility. Western inward investment, though less than in Poland and Hungary, is strong and growing.

Like her neighbours, Czechoslovakia and now the Czech Republic saw a sharp transition recession, with deep falls in GDP, industrial output and real wages. There was negative growth in industrial output in all the years down to 1994 (−7.4 per cent in 1993). The downward trend in GDP has now been arrested and there was real GDP growth in 1994 (+2.6 per cent) and 1995 (+4.8 per cent), continuing in 1996. The IMF has now attested that inflation is under control and remains modest by regional standards (60 per cent in 1991, 21 per cent in 1993, 10.0 per cent in 1994 and 9.1 per cent in 1995). The social cost of these dramatic changes has been less severe than elsewhere, as unemployment has remained below 4 per cent. In 1995, it stood at 3 per cent. Indeed, in Prague, there is a labour shortage. There are, however, serious black-spots in northern Moravia, affected by the run-down in coal mining, where unemployment has reached 15 per cent. The policy of the Klaus government has therefore been considerably less Thatcherite than its rhetoric would lead one to expect. The budget showed a surplus of 0.3 per cent of GDP in 1995.

The 1992–4 privatisation programme was relatively successful. Eighty per cent of the productive capacity of the economy has now been privatised, after reaching 50 per cent in 1993. The structure of the Czech economy has now moved close to that of western European economies, with only 7 per cent of GDP deriving from agriculture by 1993, 8 per cent from transport, 9 per cent from construction, 15 per cent from trade and catering and 35 per cent from industry. Her overall economic performance puts her within striking distance of the weaker EU economies, above Greece and below Ireland, though at present her GDP per capita is only 16.3 per cent of the EU average.

The main economic problems of the Czech Republic relate to regional imbalances created by the restructuring process, especially in Moravia, environmental damage, the imminent move to full convertibility, and the debt burden of many private firms that are technically bankrupt.

Eventually, some restructuring of the large firms that have survived into the market economy will become inevitable. A more localised problem is that of economic relations with Slovakia. The intended monetary union did not survive and nor did the initial one-to-one parity between the Czech and Slovak crowns. The depreciation of the Slovak crown has led to a Czech trade deficit with Slovakia, within the customs and labour market union. It should be remembered that trade with Slovakia was over 40 per cent of total Czech trade in 1993, though it is declining.

SLOVAKIA

With the possible exception of Bratislava and its Danubian hinterland, in close proximity to Vienna, Slovakia was the less urbanised and economically less developed part of the old Czechoslovakia, at least until the 1970s. Before 1918, Slovakia was, as Upper Hungary, an economic backwater within Hungary. However, in the period after 1968, it was the recipient of major heavy industrial investment, particularly in eastern Slovakia in metallurgy, chemicals and armaments. These industrial complexes are now redundant. Since 1993, Slovakia has adopted a much slower approach to economic reform and privatisation. The coalition that emerged from the 1994 election is slowing the process even more.

Slovakia has also been through a deep transition recession from which she is only just now emerging. GDP fell by 8 per cent in 1992 and 4 per cent in 1993. However, growth has now picked up dramatically, with +4.8 per cent in 1994 and +7.4 per cent in 1995. Industrial output fell in every year until 1995. In 1992, it fell by as much as 12.7 per cent. Inflation was 25.1 per cent in 1993, but now seems to be under control, at only 13.8 per cent in 1994 and 7.8 per cent in 1995, taking it below Czech levels. Unemployment remains serious at 14.6 per cent in 1994 and 13.1 per cent in 1995. The private sector remains relatively small. It was only 21 per cent in 1992 and broke through 40 per cent by early 1995. Her indebtedness remains fairly constant at 34 per cent of GDP and the budget deficit fell from 7.1 per cent of GDP in 1993 to a healthier 1.7 per cent of GDP by 1995.

In addition to the continuing political resistance to privatisation, there are objective difficulties relating to the complex property rights situation, deriving from earlier Federal privatisation and restitution programmes and from the heavy debt burden of the now redundant heavy industrial combines that are difficult to privatise for that reason.

Slovakia has difficulties with her trade patterns. She remains extremely dependent on trade with the Czech Republic, which still takes almost 40 per cent of her total exports, against only 35 per cent for the whole of the OECD area and a still significant 9 per cent to the former COMECON states. She has, as a result, had to make difficult decisions about the parity of the Slovak crown with the Czech crown. A devaluation would make her exports more competitive on the Czech market, but might provoke Czech retaliation. It would also stoke inflation. Despite this, the IMF is pushing this remedy. Foreign investment has been slow and reluctant due to political instability and the slow pace of economic reform. Indeed, it only reached 191 million ecu for the whole 1989–92 period. Its main provenance was Austria, Germany and the United States. Despite the fast improving economic indicators, the continuing political instability and the slow pace of privatisation are proving discouraging to investors.

HUNGARY

Hungary claims with some justice to have been engaged in a gradual and cumulative reform process, spanning almost thirty years now and straddling the political changes, thereby providing considerable continuity and stability. The reforms of 1965 and 1968 reached their outer limits within the political confines of the old system by 1989, but did prepare the ground for the creation of a functioning market economy and the establishment of the necessary public and private institutional arrangements. Trade monopolies and the old taxation system were already being phased out and replaced before 1989. Mild inflation had begun before the political changes, which was important in the process of freeing prices and wages. The process of restructuring Hungary's trade patterns towards the EU and OECD markets had already begun in earnest by 1987. By 1995, over two-thirds of her trade was with the EU.

Hungary was not able to escape the transition recession despite the gradualness of her reform process and did not emerge from it until relatively late, in 1994. GDP fell by 0.5 per cent in 1988, was static in 1989, and fell by 3.9 per cent in 1990, 11.9 per cent in 1991, 4.3 per cent in 1992 and 0.8 per cent in 1993. In 1994, her GDP grew by 2.9 per cent, but only 1.5 per cent in 1995. Industrial output was back into growth by 1993, but still only stood at 74.3 per cent of 1985 levels. But it grew strongly again in 1995 (+11 per cent), especially in export markets. It was the larger-scale enterprises employing over 50 workers that took the brunt of the restructuring. Their combined output fell by 19.3 per cent in 1991. On the other hand, agricultural output, especially for export, was still falling sharply until 1993 (–14.7 per cent), but began to recover in 1994. Private consumption and real wages are now again into growth. Agriculture and forestry remain significant employers and contributors to GDP. Engineering, chemicals, light industry and food processing are the main components of industrial production. Total production has yet to recover. Hungary is a significant importer of energy, though she also produces small amounts of oil and electricity for export. Half her electricity needs come from nuclear power. Probably due to her early start and stability, Hungary has been successful in attracting about half of all the foreign investment in central Europe, mostly in industry, transport and communications, which take about two-thirds of all foreign investment in Hungary. The main sources of that investment were Germany and Austria. Inflation is less under control than in the Slovakia and the Czech Republic. It peaked at 35 per cent in 1991, fell to 19.1 per cent in 1994 and then rose again to 28.5 per cent in 1995. Unemployment reached 12.2 per cent in 1992, but is now falling. It stood at 11.3 per cent in 1993, 10.1 per cent in 1994 and 9.5 per cent in 1995. Unfortunately, over 60 per cent of the unemployed are long-term (over one year) unemployed. The stabilisation programme and the renewed privatisation programme has reversed this downward trend by 1998. Privatisation was slow to get off the ground. The privatisation programme of the centre-right government aimed at achieving a figure of 50 per cent of privatisation by 1994, but had actually only attained 17.5 per cent. The current approach remains slow and cautious, having not yet reached the largest and most difficult enterprises.

POLAND

Poland presents far greater economic problems than her neighbours, in terms of both her domestic reform process and the related issue of integration into the EU. Poland simply has a larger economy, a larger agricultural sector and very concentrated heavy industry (on the coast, in Silesia and around Lodz). Poland was always a special case within the socialist system. The strong position of the Catholic church, the emergence of the independent trade union and the survival of private agriculture were all key factors of differentiation. Market reforms, such as they were in the 1981–2 period, had never, unlike those in Hungary, had much depth or stability, and had effectively been blocked by the political opposition of Solidarnosc. The new Solidarnosc-led Government therefore probably rightly opted to use its 'honeymoon' period to push through a radical 'big bang' strategy, involving stabilisation, cuts in subsidies, deregulation and privatisation and creation of market mechanisms and institutions all at one go.

This radical programme led to a long and deep recession in all economic indicators, including GDP, industrial production, agricultural production, employment and trade. Poland only began to recover from the very sharp drop in economic activity and living standards in 1992, perhaps a little earlier than elsewhere. Output fell rapidly in the 1990–3 period. Industrial output fell by 11.9 per cent as late as 1991. GDP fell in each year until 1991 (–7 per cent), but moved into growth in 1992 (+2.6 per cent) and a healthy 5.2 per cent in 1994 and 7.0 per cent in 1995. Agricultural production also fell, especially in the state sector, contributing to unemployment in the north and west of Poland, where state farms are concentrated. Unemployment reached a massive 15.7 per cent in 1993 and was then still rising, though slowly. It reached 16.0 per cent in 1994 and then fell to 14.9 per cent in 1995 and continues to fall, but slowly. Inflation has also been a severe problem and remains less under control than in Hungary, the Czech Republic or Slovakia. It reached 70 per cent in 1991, 35.3 per cent in 1993 and 27.8 per cent in 1995. For its size, Poland has attracted less foreign investment.

Polish agriculture was never collectivised and small peasant holdings are the norm. Only 6 per cent of all farms are larger than 15 hectares. A massive 38 per cent of the Polish population remains rural. Agriculture and related activities still account for 25.8 per cent of all employment, down, but not dramatically, from 29.9 per cent in 1985.

Her industry still shows many typical features of communist planned economies: large industrial combines, concentrated in certain regions, concentration on heavy industry, energy wastage, high pollution, over-capacity in areas such as shipbuilding, chemicals and steel that are already over capacity throughout the OECD. Heavy Engineering (27.5 per cent), tight engineering (16.5 per cent), processing (14.5 per cent) and chemicals (7.3 per cent) are the main components of industrial production in Poland on 1993 figures. As elsewhere, absolute levels of production still remain below 1988 levels for almost all sectors. In 1991, the public sector share of output was still 75.8 per cent in 1991, though this had fallen to 63 per cent by 1993. Poland was a net exporter of energy, mainly coal, until 1980, when there was a massive cut in production. Coal production remained at 131 million tonnes in 1993. She has now become a net energy importer, mainly oil and gas, whilst still exporting coal. Polish trade has considerably diversified since 1989, away from her former COMECON neighbours. Inter-regional trade remains marginal. Over 55 per cent of her trade is now with the EU. Germany is now her largest trading partner.

4 Theories of Transition

The previous chapters set out the chronology of events around the fall of communism. The aim of this chapter is to examine theories of causes of transition. It does not have the pretension to contribute to the rich and growing literature devoted to theories of transition in east/central Europe. In any case, this is an area of work in progress and the jury is out on many of the theoretical explanations offered for the transition. The aim here is more modest, being rather to present and compare the various analyses of the transition process that are, as it were, on offer and examine how they shape our view of the transition and its likely development, as a prelude to our main theme, which is the system of government and politics in the four Visegrad states. Indeed, the process of transition can offer us vital clues to the present and future problems of these countries.

It should be underlined that transition is indeed a process, which leads into a consolidation of democratic reform, which is by no means complete, nor some would argue even stable and irreversible. Indeed, one may expect some reversals within a general positive trend towards democratic reform and consolidation, though clearly this is markedly less true of the Visegrad states than of others in the region. It is above all this positive factor that justifies according them a serious degree of comparability with the broader western European universe.

Analysts who have come to the study of east/central European transitions from the background of Latin American, Iberian or Balkan transitions have made two vital points in relation to central Europe that make this last transition fundamentally different from the others. Firstly, they rightly note, there is not one single transition in central Europe, but two parallel and simultaneous transitions and perhaps even three. The transition to democracy required a social and political transition to create a functioning civil society. At the same time, unlike the other European democratic transitions of the 1940s and 1970s, the central Europeans were simultaneously engaged in a transformation of their economic systems from a socialist command economy to an open market economy. Though conceptually separate, these different transitions are closely linked and are in large measure interdependent, each requiring the other for their own success. The interlocking of these transitions is an immensely complex task that must inevitably take a long time to complete.

The factors which brought about the collapse of communism and then assisted the transition were multiple and complex. Nor is there in the literature yet anything like consensus about the relative weight of the different factors that were involved.

Causal factors can generally be subdivided into short-term conjunctural factors and long-term systemic factors on the one hand, and internal and external factors on the other. There is a degree of consensus that external factors of various kinds were more significant than had been the case in the Latin American or Mediterranean democratic transitions, though less than in the immediate post-war transitions in Italy, Germany and Austria. There is, though, less agreement about the specific weight of these external factors. Were they catalytic? Were they actually preconditions for the success of the transition process or were they necessary but by no means sufficient conditions for that success? On the other hand, were they, as some theorists are inclined to argue, no more than helpful contributions towards a development that would in any case have been inevitable? Here, the literature gives us no clear guidance. All these different conclusions are open to discussion.

Common sense would suggest that there was a degree of dialectic between internal and external factors or at least with the key external factor, the Soviet position. That immediately becomes clear if one asks why all the previous attempts at reform in Poland in 1956, Hungary 1956, Czechoslovakia 1968, Poland 1970 and 1980 all failed, whereas the 1989 reform process succeeded. What was the key difference? Some would argue that the internal erosion of the legitimation of the regimes had gone that much further. But, even so, the only dramatic difference was the changes that had already taken place in the Soviet Union. The real or imagined Soviet long-stop to the reform process had this time been removed. In any event, people remembered that in most cases, Soviet opposition to the earlier reform efforts had been real and brutal enough. Yet now, if it still meant anything, the Soviet card could only be played by reformers in favour of reform and not by conservatives against reform. In 1989, the outcome would largely be determined by the play of internal forces. These and these alone would determine whether and how far the regimes in place would be able to survive or how far they would need to bend.

What were these external factors? How did they impact on internal factors? The generalised shift in the later 1970s away from ideological legitimation towards forms of instrumentalist economic legitimation obliged these societies to become more open, and at the same time made them more vulnerable to at least the indirect effect of international market forces such as increasing real energy costs, rising interest rates, credit rating mechanisms and imported inflation. The only possible response by the régime at this point was to accelerate the process of modernisation, with all its inherent political risks. This increased their vulnerability and took them ever closer to realistic boundaries of a process of economic modernisation without political reform. By the late 1980s, Hungary and Poland were both demonstrably at or at least near that boundary.

The development of Glasnost and Perestroika in the USSR after the arrival of Gorbachev in power in March 1985 created yet more central European ironies and paradoxes in this confused pre-transition period. The messages coming out of Moscow were for the first time themselves confused and uncertain. For a time they could be read in almost any manner that factions in central Europe wished. Eventually, the message seemed to become clearer and more unequivocally in favour of reform. In time, the only message that was clearly not coming out of Moscow was that of a willingness to intervene in favour of conservative regimes in the region. Thus, the prop of the threat of Soviet intervention was finally removed. Nor, in these new circumstances, could the conservatives even claim the role of the best mediators between Moscow and the local society.

This had paradoxical effects. In the first place, up to that point the existence of the Soviet long-stop had rendered the development of indigenous political legitimation both unnecessary and virtually impossible. Now the local communist parties had to contemplate, as a matter of urgency, life without this prop. How would they react? Would they try to follow Moscow in the path of reform? Could they actually do this or was it too late? That was the key question for them. Some, such as the Polish and the Hungarian leadership, sought to adapt to the new environment and set in motion a controlled reform process. Others such as the Czecho-slovak and DDR leaderships sought to shore up the status quo and ride out the storm. There was now not just the removal of a negative restraint, but also a more positive reform model in Moscow. Indeed, if Moscow talked of democracy, how could it be wrong for Charter 77 or Solidar-nosc to talk of democracy? This created considerable ideological confusion.

In a situation where outside influences such as Moscow and the increasingly attractive European Community were increasing pressure on the system to reform and at the same time removing previous constraints upon reform, a new space and new opportunities opened up. Now, for the first time, the outcome would depend on the balance of internal forces. Could the hard-liners hold the line without reform? If so, for how long? On the other hand, could the party reformers win a race against time and establish a reformist régime with at least a minimal degree of political legitimacy, by heading off the democratic opposition? At the material time, the answer to these questions was by no manner of means as obvious as it now appears.

The start of the active pre-transition period can be set in about 1977. The regimes began to be faced with a series of broad structural changes that introduced new levels of social pluralism that inevitably undermined the existing authoritarian political systems. It was a process of gradual erosion that eventually reduced the leadership to a shell, a modern Potemkin village. There was then an internal dynamic or even a dialectical process of cooperation and competition between the party reformers and the opposition outside the party in civil society, with at least passive and from time to time active support for the party reformers after 1985. There was a significant degree of cross-fertilisation, despite the difficulty of direct communication and contact between dissidents and despite differences of history and experience. People knew what others were doing from the media – western and, after 1985, Soviet. For the first time, there was a broad, parallel movement encompassing the whole region, going in the same direction and coming to maturity within the same time scale. By the mid-1980s there was a serious chance that the long-term erosion of the old party leaderships would reach the point of no return at about the same time. Seen from the standpoint of the outside observer, looking at the facade of the system, the collapse of communism, when it came in 1989, looked like a brutal rupture with the past. The reality was considerably more subtle than that. In all three countries, but especially in Poland and Hungary, the erosion of the position of the party had reached a very advanced stage. Behind the apparent formal monopoly of political power, more pluralist forms of organisation, debate and political activity had been developing. This activity had become semi-legal or at least was tolerated by the regime, either because it had no longer any alternative or because it was a useful safety valve for dissent.

Such tolerance was a dangerous two-edged sword. It led inevitably, as the conservatives indeed feared, to the emergence of competing strands within the Polish and Hungarian party leaderships. This was soon followed by various official groups under the umbrella of the party, such as youth movements and peace councils, taking up a more autonomous and critical position. This was especially true of the peace councils which were active in the wider pan-European peace movement in the late 1970s and 1980s. At the same time, in lieu of genuine open political activity, coded critical debates were launched by experts in the influential and quite official Academies of Sciences on particular issues. Here, the debate that developed in Hungary around the Gabčikovo/Nagymaros dam project is but the most celebrated example. This was followed by spearhead groups in society that took up and 'aggregated' these various critical debates that were emerging. These took different forms: Solidarnosc in Poland, the evangelical church in the DDR, Charter 77 in Czechoslovakia and the Danube Circle in Hungary. These developments contributed to the acceleration of the erosion and delegitimation of the local communist parties. It began to create a new climate, in which there was the expectation that change was necessary and indeed inevitable in the long run. Some would go so far as to argue that these internal developments alone would in time have led to change and reform.

It is probably more reasonable to regard the simultaneous convergence of the long-term erosion of the political legitimacy of the parties and the shift in Soviet attitudes, culminating in the abandonment of the Brezhnev Doctrine in around 1988 and encouragement of reform in the DDR in 1989, as together creating the necessary critical mass that set off the chain reaction in the autumn of 1989. Could such critical mass have been generated purely internally? Perhaps; though the Czechoslovak case points up the vital importance of external factors and regional spillover. Certainly, in any event, a purely internal process would have been longer and more uncertain in outcome.

The removal of the Soviet veto on reform was crucial in another way. It altered radically the dynamics of the internal situation, transforming the strategic calculations of the various groups in contention. In that sense, if in no other, the Soviet Union was still a key factor. As long as the Soviet Union remained a likely long-stop to any reform process, the party reformers held a key strategic advantage and could control the agenda and pace of reform. They could afford to allow the process to develop gradually, without envisaging an immediate transition to full pluralist democracy, precisely because they could credibly argue that this last option did not exist at all. They were also in the position to argue, as did Jaruzelski in Poland, that their political survival in any new power-sharing arrangement was a touchstone for the Soviet leadership. Once the Soviet Union disappeared as a factor in these calculations or even appeared to be on the side of reform, time was no longer on the side of the party reformers.

Initially, party reformers and the opposition had been objective allies against party conservatives. At first, they needed each other. For the opposition groups, the existence of party reformers made political debate possible and enlarged the amount of pluralist space available in society. They, as it were, made a breach in the wall that the opposition could then climb through. For the party reformers, opposition interlocutors outside the party in civil society were vital to their strategy; without such a dialogue, their efforts would never increase the legitimacy of the system. Political dialogue, let alone elections without non-party players would never impress society at large. But once the option of full democratic pluralism became available, these two groups became competitors, engaged in a race against time, especially in Hungary.

This brought about a new central European paradox that was to be at its most acute in Hungary, but was not entirely absent from calculations in Poland. At this point, it was the party reformers who wanted to accelerate the pace of reform and were resisted by the opposition. This was of course not at all the case in Czechoslovakia where the leadership adopted a quite different strategy of immobilism. For the Polish party leadership, it was essential to conclude an agreement with Solidarnosc whilst it remained weak enough to be prepared to concede a continuing role to the party and whilst there remained at least an element of lingering uncertainty about the likely attitude of the Soviet Union towards a more radical arrangement than that under discussion. In Hungary, the reform wing around Imre Pozsgay sought to establish a strong directly elected presidency as the coping-stone of a new constitutional arrangement. The presidential election would be held before parliamentary elections, installing their candidate in a key gate-keeping function before the opposition could organise. This would enable the reformers to take advantage of the much greater public recognition of their leaders. Pozsgay himself was no doubt the intended presidential candidate. Opposition leaders were in the nature of things too unknown to win a direct presidential election at this stage. They would be defeated in a too early election. Furthermore, they were split into liberals and conservatives. Some of the conservatives in the MDF were prepared to give the party reformers a fair wind at this period. The liberal opposition favoured a slower and more measured approach to reform, based on a parliamentary system and with parliamentary elections taking place first. As we have seen, they countered the party reformers with a referendum, but it was a close-run thing. In Czechoslovakia, the situation was different. When the collapse came in November 1989, there was a political void. There were no party reformers. Equally, there was no well-structured opposition as in Poland and Hungary. In that void, it was easy for dissident personalities such as Havel, Dienstbier and Klaus to step into the ring and assume power even without a pre-existing structured organisation.

These considerations all played a role in determining the nature of the post-communist political system and the nature of the political parties that came to be established. The manner in which the transfer of power took place was also an important factor. Despite the apparently radical nature of the change, the long-term erosion process, the commitment of the opposition to non-violence and high ethical standards made for a 'soft' transition using the forms and instruments of the old regime to effect that change. Havel was, for example, elected President of the Republic by the old communist National Assembly. The term 'velvet revolution' invented in Czechoslovakia was equally apposite elsewhere. There was no brutal revolutionary change. As it was, the actual process of transfer of power involved some degree of cooperation between the old and the new power holders, articulated through the device of the Round Tables. This involved such a degree of compromise and even complicity that it precluded radical purges or repression. This was indeed the tacit bargain. The former power holders abandoned those still important levers of power that remained in their hands, including significant military force, with which they could have seriously impeded the transition and raised the cost of removing them, but that would have burnt all bridges between them and the opposition and altered the nature of the process to their detriment, making a more radical settlement inevitable. These considerations had important consequences – positive and negative – for post-1989 politics and constitution building, to which we will now turn in the next chapter.

5 Constitution Building

In this region, as often elsewhere in continental Europe and of course in the United States, constitutions and constitution building is of highly symbolic significance. It is part of nation and regime building. A new constitution is often a kind of rite of passage from one situation to another. In this region, only Hungary that had been an autonomous part of the old Habsburg Dual Monarchy between 1867 and 1918 had any continuous modern constitutional tradition. Poland and Czechoslovakia had not existed as nations before 1918, though Czech and southern Polish deputies had played an active part in imperial politics as members of the Reichsrat in Vienna. The Slovaks, as a backward and oppressed part of Hungary, had been politically disenfranchised before 1918.

In the inter-war period, Poland found it difficult to establish a solid and stable parliamentary system and successive attempts to do so failed by the time of the Pilsudski coup in 1926. Hungary and Poland adopted successively more authoritarian constitutions as the 1930s advanced, which clearly offered no usable model for the post-war period. Only Czechoslovakia was able to establish a workable parliamentary constitution that functioned more or less effectively until the state was dismembered in 1938–9. It did offer a model for the short, uneasy democratic period between 1945 and 1948. Features such as the presidency were carried over into the communist period whereas elsewhere a Soviet-style collective head of state became the norm. It was also able to serve as a model after 1989.

In the communist period, the constitution was a formal facade, a democratic fig-leaf of little importance. The real power relations in the system bore no relation to the formal provisions of what might be, on paper, exemplary democratic constitutional structures that often at least formally retained considerable continuity with previous traditions. The real locus of power was in party organs such as the Politburo and Central Committee, not in state bodies such as the cabinet and parliament. This relation of subordination of state organs to party organs may or may not have been formalised by some generalised coded reference in the constitution to the 'leading role' of the party and its organs.

What happened in 1989 bore little relation to earlier revolutions such as the French revolution, American revolution or the Bolshevik revolution in that there was no violent break, no rupture. The old power as it were ebbed out and faded away, almost without resistance, but it was still there, though headless and impotent, almost pathetically eager to do the bidding of the opposition in carrying through the transition. Hence the term 'Velvet Revolution', applied in Czechoslovakia, but was equally applicable elsewhere. This situation, though it had obvious and undeniable advantages, did pose an almost existential dilemma for the opposition leadership. Of course, on the one hand, it was difficult to look a gift-horse in the mouth. Thinking of the past (1953, 1956, 1968, 1981,...) and looking at Romania, it was almost too good to be true that the old system, which still controlled the levers of military and police power, gave up without recourse to violence. This willingness and the implicit bargain of subsequent moderation obviously could not be rejected. However, everything has a cost. There was a clear down-side to this type of velvet transition. There had been no or very little symbolic smashing of the old order. New institutions were not needed to hand over power, since the old order had handed over power already through the various Round Table type processes. The new leadership inherited the machine largely intact, rather than smashing it. This also had an obvious operational advantage in a complex modern state. However, it meant that the first political task of the new order was not to take power – since it already had it – but to legitimise the hand-over that had already taken place. This was urgent. As a result, it was obviously tempting to move to elections largely within the existing structures, altered only as much as necessary to enable what was ostensibly a multi-party election but in reality a plebiscite on the old system, whose result was a foregone conclusion, to take place. This of course in reality precluded the option of a complete constitutional rethink during the first phase of the transition.

It was also tempting to use the still extant but demoralised machinery of the old system to do the dirty work of dismantling the old system. This clearly had advantages in terms of speed and avoiding divisive debates within the reform movement itself. However, it terms of symbolism and democratic legitimation it was not without risk. It actually showed the illegitimate institutions of the old regime 'legitimating' the change, as an elite process, without any broad democratic debate within the reform movement, let alone within the wider civil society. Inevitably, as we have seen, a degree of compromise and moderation towards the old system and its less compromised leaders was a natural and indeed implicit if not at times explicit bargain within the Round Table process. Perhaps it could not have been otherwise and certainly the benefit of a non-violent transition was inestimable, but a price there was.

As a result, despite the geopolitically far-reaching nature of the changes that indeed amounted to a 'remake' of the continent on a scale with

1648, 1818, 1919 and 1945, the immediate constitutional changes were perhaps less than might have been expected and the degree of continuity greater. There was not, as it were, any 'Jahre Null' or 'l'An Un de la République'. There was no immediate or drastic dismantling of the old structures, nor were there any symbolic constituent assemblies. One ironic and useful consequence of the old communist doctrine of theoretical parliamentary supremacy was precisely that the old parliaments were indeed 'constituant' (legally entitled to amend the constitution) when they needed to be. In some other type of system that might not have been the case. For many months, the old communist parliaments continued to sit and work intensely, sometimes with limited changes in membership, also ironically only made possible by the old doctrine of parliamentary subordination to the party, which permitted recall of deputies and appointment of new ones without election. Of course they were under new management and singing to new tunes. Indeed, they were acting as agents of the new leadership, removing the main symbols of the old system from the constitutions and opening the way for early elections, but nothing more radical. This mainly covered symbolic issues such as the name of the state (Peoples Republics disappeared), the state flag and arms, and removal of references to the 'leading role of the communist party'. With these changes, the constitutions though still imperfect in many regards were serviceable for the most immediate needs. Only the most urgent reforms were undertaken piecemeal, under day-to-day pressure of events and needs, without an overall coherent alternative design. Often, perhaps unintentionally, these early decisions prejudiced future options. In a pithy pun, often the 'tabula ronda' prevented a 'tabula rasa'!

Nor did the semi-democratic elections held in Poland in June 1989 and the fully democratic elections held in Hungary and Czechoslovakia in the spring and summer of 1990 change this situation fundamentally. The new parliaments, though democratically or partially democratically elected, closely resembled the old parliaments in form, powers and even in procedure. The plebiscitary nature of the elections also meant that with the possible exception of Hungary no durable party system and hence model of parliamentary behaviour emerged at these founding elections. The elections were simply won by the most effective exponents of reform in each case: Solidarnosc, OF/VPN and MDF in Hungary. The assemblies composed by this basic, rather crude principle were not obviously equipped to conduct the broad constitutional debate needed to create new constitutional and political models of governance. Nor were the governments that then emerged able or willing to impose any coherent model of constitutional reform on the parliamentary assemblies, which might otherwise have been an alternative route to a coherent reform. As a result, none of the countries was able, as optimists had at first hoped, to pass a coherent constitutional reform package during the term of the first legislature. All retreated into the more piecemeal approach of a series of iterative and corrective mini packages.

Nor in a sense were these wider constitutional issues the most important priorities for the new regimes. They had to deliver the beginnings of economic change very rapidly. The revolutions had been based on an unrealistically negative critique of the past and excessive expectation of what a market economy could deliver in the short term. They unleashed pent-up expectations and hopes that no one could fulfil in a short time. Excessive hopes were placed in the miracle-working ability of the new leaders, who had to run before they could walk and run to keep still. They certainly did not have the luxury of a period for calm reflection. They were forced to deal with contradictory needs. Their critique of communism from the underground had centred on its excessive concentration of forms of totalitarian power, its destruction of civil society and effective deresponsibilisation of citizens, and its weakening of all independent intermediary institutions, all of which created a void into which strong and charismatic personalities, benign like Havel or less benign like Mečiar, Iliescu or Milosovic, were projected, almost whether they liked it or not, and in which new forms of collectivist identification such as nationalism tended to develop. The ideology of the reformers would have suggested a weaker, more decentralised, pluralistic state, based on norms of compromise and tolerance. Yet this was a luxury that pressure to deliver made a very difficult option. Now the state was expected to deliver, and now people actually believed that it would. This was a heavy burden. Inevitably, the temptation was considerable to use the machinery and levers of power that were to hand to achieve or try to achieve what was being demanded. Clearly, it was not an easy moment to give out a kind of Thatcherite lesson that people should expect less from the state, stand on their own feet more and take more responsibility for their own lives. The communist legacy of statism trapped the new leaders in a dangerous way and made their task more difficult and increased pressures on them to use whatever machinery was to hand. This made for a very prudent and even conservative approach that led to keeping as much institutional familiarity from the past as possible.

This is what is meant by the often used metaphor of 'rebuilding the boat in the open sea'. They did not have the luxury of a Philadelphia Convention, Etats Généraux of 1789 or the German Parliamentary Council of 1949, working in relative isolation from day-to-day pressures of govern-ance. What has emerged to date therefore remains partial, incomplete, often technically deficient, ambiguous and contradictory, but it would have been difficult to have achieved better. In any case, as we shall see, the process is continuing.

The process – to continue with the boat-building analogy – started with such sound timber as remained in the existing texts, added sound timber stored in reserve from the past in the form of older, traditional constitutional ideas (a strong presidency and Senate in Poland for example), grafting on new and sometimes green unseasoned timber from the ideas of reformers (constitutional courts and charters of minority rights) and finally overlaying imported foreign timber in the form of foreign constitutional models such as the German constructive no-confidence system or the French Fifth Republic presidency. Between competing ideas, the status quo often became a bottom line or a *via media* in a confusing debate.

We shall now turn to make a brief survey of the constitution-making efforts in the four states.

POLAND

Poland deserves the most detailed attention because it was the earliest case and pioneered the Round Table method which was then applied in one form or another elsewhere, and because Poland has also exemplified the piecemeal method that also came to be applied elsewhere.

The 1952 Polish constitution was modelled on the Soviet 1936 consti-tution. It had introduced a spurious form of total parliamentary sover-eignty, which actually facilitated control by the party, using parliament as a rubber-stamp for decisions taken elsewhere in party organs. The Round Table negotiations conducted in the spring of 1989, very early in the reform process in the region as a whole, created a cautious com-promise on political reform, involving the dismantling of only the most immediately obnoxious trappings of the old system and the creation of some form of limited power sharing between the so-called 'Contractual Sejm', which was not to be fully directly elected, and the Senate, in which Solidarnosc-supported candidates eventually won all but one seat. This then led to an unexpected form of power sharing, encapsulated in the pithy formula: 'Your President (Jaruzelski) and Our Prime Minister (Mazowiecki)'. Constitutional reform remained strictly limited and functional at this stage.

The Contractual Sejm might well have still been able to push through a broad constitutional reform if there had been a coherent will to do so. On the one hand Mazowiecki and then later Walesa were in principle opposed to using that Sejm, in which the communists remained predominant, for that purpose, even though it is not likely that the communists would have proved greatly obstructive. However by the time of the election of Walesa as President in November 1990, the moment had probably already passed. Solidarnosc was less and less united and increasingly split into warring and irreconcilable factions. The presidential campaign itself, opposing Walesa and Mazowiecki in a bitter struggle contributed to the divisions. These divisions also became reflected in approaches to the issues confronting the framers of a new constitution. Widely divergent drafts were developed in the two Houses of Parliament. The Sejm draft, produced in its Constitutional Committee, was more parliamentary in approach and hence was opposed by Walesa. The Senate draft proposed a stronger presidency. The debate between these two approaches bogged down and no result was within sight when elections were called in 1991.

The fragmented Sejm elected in 1991, which gave rise to a series of short-lived, weak and divided coalition governments of up to seven parties, was in no condition to resolve these issues and generate a new constitution. It did however work along a twin-track approach. It set in motion a long-term exercise. In July 1992 an Act was passed laying down the procedure for the drafting of a new constitution. The Sejm overruled the Senate and rejected the amendments of the Upper House. This Act established a Joint Committee of Sejm and Senate. Each House was represented by a delegation equivalent to 10 per cent of its membership. Thus, there were 46 deputies and 10 senators. The President, Government and Constitutional Court were entitled to delegate non-voting observers to the Committee. Final adoption of a draft required a two-thirds majority in a joint sitting of both Houses, i.e. two-thirds of the 560 deputies and senators (460 + 100). The text adopted would then have been put to a national referendum for final approval. This Act was passed almost at the same time as the other short-term track was coming to fruition, leading to the adoption of the so-called 'Little Constitution' on 17 November 1992. Although this might appear contradictory, it was fully in line with Polish tradition, where there were earlier examples of 'little constitutions' being adopted as partial or interim measures in parallel with wider constitution-making efforts. The most controversial issues were the powers of the presidency, the reform of local government, civil rights (President Walesa submitted a draft bill of rights in

November 1992) and continuing bicameralism. Only limited progress had been achieved before the 1993 general election.

This second and less ambitious track finally led to the adoption of the so-called 'Little Constitution' on 17 November 1992, in line with Polish constitutional traditions. It arose from an initiative of President Walesa, as a response to the problems that the ambiguities of the 'Round Table' constitution were causing. It limited itself to spelling out the relationship between President, Government and Parliament. Walesa and his advisors drew up a proposal aimed at creating what would have been ostensibly a semi-presidential constitution under which the president would have had important powers in relation to defence and foreign policy, over the appointment of the Prime Minister, a legislative initiative and veto and a power of dissolution of the Sejm. This proposal had no chance of adoption as it stood, but it probably actually represented an opening gambit, which even watered down as it was would give the president real powers.

The Sejm Committee rejected the key points in this draft, leading Walesa to withdraw his proposal. At this point, an alternative proposal came into play from the Democratic Union (DU) (now Union of Liberty, UW). In the course of debate modifications were made to three key areas: the procedure for the formation of the government; the role of the Senate; and the electoral system. These compromises were made to build a strong coalition in favour of the proposal. The DU draft was considerably less presidential than the Walesa draft, but even so, a coalition of the anti-Walesa Centre Union and the former communist SLD watered the text down even further on the issue of appointment of the government, creating thereby a very complex, multi-stage procedure that evenly balanced the powers of the President and those of the Sejm. The Senate was retained, but with weaker powers in most cases. A two-thirds majority was no longer needed for the Sejm to overrule the Senate. The proportional electoral system was enshrined in the constitution as a deal with the PSL.

After the 1993 elections, the other track was taken up again. The new SLD/PSL coalition had close to the necessary two-thirds majority and could attain it with the added support of the leftist-leaning UP. It needed however to build a stronger consensus, including part of the centre and even part of the extra-parliamentary right of almost 30 per cent of the electorate that was unrepresented in the Sejm due to the electoral system, if it was to be sure of carrying the referendum that was required after the parliamentary vote.

The basic procedure and structure of the constitutional committee remained as it had been in the previous legislature, as laid down in the 1992

Act. Procedural jousting dominated the first phase of the new committee's work. The unrepresented parties of the right, the Church and other social organisations demanded seats in the committee and even formed their own shadow committee. The UP wanted a referendum to settle some prior questions of principle before the committee even began its work. President Walesa wanted a right of popular initiative. This was accepted, but with a threshold of 500,000 voters, enabling only Solidarnosc to table such an initiative, joining the six others before the committee. A compromise was reached to allow the various extra-parliamentary organisations to send observers to the committee. The joint committee was chaired by Aleksander Kwasniewski until he became President of the Republic in 1995, with a PSL vice-chairman. There were six sub-committees and a final drafting committee. In all, seven proposals were put before the committee: one from President Walesa, one from the Senate, one from Solidarnosc (a popular initiative) and four from political parties. The Church has played an important part in the debate, with its demand for a specific Christian reference 'invocatio dei' in the constitution, a constitutional grounding of Christian values, and its rejection of a strict separation of Church and State. These demands would also, in the eyes of the Church, be underpinned and given practical expression by the Concordat, signed in 1993, but not yet ratified by the Sejm. The Church was initially critical of the developing consensus in the committee, though there has now been a relatively favourable compromise on church–state relations as such. This was based on a proposal made in the committee by former Prime Minister Mazowiecki (UW) that indeed did not provide for a strict separation of church and state, but nor did it provide for the 'invocatio dei' or other 'philosophical' reference in the constitution. During the course of the discussions, Walesa's representatives withdrew from the committee and he put his support behind the most presidential of the other proposals before the committee, those from the Senate and from Solidarnosc. The other drafts from the various political parties, including that from UW, though excluding that from KPN, are more parliamentary in form. There was never any real likelihood that a more presidential proposal would pass, and that possibility has diminished even more with the defeat of Walesa. Now, even the KPN and other extra-parliamentary groups may be less eager to see a presidential system put in place. At the drafting session in January 1995, following on the vote of principle in 1994 rejecting a pure presidential system, the committee agreed not to include any 'philosophical' reference and on an essentially parliamentary, bicameral system. The President would be 'the guarantor of the executive power and not the head of the executive branch'. The committee's work was practically suspended during the long presidential election campaign. Then with Kwasniewski's election it lost its chairman. It continued work on other important, though less central issues during the early part of 1996, finalising provisions on the Constitutional Court, that would remove the power of the Sejm to overrule decisions of the court, as well as provisions on the independence of the media.

The long-drawn-out saga of the revision of the constitution came to a successful close. It could be regarded as a monument to the SDL-led coalition since 1993 just before it was defeated. The final version of the constitution owed much to the skilful brokering work of former Prime Minister Mazowiecki, especially on issues such as the symbolically important and controversial preamble. His party, the UW, played a key role in the adoption of the constitution, to which it attached symbolic importance. It provided the SDL–PSL coalition with vital external support from a non-communist standpoint. This was vital in winning the referendum, given that the Sejm elected in 1993 significantly under-represented opponents of the constitution. The draft was approved in the Sejm on 2 April 1997, by an overwhelming but unrepresentative vote of 451/40/6. It was then put to a referendum on 25 May, just before the Pope's visit, so that he would not become involved in the controversy. In the campaign, the constitution was opposed by AWS and Movement for the Reconstruction of Poland (ROP) and supported by SDL, PSL and UW. In the later stages of the campaign, the Church appeared to switch from neutrality to near opposition. Earlier, the Church had appeared satisfied with generous concessions on the content, though stopping short of its full demands on the preamble and abortion. During the campaign though, the Episcopate expressed its 'moral misgivings' about the text. Turnout was low at only 42.9 per cent. The constitution was passed by a small but adequate margin of 52.8 per cent in favour.

HUNGARY

Hungary has had the longest, most gradual and iterative constitutional reform process. It began well before the final end of communism in Hungary, let alone elsewhere in the region, and was indeed an integral part of the process itself. Unlike Poland and Czechoslovakia, the process of constitutional change was set in motion by the reform communists themselves rather than by a triumphant opposition, as a deliberate part of its survival strategy. As early as 1987 informal proposals for reform began to circulate and be debated. Party reformers such as Poszgay and Nemeth began to work with non-party reformers in the moderate opposition that was later to become the MDF. Poszgay actually proposed to move to multi-party pluralism as early as January 1989, a move subsequently endorsed by the MSZP leadership. Following the rehabilitation of Imre Nagy in June 1989 and the reform congress of the old party that gave birth to the 'new' MSZP, parliament began to dismantle the 1949 Stalinist constitution, modelled on the Soviet constitution of 1936. Thus, on 18 October 1989 over one hundred amendments were adopted by 333 votes to 5 with 8 abstentions. A provisional President was elected to pave the way for multi-party elections.

At this point, the reform communists lost the initiative and in a close referendum forced by the more radical opposition groupings, in particular SDS and FIDESZ, their game plan for an early popular election of a strong presidency was blocked. This meant that the new system would be a parliamentary system. After the April 1990 elections, the victorious MDF and the main opposition party, the SDS, agreed a broad deal, under which the SDS candidate for the presidency was elected to a weak presidency and about 20 types of legislation would require a two-thirds majority in parliament. Thus, by a piecemeal, iterative, default process of mutual checks and balances, the contours of the new system were put in place, like a jigsaw puzzle.

Though not perfect, this was initially enough. The 1990–4 parliament was certainly unlikely ever to write a new constitution, as the coalition did not have the necessary two-thirds majority and in any case was likely to have divided on some detailed issues. Nor could it expect to build a consensus with the opposition. Indeed, it did not seek to do so, and from about 1992 even ad hoc constitutional revision petered out. In the earlier period, especially during 1990, correctives were undertaken to the hasty amendments of 1989. These were then consolidated in 1990. The overall effect of the 1989 amendments had been to create a weak presidency and government and a strong parliament. The 1990 amendments, especially the introduction of the constructive no-confidence model, strengthened the position of the government. In addition, during this period, a number of 'constitutional laws' requiring a two-thirds majority were adopted, implementing various revised constitutional provisions, such as for example the new Local Government act of 1990.

The MSZP–SDS did of course enjoy a two-thirds majority and the coalition programme of June 1994 contained a commitment to rewrite the constitution. The aim would be to consolidate, update and revise the 1990 text in the light of experience, and more specifically to consolidate and develop the separation of powers by strengthening the executive powers of government, the supervisory powers of parliament, and the independence of the judiciary, and stabilising the constitution by making revision more difficult by requiring amendments (as in Denmark) to be passed in one parliament and then passed again in the new parliament after an election.

The new constitution is being drafted by a special 27-member parliamentary Constitutional Committee (CC). This CC was only established in June 1995, after protracted negotiations about the procedures to be adopted for the revision of the constitution. The coalition made extensive and in western eyes frankly exaggerated concessions to the opposition. Initially, it had been proposed that the CC should be chaired by the Justice Minister. This was opposed by the opposition, probably their most reasonable criticism. The government accepted that the Chair of the CC should be the Speaker of the National Assembly (actually also MSZP). All Standing Orders relating to the working of the CC need a four-fifths majority on the floor of the house, requiring the support of several opposition parties and certainly MDF. The CC is required to report at the latest by the end of the parliamentary term in 1998, otherwise it will be foreclosed. Each of the six parliamentary parties has an equal delegation on the CC, despite the fact that the MSZP alone has an absolute majority of the seats in parliament. Each party delegation has one vote, and the vote of at least five of the six delegations is needed for *every* CC decision. These five delegations must together represent at least two-thirds of the seats on the floor of the house, giving MSZP, as well as any two opposition parties, an effective veto. The junior coalition partner does not of course have a veto, nor can it form a veto group with opposition parties, as the coalition agreement forbids it to vote differently from MSZP, but equally the reverse applies. The two coalition parties must agree on a prior common position. The final result must be approved by the full house and put to a national referendum. The mainstream parties, MSZP, SDS, MDF, favour a gradualist, organic approach, tidying up and building on the 1990 constitution, rather than looking for radical departure as some on the far left (including some MSZP) and the ultranationalists and the populist smallholders party would wish, favouring a stronger presidency and weaker government, with direct popular election of the president and abolition of the constructive no-confidence procedure.

In any event, this extremely complex revision procedure, coupled with the time limit and the fact that meanwhile no more ad hoc amendments can be adopted by the existing procedure without breaking the consensus, make radical change unlikely. Indeed, it may make any change at all unlikely, as the procedure maximises the capacity of minorities to block and drag out the process. Another unfortunate side effect has been therefore to greatly strengthen the hand of the Constitutional Court, as its decisions can no longer in practice be overturned by constitutional amendment adopted by the coalition's two-thirds majority. In the present situation, some might applaud that, but as a longer-term consequence it may be less desirable.

Despite the complex and highly, perhaps excessively, consensual procedures laid down in 1994 for the drawing up of a new Constitution, the 1994–8 legislature failed to adopt a new Constitution. The reasons did not lie with the extra-constitutional veto that these procedures gave to the opposition, but with MZSP, who defected from the consensus at the last minute. Even Prime Minister Horn did not vote for the draft when it came to plenary on 17 December 1996. MSZP had always been lukewarm towards the enterprise, regarding it at best as unnecessary and at worst dangerous, as seen from its own point of view. On the one hand, it would in future become very difficult to amend the Constitution, especially to overturn Constitutional Court rulings. The existing ad hoc use of 'two-thirds majority' laws seemed preferable to MSZP. For MSZP, the provisions on the voting rights for Hungarians living abroad (liable to be violently anti-communist) were also definitely not in the party's interest. The party also wanted to retain the socio-economic rights that are still enshrined as a residue from the old Communist Constitution. This behaviour by MSZP was bizarre in the extreme and represented an astonishing breach of faith, but was accepted with relative equanimity by all the other supporters of the draft, including SDS, the smaller government party. None of them was prepared to die in the ditch for constitutional reform. It was not a major political priority. Only the populist Smallholders Party regarded it as an important political issue. They had not been part of the consensus, arguing for a more presidential form of government, with direct election of the president and a bicameral Parliament and more direct democracy through wider use of the referendum.

Picking up the pieces, the Committee proposed a new draft with a few modest proposals that might prove generally acceptable. These involve reducing the number of MPs from 386 to 352; increasing the number of signatures required to call a referendum from 300,000 to 400,000; increasing the term of office of Constitutional Court judges from seven to twelve years. Some minor ad hoc changes on judicial reform, immunity of MPs and restricting the issues on which referenda can be called whilst making them binding were enacted outside the 'grand reform'. No more progress was made in the 1994–8 term.

THE CZECH REPUBLIC

Clearly, the constitutional system in the Czech Republic was almost completely conditioned by the long and ultimately unsuccessful attempts to write a new federal constitution for Czechoslovakia that would be acceptable to both Czech and Slovaks. By the time of the 1992 elections for the Federal Parliament and the two Republican Legislatures, these efforts had already virtually reached the point of no return. The elections only sharpened the latent conflict and led to both sides digging in around irreconcilable positions. The outcome of the elections reinforced this general impression, with the emergence of two diametrically opposed and hegemonic victors in each Republic – ODS in the Czech republic and HZDS in Slovakia. Separation soon became the least worst and probably the only option.

The constitutional debate in the 1990–2 Federal and Republican Legislatures had not only concentrated on how to rebalance the federation. Other matters such as the role of the president, bicameralism, the powers of the Constitutional Court and local and regional government had all been important areas of debate, but soon the nascent conflict between Czechs and Slovaks drowned out all other issues. Czechoslovakist, transversal voices such as that of President Havel lost out and could no longer make themselves heard.

The Federal Assembly elected in June 1990 was both a constituent assembly and a working Parliament. It could amend the constitution piecemeal, write a new one and act as the ordinary legislator and controller of the Government. It was supposed to draw up and adopt a new constitution during its two-year term, which it failed to do. The OF had not wished to take what might have been the easiest option that was followed to some degree both in Hungary and Poland, namely that of using the old partially revamped parliament that continued to sit between November 1989 and June 1990, essentially as the uncritical agent of Civic Forum (OF). It was felt that such a body lacked any legitimacy to undertake the task of drafting even a Czech-style 'Little Constitution'. With hindsight, this may have been a missed opportunity, even if it was passed up for the best of democratic reasons. It may have been indeed the only chance to save the federation. A draft could have been drawn up and held over for final adoption immediately after the first democratic elections.

As we have seen, the 1990–2 legislature was dominated by efforts to reform the federation. Alongside that, a parallel debate was going on about the future form of the three constitutions, federal, Czech and Slovak, that were supposed to be adopted within the two-year period.

The most important immediate changes needed to create a democratic state were passed in 1990 and 1991: removing socialist elements, laying the ground for a pluralist, parliamentary system of government and ensuring civil and property rights. However, this piecemeal approach was frequently deficient and in any case resolved neither the problems of relations between the Czechs and Slovaks within the Federation, nor removed the need for a more coherent, global constitution-building effort.

The new Federal Assembly elected in 1990 set up a Constitutional Committee and began work on the numerous proposals that were put forward. The most important came from a cross-party group of deputies which favoured a form of balanced parliamentarianism in which there would be a system of checks and balances between the president and parliament. The civic Democratic Party (ODS) soon put forward a proposal for a prime ministerial system; President Havel made proposals for a stronger presidency, able to intervene to resolve political crises or deadlocks, especially in the event of a disagreement between a simple majority in parliament and the president. The balanced proposal would have limited the sovereignty of parliament both through the presidential powers of dissolution and veto and by the Constitutional Court. These proposals were never synthesised or composited and no compromise emerged. Nor did the government itself seek to take the lead by making its own proposals that might have broken the deadlock.

In 1991 these debates, important though they were, came to be sidelined more and more by the single urgent issue of reform of the federation before the legislative term and with it the Constitutional Committee ran into the buffers. This issue was also increasingly shifted into other fora such as presidential talks and direct bi-and multi-lateral party talks outside parliament. As a result, there was never an adequate consensus in the Federal Assembly to bring any proposals to a vote on the floor. After the 1992 election, it became clear that dissolution of the Federation was the only possible solution. Constitution building now shifted from the Federal level to the two Republican legislatures that were now charged with drawing up constitutions for the two new sovereign states that would emerge from the old Federation on 1 January 1993.

The parliament of the Czech Republic that had not of course been elected as the constituent assembly of a sovereign state now inherited the task of writing the Czech constitution. Its Constitutional Committee put forward a draft, based on the work in progress in the old Federal constitution and the existing provisions of the old Federal constitution. This draft was adopted in December 1992. It is close to the old ODS proposal for a parliamentary system with a weak President and a strong Prime Minister.

SLOVAKIA

The process of constitutional reform in Slovakia was closely tied up with that in the old Federation. In the 1990–2 legislature a constitution for Slovakia, as part of the Federation, had been drawn up, with sharp conflicts within the ruling VPN and Christian Democrats. At the same time, a Declaration of Slovak Sovereignty had been adopted, though not by the two-thirds majority that would have given it full legal force. Following the 1992 elections and the decision to split the Federation, the Slovak National Council (Parliament) adopted a formal Declaration of Independence on 17 July 1992. The new constitution for the Slovak state was drawn up and adopted by the Slovak National Council on 1st September 1992 and entered force on 1 January 1993. Not surprisingly, the Slovaks moved to write a completely new constitution, *ex novo* unlike the Czechs. The final vote was preceded by a widespread process of public consultation and public debate in which there were many critical voices. It was opposed in parliament by the Christian Democrats and the Hungarian parties. Critics argued that it was too imprecisely drafted in regard to such matters as the powers of the President *vis-à-vis* the Government, created a too strong executive, centralised power in the hands of the Prime Minister, subordinated the President to parliament and inadequately protected the rights of minorities and in particular those of the Hungarian minority.

6 The Presidency

Though none of the four states has a presidential system and hence an executive presidency, nor had one in the past, both the presidency as an institution and the Presidents who have occupied the office both between the wars and since the revolutions of 1989 have been of considerable political importance, and this merits examination as part of the political systems of central Europe. In the hasty constitution building that took place in 1989–90 and again in 1992–3 in the Czech Republic and Slovakia, it was necessary to consider the role of the presidency and hence its role *vis-à-vis* both Parliament and the executive.

Clearly, before 1989, this had not been a matter of any importance, in the sense that whatever might have been the formal constitutional position, the real locus of power in the system lay with the General Secretary of the Communist Party, who might or might not also have held the position of head of state at the same time. In any event, his power derived from his party function and not from his position as president. Where the presidential office was held by another person, then that person was clearly politically subordinate to the General Secretary. Furthermore, in some countries, there was at various times no President as such, but rather a collective body that formally exercised the function of head of state.

As we have seen – and we shall return to this – the exact balance of power between President, Government and Parliament in each country was determined by the dynamics of the transition power struggle itself and also to a considerable extent by the personalities involved. In all the three (later four) countries the option of an executive presidency was virtually ruled out by the fact that it was the preferred option of the reform communists and because of real and legitimate fears about recreating strongmen and new cults of personality. Indeed, rejection of this had been a major strand in the 1989 revolutions.

In Hungary, the idea of a strong, popularly elected presidency on the French model was central to the strategy of the reform communists in their efforts to retain control of the process of change. An early direct popular election of the President would have constituted their best hope. As we have seen, the opposition saw through this and thwarted their strategy. As a result, Hungary has the weakest presidency in the whole region and its already limited powers were further limited in practice by the emergence of clear parliamentary majorities after both elections.

Poland lies at the other extreme. Here, a strong presidency was tailor-made for the communist strongman General Jaruzelski as part of the Round Table compromise settlement in 1989 at a time when the opposition thought that it needed to make such major concessions both to the old regime and to Moscow. The decision of Lech Walesa to seek the office in 1990 and his refusal to be elected by the only semi-democratic, so-called 'contractual Sejm' led to the institution of direct popular election and continuation of a strong presidency in what then became a semi-presidential system, with some similarity to the French model. Indeed, just as the constitution tailor-made for General De Gaulle later fitted Mitterand, who had criticised it, the Jaruzelski presidency suited Walesa, who even sought to strengthen it more.

Czechoslovakia and later the Czech and Slovak Republics were intermediate cases. There was a tradition of a non-executive presidency in a parliamentary system, similar to that of the French Third Republic, inherited from Masaryk, the first Czechoslovak President and founder of the state, into which Havel easily fitted. Even under communism, the office of president had been retained and some of its traditions had even revived during the presidency of General Svoboda during the Prague Spring, with the idea of the President as a powerful moral leader. Vaclav Havel did not seek to be an executive president and was probably not suited to such a role anyway. In any case, reformers, including Havel, were rightly fearful of the dangers of establishing any new 'cult of personality' or strongman regime. This had indeed been an important part of their ambient 'anti-politics' credo. A parliamentary system therefore best suited tradition, the personalities concerned and the situation that prevailed at the time.

These concepts were later carried over into the new Czech and Slovak constitutions after 1993, with constitutional monarch type presidencies in parliamentary systems, with limited though important (more in Slovakia) powers to act as an arbiter and guarantor of the constitutional order and human rights.

FOUR PRESIDENTS

Notwithstanding the obvious fears throughout the region about creating an over-mighty presidency, it soon became apparent that there was a need for a presidency that could, in this extraordinary period of political turbulence, represent a centre of stability in shifting and often unstable parliamentary situations. There was also a need for a moral symbol in difficult times and for a respected national representative towards the outside world who could be an asset on the European and world stage, especially in the battle for membership of the IMF, Council of Europe, NATO and EU.

All four Presidents – Walesa (Poland, until 1995), Havel (Czech Republic), Göncz (Hungary), Kovac (Slovakia) – despite their very obvious differences in origin and personality, do, each in their own way, respond to some or all of these needs and have been successful in so far as the system in which they operate has allowed.

Vaclav Havel is clearly the most respected of the four, though like many earlier Czech leaders he was never so popular in Slovakia. He came from a respected Prague upper-middle-class family. His father was a well-known architect between the wars. Havel became a critical writer and playwright during the communist period and spent several periods in prison. He was active in developing the post 1968 'anti-politics', based on the concept of creating areas of space for a civil society independent of the party, in which, in one of his most telling phrases, people could 'live in truth'. He was a founder and later spokesman for the dissident organisation Charter 77, founded in 1977. He has developed a style and informality all his own. As President, first of Czechoslovakia and then of the Czech Republic, he has made a number of issues his own. He fought for the unity of the Czechoslovak state. He has worked for reconciliation between Czechoslovakia and Germany and with the expelled Sudeten Germans. He has been active in defending a broad conception of democracy and human rights. His liberalism has often brought him into conflict with his hard-line market-orientated Prime Minister Vaclav Klaus. After the 1996 elections, he became more politically active, arguing for some political change in response to the outcome of the election and later in response to the economic crisis that hit the Czech Republic in 1997. His remarriage to a younger actress after the death of his first wife Olga and his illness weakened his position and popularity. However, he was re-elected in January 1998, with the aim of helping to achieve early Czech membership of the European Union.

Hungarian President Arpad Göncz elected in 1990 and re-elected in 1995 is older than his colleagues. He was condemned to death after the 1956 rising and spent years in prison. He too is an intellectual and has translated English and American literature into Hungarian. He became a leading figure in the liberal opposition grouping, the Alliance of Free Democrats, and then became President, as it were, from the opposition benches as part of a broad compromise between the conservative MDF-led governing coalition after 1990 and the Free Democrats, required to mobilise the two-thirds majority needed for the election of the president and the passage of numerous constitutional laws. He became a respected national father-figure and guardian of the constitution, and as such has been active in matters relating to the rights of minorities, pluralism in the media and relations with Hungary's immediate neighbours where Hungarians also live (Slovakia and Romania).

Michael Kovacs, President of Slovakia since 1993, is a Protestant in a mainly Catholic country. Originally, he emerged from Public against Violence (VPN) and then moved with Vladimir Mečiar over to the Movement for a Democratic Slovakia (HZDS). He was Mečiar's candidate for the presidency in 1993, when Slovakia became independent, but rapidly came into conflict with Mečiar over the latter's style of government and Mečiar has made repeated efforts to remove him from the presidency. The two have now become bitter rivals for supremacy in the young Slovak democracy and their rivalry remains a serious destabilising factor. Kovac has tried to oppose authoritarian tendencies and uphold constitutional principles.

Lech Walesa was the most controversial of the four. He is not an intellectual. He was an electrician at the Lenin Shipyards in Gdansk and became active there as leader of the 1980 strike movement on the coast that was to oblige the government to recognise an independent trade union that was to become Solidarnosc. He was briefly interned after martial law was declared in December 1981, but remained the informal leader of the now underground Solidarnosc. He is an ardent Catholic and has been closely associated with the Polish Pope John Paul II. He was awarded the Nobel Prize and has been much honoured abroad. His relations with the more intellectual wing of Solidarnosc around people such as Kuron, Michnik, Geremek and later Mazowiecki, many of whom founded the KOR (Workers Defence Committee) and became advisors to Solidarnosc, were often stormy. He needed them, but they needed him as a populist tribune and a link to the working class from which he came and which he understood much better then they did. He alone was able to hold together the turbulent and fractious groupings that made up Solidarnosc, at least until it achieved power. After Mazowiecki became Prime Minister – he had been made so by Walesa – he tended to ignore Walesa, which was a serious error. In response, Walesa wandered off the reservation, voicing a populist critique of the new Solidarnosc government for making too many compromises with the old power holders and for moving too slowly on reform. He then defeated his own Prime Minister in the presidential election in 1990, causing Solidarnosc to split into two broad groupings – liberal and populist – which then in turn split further. As president, he has sought to maximise his powers and has not always done so wisely. He has posed as the main opposition to the post-communist coalition elected in 1993. He has shown that his old political abilities have not deserted him. Initially his popularity fell drastically and he seemed unlikely even to make it into the second round of the 1995 presidential election against the post-communist Kwasniewski. However, in the end he came through, mobilising opinion and presenting himself as the only candidate able to prevent the election of Kwasniewski, but was defeated in the second round. His pugnacity, and emotive, intuitive, populist and uncompromising, even arrogant and authoritarian style were at one and the same time his worst enemy in governing but his best asset in adversity. This has made him a real 'come-back kid', but not enough to defeat Kwasniewski in the second round.

PRESIDENTIAL POWERS

Poland

(i) Mode of Election

The President of Poland is elected by universal suffrage for a term of five years (1990, 1995, . . .) and an incumbent may only be re-elected once. Therefore, Lech Walesa, even if re-elected in November 1995 would have had to stand down at the end of that term. Elections shall be held no sooner than four months and no later than three months before the end of the current term. Elections are normally held on Sundays. In order to stand, candidates must present 100,000 voters' signatures on an election petition. This has not proved a serious obstacle, though some of the smaller right-wing groups have cooperated in collecting signatures by asking voters to sign for several parties at once, which they are entitled to do. There were 13 candidates in 1995 of which only five obtained more than 5 per cent of the vote in the first round.

Should no candidate obtain an absolute majority in the first round (50 per cent + 1), then a run-off takes place two weeks later between the top candidates remaining after any withdrawals. Normally, the top two will simply both remain in the field, though tactical withdrawal is possible. This is near to the French system. Discipline is much weaker and poll ratings much softer and more fluid than in France. Indeed, several candidates who had shown sustained significant poll ratings before the campaign actually obtained a derisory vote. In 1995, the various candidates of the right opposed to Walesa were unable to agree on one standard-bearer who might have relegated him to third position and have won a place in the run-off. There is no Vice President. In the event of a vacancy, a new election must be held. Results for the main candidates in the 1995 election are shown in Table 6.1.

Table 6.1   Results of the 1995 presidential election

	First round (%)	Second round
Kwasniewski (SLD)	38.0	
Walesa	31.0	
Kuron	9.0	
Olezewski (Conservative)	6.5	
Pawlak (PSL)	5.2	
Ms Gronkiewicz-Walz	3.8	
Others	6.5	

The election was interesting. It showed the emergence of a strong left bloc and the eclipse of the Peasant Party, the failure of the centre (Kuron) and the continued splitting of the anti-Walesa right. It also showed, both with Kwasniewski and Walesa, that the presidential elections are dominated more by personalities than by party. Two clear political camps which could mobilise and concentrate support between the rounds, which exist so effectively in France, and would have ensured the re-election of Walesa, do not exist in Poland. At the next election, though, the way will be open for a polarised two-camp system on the French model, as Walesa will not be able to stand again. There was, though, to be a battle for the Walesa inheritance, which has now, at least provisionally, been won by the led Solidarnosc groupings rather than more right-wing conservatives.

(ii) The Powers of the Presidency

There has as yet been no comprehensive revision of the 1952 Stalinist Constitution, though successive amendments, including most importantly the so-called 'Little Constitution' of 17 October 1992, have left little of the original intact. At the moment, the process of writing a new constitution is continuing and will eventually culminate in a national referendum. The role and functions, mode of election of the President and his relations with Government and Parliament were key issues addressed both in the 'Contractual Sejm' and in the Little Constitution.

The President is declared to be 'the supreme representative of the Polish State in internal and international relations' [§ 28(1)] and is charged with ensuring 'Observance of the Constitution...as well as upholding international treaties' [§28(2)]. He is also responsible for exercising 'general supervision with respect to the internal and external security of the state' [§34]. These vague, general powers of arbitration and oversight, similar to those of the French President, are, as in France, enhanced by popular election and have been used by President Walesa as the basis of strong presidential reading of the constitution and as a justification for an extensive – at times too extensive – use of his more specific powers independently of the government.

The President has all the classic powers of the head of state, appointment of Ambassadors and senior officials and the position of Commander-in-Chief of the armed forces, but here he cannot act independently of the government. There are exceptions. He can appoint the Chairman of the National Bank and three of the nine members of the State Broadcasting Commission on his own initiative. He can also exercise clemency without ministerial countersignature.

He does not normally chair the cabinet, though he can do so in important matters. He may require reports from ministers and the government has a general constitutional obligation to keep him informed about government business.

He has an important role in the legislative process. On the one hand, he can introduce legislation, and table amendments to his own bills in the course of their consideration. Interestingly, he may appoint representatives to defend bills that he sponsors before the Sejm and Senate and their committees. He may also address the Sejm. On the other hand, he can refer bills adopted by Parliament to the Constitutional Court for a binding opinion on their constitutionality, though, as always, the Sejm can override this opinion by a two-thirds majority. He also can exercise a presidential veto on any bill, including the budget. This veto can only be overridden by a two-thirds majority of the Sejm, as in the United States. Usually, the government coalition will not have a two-thirds majority on its own and would therefore need some opposition votes to override. Walesa has made ample and effective use of both the power of reference to the Court and the presidential veto. For example, he vetoed a liberal abortion bill and retrospective tax measures in the 1993 budget. He may also propose a national referendum.

Probably, though, his most important powers relate to the closely interlinked issues of government formation and dissolution of the Sejm. Here, his powers are weaker than those of the French President. He does not have an unfettered right to appoint the Prime Minister nor to dissolve the Sejm. He has an important role in both matters, but can only act when certain conditions are fulfilled. The constitutional provisions on cabinet appointment and dissolution of the Sejm are very complex and combine elements of the French system of considerable presidential discretion with the German model of constructive no-confidence and severe limits to the power of discretionary dissolution of the Sejm. Firstly, a new government must be formed after each Sejm election (German model) or obviously in the event of the resignation or defeat of the Prime Minister. In the first round, the President nominates a candidate at his total discretion. The Sejm then has 14 days to act on his nomination. Should the Sejm reject the President's nomination or not act on it within the time limit, it may then itself elect the Prime Minister by a majority of its membership, within a further time limit of 21 days. Should it not do so, the initiative reverts to the President, who can then nominate the same or another candidate, who he can then formally appoint if the nomination is approved by a simple majority of those voting within 21 days. If this candidate also fails, the Sejm may then elect its own candidate by a simple majority again within 21 days. Finally, if still no one is appointed, the president may either dissolve the Sejm, or appoint his own candidate for a six-month period. If such a Prime Minister is neither defeated nor given a vote of confidence within this six-month period, the President may also dissolve the Sejm, which has indeed been done on one occasion.

Normally, the Sejm must pass a constructive motion of no-confidence if it wishes to censure the government, indicating the new Prime Minister at the same time. This person must be appointed by the President. However, should the Sejm fail to elect a new Prime Minister, it then opens the way for the president either to accept the resignation of the Prime Minister or exercise the alternative option of a dissolution of the Sejm. If the annual budget is not adopted within three months after it is tabled, then the President may also dissolve the Sejm. Walesa has sought, so far unsuccessfully, to create such a situation by a late veto. Clearly, if the Sejm failed to override the veto it could open (by a two-thirds majority required) the way to its own dissolution by the President. Here, Walesa used this lever in 1994 to provoke a change in Prime Minister, though with the same coalition.

Other ministers are proposed by the Prime Minister and must be appointed by the President – the exception was the three constitutionally specified so-called 'presidential ministers', the ministers of foreign affairs, defence and interior (hence police and internal security). These ministers could only be appointed after consultation with the President.

This does not amount to a formal veto, let alone a right to impose a person, but, in practice, Walesa has achieved that result. Hence, particularly in the coalition of post-communist parties between 1993 and 1997 these presidential ministers did not come from the coalition parties and represented potential cuckoos in the nest for the government, and have now been abolished.

The constitution as adopted is a much more parliamentary text than the 1992 Little Constitution. The President's powers have been significantly reduced. This was the goal of SLD at least as long as Walesa remained in power. By the time roles were reversed, with Kwasniewski elected as President and the SDL likely to lose its parliamentary majority, it was too late for SDL to change direction and argue for a more presidential system. Compared with the Little Constitution, the President has lost powers in several key areas. He can now only dissolve the Sejm in two very limited cases either where the Sejm fails to approve his nominee for Prime Minister or elect an alternative, or where the Sejm rejects the Budget. Furthermore, where the first condition is met, he must now dissolve the Sejm and may not appoint a 'presidential cabinet'. His veto can now be overridden by the lower Sejm majority of 60 per cent. He is no longer actively involved in the day-to-day work of the Government and no longer has decisive influence on the three former so-called 'presidential ministers'. Even where he can act, he must now do so with a Prime Ministerial countersignature. The role of the Prime Minister has been clarified and significantly uprated. He has now become a real head of Government. The position of the executive has also been strengthened by the new provision that it can only be removed by a constructive no-confidence vote and by the weakening of the Senate. The former right of the Sejm to overrule judgements of the Constitutional Tribunal by a two-thirds majority vote will disappear after a two-year phasing out period. The wide range of social and economic rights contained in the 1952 communist Constitution has been retained. Some commentators now ask whether the balance has not gone in terms of reducing the powers of the President and whether the new more symbolic President should actually be directly elected.

Slovakia

(i) Mode of Election

The Slovak President is not directly elected by the people. He is elected by Parliament (unicameral) by a three-fifths majority (at least 90 votes) for a five-year term. Unusually, he may be removed at any time, equally by a three-fifths majority, by a purely parliamentary, non-judicial process. Thus normally some opposition votes will be required for election or removal, though the additional margin may not be very great. For example, the present three-party coalition disposes of 83 of the 90 votes needed.

(ii) Powers of the President

The powers of the Slovak President make him the second most powerful head of state in the region, after his Polish colleague. The Slovak system was no doubt intended to be a parliamentary system, with a figurehead President. The constitution was drafted in extreme haste in late 1992 and it omitted to specify that the president was subordinated to the government in the exercise of his powers. Thus, there is no provision for counter-signature nor any requirement to act automatically on a government proposal. He can exercise all his powers independently, though on appointments there must be a Government proposal, but he need not accept it. This interpretation has been confirmed by the Constitutional Court. President Kovac has on at least two occasions refused ministerial nomination of the Prime Minister or has refused to sack ministers. He can chair the cabinet and require ministers to submit reports to him. He is therefore in a strong position *vis-à-vis* the Government.

On the other hand, he is in a much weaker position *vis-à-vis* parliament. He cannot normally dissolve parliament. He can only do so in the very unlikely situation that the government's programme is rejected three times within six months. However, of course, were such a situation to arise he could dissolve Parliament without the approval of the government, as for all other actions. He can submit bills and attend parliament. He can refer matters to the Constitutional Court. He has a weak suspensive veto on bills. There is no special majority required to override, only a second parliamentary vote. Most seriously, he can be removed at any time by a three-fifths vote in Parliament, and Mečiar is actively seeking to achieve this at the moment.

The Czech Republic

(i) Mode of Election

The Czech President like the Czechoslovak President is elected by Parliament and not by the people. In theory the Czech Parliament is bicameral, with an Assembly (200 members) and Senate (81 members).

Until the Senate was created, the Assembly combined the powers of the two chambers. Under the bicameral system, the President is elected in a joint sitting of both chambers. Nominations can be made by ten Deputies of Senators. In the first round of voting, any candidate who obtains an absolute majority among both Deputies (101) and Senators (41) is elected. If no candidate achieves this 'double majority' a second round is held between the candidates having achieved most votes in each chamber. If still no one wins a majority of both Senators and Deputies, a third round with new candidates is possible 14 days later. At present, the Assembly alone elects the President – Vaclav Havel was elected Federal President in 1992, but could not be re-elected in the Federal parliament after the 1992 elections due to Slovak opposition. He was then elected Czech President in 1993, with the support of Prime Minister Vaclav Klaus and he was re-elected in January 1998. No one can serve more than two consecutive terms.

(ii) Powers of the President

Prime Minister Vaclav Klaus certainly did not want a strong presidency. The new Czech presidency is actually weaker than the old federal presidency. For example, the Czech President no longer has the right of legislative initiative. The formal powers of the President are quite limited and resemble those of a constitutional monarch in a parliamentary system. He formally appoints the Prime Minister, and on his proposal the other ministers, but this is more in the nature of a formality, since the counter-signature of the Prime Minister is required. He has all the other classical functions of the head of state, special appointments, where a ministerial counter-signature is always required (§62). He may address messages to Parliament, but has no formal right of legislative initiative. Vaclav Havel has used this power to recomend variously a creation of a constitutional court, establishment of the Senate, and creation on regional authorities, especially in Moravia. He has a suspensive veto on legislation, which forces Parliament to vote again, but only requires an absolute majority (101 votes) to override. On occasions, such as in relation to the discriminatory bill on compensation of Second World War resistance fighters, this veto held up, as only 78 votes were cast to override. The weak state of both party and even coalition discipline in the Czech Parliament gives this veto power more potential bite than might appear on paper. He has a very limited power of dissolution of Parliament. This can only be activated under four restrictive conditions. Where the President's nominee for Prime Minister is rejected a second time, then the President shall appoint a nominee of the Speaker of Parliament. If this nominee fails to win a vote of confidence, then the President can dissolve Parliament. Equally, he may dissolve parliament if after three months Parliament has not acted on a bill that the Government has declared to be a matter of confidence. He may also dissolve if there has been no quorum in Parliament for three months, which is very unlikely. He can also refer matters to the Constitutional Court. Despite his limited powers, President Havel is an important moral authority and a popular symbolic figure. As such, the Klaus government, which often disagreed with him on issues and opposes a stronger presidency, considered him to be an important international asset, in terms of the image of the Czech Republic in the EU and the United States.

Hungary

(i) Mode of Election

The Hungarian President is also indirectly elected by parliament. Indeed, as we have seen, the option of a directly elected presidency was promoted by the reform communists and explicitly rejected by the liberal opposition Free Democrats. The President is therefore elected for five years (one year longer than the term of the parliament) by parliament. Nominees require the support of 50 Deputies to stand. Clearly, this restricts the number of candidates. Ferenc Madl, a former MDF minister, who stood against incumbent president Arpad Göncz in June 1995, had to stand as the candidate of several centre-right opposition parties. A two-thirds majority is required for election. If no one wins with the necessary majority in the first two rounds, in a third round there is a run-off between the top two contenders. The whole process must be completed within three days. At present the ruling coalition controls a two-thirds majority, but usually, as in 1990, some opposition support will be needed to elect the president.

(ii) Powers of the President

The Hungarian President has few independent powers. He is more in the nature of a father figure, above ordinary politics, than an active political figure, though his reserve powers can be important. He nominates a Prime Minister, who must be elected by Parliament. This power is severely restricted by the stability of the Hungarian party system and by the fact that the two elections (1990 and 1994) have produced clear majority coalitions. He has in reality had no discretion in any of three

Prime Ministerial nominations that he has been called on to make (Mr Antall in 1990, Mr Boross in 1994 on Antall's death and Mr Horn in 1994). The constructive no-confidence system introduced on the German model in 1990 also means that the President would have no discretion in the event of a no-confidence motion. He can only dissolve parliament after four no-confidence votes in 12 months or if parliament fails to act on his nominee for Prime Minister within 40 days. He makes all senior appointments, but is bound, closely, as the Constitutional Court has ruled, by the proposals of the government. Clearly, in some limited cases, especially in relation to judges and heads of broadcasting bodies, he could exercise a degree of discretion, and has done so.

In conclusion, it may be said that the presidents of the region have played an important diplomatic and symbolic role, initiating the Visegrad Co-operation Process and holding annual informal meetings. They have also been important factors of stability in the difficult transition period, more by the force of personality, contribution to the collapse of communism and example than through their formal powers. Even in Poland a fairly strong presidency was not institutionalised beyond its first 'historical' incumbent, Lech Walesa.

7 The Governments

All four countries have what is basically a parliamentary system, which means that the Government, responsible to Parliament, is the locus of executive power. Even in Poland and Slovakia, where the President of the Republic exercises real political power and has a strong constitutional position and the system thus exhibits some semi-presidential features, day-to-day executive power is very much in the hands of the Government. Formally, and to outward appearances, that had also been the position during the communist period, though the official state machinery had in reality been subordinated to the parallel party organs. After 1989, the state had to rediscover its autonomy and capacity for independent action. The new political leaders that came to power then had to take control of the state machine and make it operate in pursuit of new objectives and with new methods. Western modes of governance, the rule of law, political and legal accountability, open and democratic political debate, compromise and coalition politics all had to be discovered or rediscovered in a short period of time in societies that were quite unfamiliar with these concepts.

The executive branch, that is the Government, soon became the natural focus of leadership in the reform process. The new political leaders, catapulted often literally overnight from prison cell to ministerial office, had to make the difficult transition from a sceptical dissident, rightly suspicious of political power, to a wielder of political power, a decision-taker. They had to make the government machine dance to a new democratic and market-orientated tune, without destroying it. Only the total, disorientating and demoralising collapse of communism made this possible, minimising the latent obstructive friction from the still extant old bureaucracy. Inevitably, though not openly hostile, the old cadres could hardly be expected to show much initiative, imagination or risk-taking in favour of the new political course that was imposed on them by their new masters. What new structures and what reforms were needed?

POLAND

The Polish Council of Ministers (Cabinet) is the executive branch. It is given specific powers and duties under the Little Constitution of 1992. It is stated that 'it shall conduct the internal affairs and foreign policy of the

Republic of Poland' [Article 51(1)], and shall 'manage the entire governmental administration' [Article 51(2). The Government is also em-
powered to ensure the implementation of the laws; issue regulations with
the force of law, where authorised by the Sejm to do so; draw up budgets
and submit them to the Sejm and then implement them when passed;
direct, coordinate and control all the organs of the state administration;
supervise local government; conduct foreign and defence policy and
draft legislation for submission to the Sejm.

The Council of Ministers is made up of the Prime Minister, Deputy
Premiers and Ministers. There are currently 20 ministers. Rather unusually, certain office holders who are not Ministers may also be members of
the Council of Ministers. These include the heads of certain commis-
sions and agencies. The Council of Ministers collectively and the individual
ministers are responsible to the Sejm, though not to the Senate.
The Sejm may remove the Government or individual ministers by a
vote of no-confidence passed by an absolute majority. A minimum of 46
Sejm deputies (10 per cent of the total) is required to table a motion of
no-confidence.

As we have seen, the Prime Minister is appointed by a complex inter-
action between the President of the Republic and the Sejm. A new
Government is in any case formed after each election to the Sejm, but
not necessarily after a presidential election. The other ministers are
appointed by the President on the proposal of the Prime Minister. A new
Government takes office after receiving a vote of confidence from the
Sejm on its programme, except where the Sejm fails to act within the
time-limit laid down in the Constitution. The President does not have a
generalised power of dismissal of the Prime Minister or other ministers.
The Prime Minister may propose to the President the dismissal of certain ministers. However, the agreement of the President is not always a
formality here. The Prime Minister fixes the functions of each ministry.
He chairs the cabinet and sets its agenda. However, the President may
summon, attend and chair the Cabinet on matters of extreme importance. This is very rare. The Ministers of Foreign Affairs, Defence and
the Interior are so-called 'presidential ministers' on whose appointment
the President must be consulted and to which he must in practice agree.
This was important between 1993 and 1996, when there was conflict
between the then President Walesa and the SLD/PSL coalition; then,
these ministers were outside the government parties and could not be
dismissed without the President's agreement. Now, under SLD President Kwasniewski, these presidential ministers become less important,
and have now been abolished under the new constitution adopted in 1997.

The Prime Minister is much more than a mere *primus inter pares*. He may propose the removal of ministers to the President, or reshuffle the Cabinet, with the approval of the President. He chairs the cabinet and may ask it to revoke decisions of individual ministers, though he may not instruct a minister to act. Individual ministers are constitutionally responsible for directing their ministries and are politically responsible to the Sejm. They may be assisted by state secretaries, appointed by the Prime Minister on the recommendation of the minister concerned. There are permanent cabinet committees on Economic and Social policy, Foreign Policy and Defence and Security. Other committees may be created. Some key ministers, such as the Finance Minister, sit on all cabinet committees. These committees prepare the work of the full Cabinet, which meets weekly. The Cabinet Office, headed by a minister of cabinet rank, coordinates the work of the cabinet and its committees.

There is no formal coalition committee, as there is for example in Hungary, though representatives of the two coalition parties (SLD and PSL) meet weekly and indeed coordination between the two parliamentary groups of the majority remains weak. It is not unusual that even SLD deputies – one of the more disciplined parties in the Sejm – do not all vote together, even on government bills. Formal whipping decisions are rarely taken, unless it is essential. The SLD and the PSL groups can and do actually vote differently. The bill on the privatisation of the tobacco industry was a case in point: here, 26 PSL deputies voted against this government measure. Thus, the Government's majority is much less solid and predictable than it would appear on paper. Majorities often have to be built or shored up on a case-by-case basis, though the reservoir of 298 SLD and PSL deputies normally can provide the bulk of the necessary 231 votes for a majority.

HUNGARY

Hungary was the first country in the region to establish a fully parliamentary Government, based on a coalition between several parties, confronted by a credible, non-communist opposition. The first government after the fall of communism was a three-party centre-right coalition of the MDF, Christian Democrats and Smallholders. The government formed after 1994 was a two-party social-liberal coalition of the MSZP and the SDS. Hungary also established a stable and effective system of 'gouvernement de législature'. The Prime Minister is elected by Parliament on a proposal from the President of the Republic, after debating the new government's proposed programme. The other ministers are then appointed by the President on the recommendation of the Prime Minister. The government remains accountable to Parliament and may be dismissed by a vote of no-confidence. Hungary has however copied the German model of a constructive no-confidence vote, which makes toppling of a Government by purely negative majorities impossible. The motion must also at the same time propose an alternative Prime Minister. As a result, few no-confidence motions are tabled and none have passed. The assumption of government and opposition alike is that a government once in place will last for the full four-year term. The government remains accountable to Parliament and must keep it informed on all policy measures.

Several new ministries were established in the early period after 1989, such as a Ministry of Industry and Trade and a Ministry of International Economic Relations, both of which had a key role in the process of economic transformation. The total number of ministries was kept small, though state secretaries were appointed in most ministries. There were only 13 ministers in the Antall government. The Horn government comprises 12 departmental ministers and one minister without portfolio. The Ministry for International Affairs was abolished and its functions transferred to other ministries. Numerous independent, semi-independent specialised agencies were formed.

The present MSZP/SDS coalition government's composition, structure, policy and *modus operandi* is laid down, often in great detail, in a formal coalition agreement between the two parties, which was ratified by congresses of both parties. This was not the case in 1990, but no doubt will now be the future pattern. This coalition agreement was drawn up in a series of bipartite committees, including one on the structure of government and another on operating rules for the government and a plenary negotiating committee composed of heavyweight delegations from both parties.

Given the fact that the MSZP alone has a majority both in Parliament and in the Cabinet, SDS attached the greatest importance to laying down formal rules that would ensure that the parties would each have a mutual veto on all major decisions. Thus, the agreement states that the two parties intend to 'govern jointly', which means joint decision-taking. The agreement establishes a procedure of permanent consultation between the Prime Minister Horn (MSZP) and his 'Coalition Deputy' Interior Minister Kuncze (SDS), equivalent to a Vice-Premier. They are required to confer in the first instance to resolve inter-party differences. Clearly, the Cabinet cannot operate by formal vote, as the SDS has only three ministers. The coalition parties must reach agreement on policy programmes, bills, treaties, privatisation measures, budget targets and on the exchange rate. They can also only act by consensus on all major appointments, listed in an appendix to the agreement. This list includes the heads of the security forces and the secret service. Both parties must be represented in all cabinet committees that may be set up, though none is directly specified in the agreement itself. State secretaries are provided for in all ministries. As a rule they are drawn from the same party as the minister, though the SDS does have a state secretary in the MSZP-led Foreign Ministry. The college of administrative state secretaries (senior civil servants in each ministry) is established as a preparatory body for Cabinet meetings. There are three inner cabinets: the political inner cabinet, composed of the Premier, his coalition deputy and the Finance Minister; the economic cabinet, involving the economic ministers and the SDS Minister of Transport and the President of the National Bank; and the national security cabinet chaired by the SDS Interior Minister. This keeps a delicate balance of representation and chairmanship between the parties.

The coalition agreement also established the ground-rules for co-operation between the two parliamentary parties of the coalition, envisaging far tighter discipline than in Poland or even the Czech Republic. A Coalition Coordination Council involving the Prime Minister, his SDS Deputy, the two group leaders, the two party chairs and one other representative of each party has been established to settle disagreements regarding parliamentary business by consensus. Parliamentary offices are also shared out in the agreement, not only between the MSZP and the SDS, but also with the opposition parties, according them a degree of over-representation. The agreement commits the two parties to support bills in Parliament only on the basis of a prior joint agreement and to consult on all parliamentary activities and initiatives. They are also pledged to vote together and to provide the necessary majority backing for all agreed measures, including of course government measures. This formula gives the SDS a *de facto* veto and allows for some permitted dissidence in each group, provided that it does not endanger the required majority.

The centre-right opposition parties have reached a preliminary agreement to act together to form a Government after the 1998 election, if they have the necessary majority to do so. They will undoubtedly draw up a fairly detailed joint platform and then if they go into government a detailed coalition agreement like the present one. Hungary has therefore achieved a stable executive and tight party discipline, but with clear and operative provision for alternation in government, which is a sign of political maturity.

THE CZECH REPUBLIC

The Czechoslovak Federation had three governments, a Federal Government and separate Czech and Slovak Governments. After separation became inevitable in 1992, a short-lived transition government, with equal numbers of Czech and Slovaks, was set up to oversee the separation. The theatre of political action then moved to the republican governments that became fully-fledged sovereign governments on 1 January 1993. Thus, from June 1992, Vaclav Klaus, the ODS leader, who had been Federal Finance Minister, left the Federal Government and became Czech Prime Minister, which he remained after January 1993.

The Czech Republic has a parliamentary system, with a strong Prime Minister. The Prime Minister is formally appointed by the President of the Republic and must win a vote of confidence in the lower house within 30 days. Though the President can and does undertake some exploratory discussion with political leaders before he makes a nomination and undoubtedly can seek to exercise some influence on the government formation process, his discretion remains limited, even where there is no clear majority. The process after the 1996 election is instructive. The outgoing coalition only won 99 out of 200 seats. It needed the support or at least toleration of the CSSD opposition, the main gainers in the election. President Havel consulted widely. It was an open secret that he would have preferred a coalition under the (Christian Democratic Union–Czech Peoples Party) KDU–CSL leader or under an ODS politician other than Mr Klaus. But he could not achieve this, even though Mr Klaus was obliged to take on board some of the desiderata of both his KDU–CSL and ODA coalition partners and of CSSD. The Constitution does not specify that an absolute majority is required to endorse the nomination, only a relative one. Hence, a minority government could survive with some deliberate abstentions. The Government as a whole is accountable to the Chamber, but not the Senate. It may pass a motion of no-confidence by an absolute majority or refuse a motion of confidence. However, such a motion can only be tabled by a minimum of 50 deputies. In the last legislature no opposition party could muster this support alone. Now CSSD can do so.

The Government is relatively small with only 17 members. It was dominated by ODS during 1992–6. Now, ODS had been obliged to relinquish its majority in the cabinet and sign a more binding coalition agreement. In the last term, the coalition held all chairs of parliamentary committees. This has now changed. CSSD Chairman Zeman has become Speaker of the Chamber and CSSD has obtained some committee chairs, including the Budget Committee. The Prime Minister and other ministers are active in their parliamentary groups. Klaus attends the ODS group once a month. Voting discipline within the coalition is strong, though cases of divergent voting do occur. There is a 13-member Coalition Committee including 9 coalition MPs. In the new situation after the 1996 election, where the coalition parties are a minority, they will have to include CSSD in policy deliberation.

SLOVAKIA

The new Slovak Constitution of 1993 lays down fairly detailed rules in relation to the Government. It provided that the President of the Republic appoints the Prime Minister and on his proposal the other ministers and fixes their departmental competences. The government automatically resigns after an election, though it remains in office until replaced. The requirement of presidential appointment is not, as the Constitutional Court has confirmed, a mere formality. The President can and has withheld his agreement. Once appointed, the new government must obtain a vote of confidence by a simple majority within 30 days, as in the Czech Republic. The National Council (Parliament) can dismiss the government as a whole or indeed individual ministers by an absolute majority on a motion proposed by at least 30 deputies. Ministers are accountable to Parliament and must report to it on their activities. Both the plenary and committees can require the attendance of ministers. Ministers must, as in France, give up their seats in Parliament. Currently there are 14 ministers in a three-party coalition Movement for a Democratic Slovakia, Slovak National Party and Workers Party. The HZDS of Prime Minister Mečiar is the dominant partner in the coalition. In this young Republic, the structure of Government has far from stabilised and change is likely to continue for some time to come, as elsewhere in the region.

The Constitution enumerates (article 119) a number of key items on which the government (rather than individual ministers) must decide collectively, by an absolute majority vote. These include: presentation of bills to Parliament, tabling of the budget, treaties, major appointments and dismissals of officials, policy programmes, requests to Parliament for a vote of confidence, government regulations and decrees that require the signature of the Prime Minister. The President of the Republic may attend and chair the Cabinet, but does not do so as a rule. Indeed, relations between the present incumbent and the Prime Minister are so cool that this would cause a major embarrassment.

The working of the Slovak government has been something of a paradox. The Government has itself has been dominated for most of the time both before and after independence by the centralising and autocratic Prime Minister Mečiar. However, structurally and politically, the executive has appeared weak in relation both to Parliament, the President of the Republic and the Constitutional Court, all of which have sought and indeed obtained some control over the Government. When the Constitution was being drafted, it was assumed that the Prime Minister's apparent power to appoint or dismiss ministers freely, to return bills to Parliament for reconsideration and to link (as in France) a vote on a bill to a vote of confidence in the government, gave him the levers of strong prime ministerial government, especially when linked with Mečiar's personality. In reality, his autocratic tendencies have provoked an opposite reaction, in the form of conflicts, splits and on two occasions his removal from office. Party and coalition discipline remains weak and other bodies have set the limits of prime ministerial power.

8 Local Government

The reform, reconstruction and revitalisation of local government was just as urgent and difficult a task in 1989 as reform at national level. Indeed, the revitalisation of local government was one of the key conditions for creating a new civil society and political space that would make the new democratic institutions function. Under communism, local government had for all practical purposes lost its autonomy and become part of the transmission belt system of the regime. However, it was, in 1989, potentially a vital tool in the reform project. It was at the cutting edge of delivering services to the citizens; it was their first and most immediate contact with the state, demonstrating to them at first hand the new and more human face of the democratic system; it was the laboratory and school of democratic politics. Local party activists, councillors and local NGOs could represent a larger and more widely distributed network of civil society then central government elites, and initiate a large number of people into some form of political activity and public responsibility, learning the need for personal commitment and responsibility, dialogue, compromise and tolerance that had not existed under communism.

Before 1989, the central European states had been highly centralised in practice, even Czechoslovakia which was theoretically at least a Federation. Federalism was only skin deep and had always been seen as 'unequal' by Slovak nationalists and in any case disappeared after 1993, with the break-up of Czechoslovakia. References to an attenuated form of federalism or regionalism in the form of autonomous bodies for Moravia and Silesia remained in the Czech Constitution, but were not immediately implemented, as ODS opposed all form of decentralisation. Since the inconclusive 1996 elections, it is conceivable that these constitutional provisions will be implemented, as all other parties now wish to see progress on this issue. The other three states are all highly centralised.

What were the problems faced in reforming local government? Firstly, as with other reforms, there was a degree of urgency. Local government could not be left for too long in a time warp, as an unreconstructed bastion of the old system. Without fairly radical action, especially in the countryside, the old local elites might even survive what were formally at least democratic elections. The new Governments needed more than simply neutralising local government. They needed the active support of local government in carrying through the reform process. On the other hand, too early elections might bring in inexperienced people or legitimise the old guard in power. It should not be forgotten that significant resources in terms of buildings, housing stock, enterprises and between 10 and 20 per cent of all public expenditure was in the hands of local government. It was also important to establish special new structures in the capitals, Warsaw, Prague and Budapest, as it was an important matter of political symbolism who controlled the capital. All capitals showed the same particularity. The most liberal wing of the reform movement (the Dienstbier wing of OF in Prague, SDS in Budapest and UW in Warsaw) were much stronger than average in the capitals. Mayors often came from the liberal opposition groupings. It was therefore vital to establish early democratically and operationally viable structures, anchor principles of autonomous local self-government in the Constitution or basic laws and find a balance between adequate financial autonomy and necessary compliance with national spending controls.

HUNGARY

Under the Constitution, all local government legislation requires a two-thirds majority in Parliament, which during the 1990–4 legislative term required cooperation between the centre-right coalition and the liberal opposition parties and in particular the SDS. Nevertheless, important local government reforms were enacted during the first part of this parliamentary term. There were six major statutes enacted in 1990 and 1991, dealing with the election of local councils, powers of local authorities, financing, relations between local and central authorities and the reorganisation of local government in Budapest. The old system of central tutelage was abolished. The powers and responsibilities of local government were significantly widened and the system of local government finances was reformed. At the same time, the structure of local government was streamlined. In the pre-1989 structure, there had been no less than eight different types of local authority, which has now been reduced to four, but there has been a doubling of the number of authorities from 1,542 in 1989 to 3,089 now.

As elsewhere and not only in central Europe, the two most difficult areas have been financing and coordination. The reforms have evidently greatly strengthened Hungarian local government and given it a degree of autonomy, but in the first flush of enthusiasm for freeing local government from its shackles, inadequate attention was paid to the need, even in a democracy, for some degree of central coordination to ensure that minimum standards and minimum competence in administration are met and that local policies do not breach national policy dictates. Thus, the Counties no longer have supervisory powers over the lower tiers of authorities in their areas, which can lead to very real difficulties. The thrust of the reforms, with at times unfortunate results, has been to progressively separate devolved central state functions from the functions of autonomous local authorities, which had in Hungary as elsewhere in the region, previously been fused in all-purpose People's Committees.

There now 3,092 municipalities (2,915 villages and 177 towns); 1,663 have under 1,000 inhabitants and only 9 over 100,000 inhabitants. There are also County administrations, which provide regional services and deal with the coordination of physical planning and socio-economic policy. The second tier above the municipalities was abolished. There are also decentralised state administrative offices at County level, supervised by seven regional Commissioners of the Republic and one for Budapest. These Commissioners, equivalent to the French Préfets, are appointed by the President of the Republic on the proposal of the Prime Minister.

At the County level, a mixed system of election has been introduced. Alongside County Councils, appointed Regional Councils, representing the various socio-economic interests and public bodies have been set up. These bodies are responsible for drawing up regional development plans and allocating block grants. This achieves, by the back door as it were, a partial reintegration of the decentralised national authorities and the elected local authorities. For its part, Budapest has a two-tier local government structure.

Municipalities are responsible for providing general local services. They may also undertake any functions or tasks delegated to them by other state authorities and any activities not prohibited by law. In that sense, they are all-purpose authorities. They have therefore a hard core of mandatory tasks undertaken on behalf of the central state. Key areas of responsibility are civil defence, education, hospitals, primary health care (shared with the central government), nursery education, town planning, sanitation, leisure and cultural activities, roads and district heating provision. Municipalities may cooperate with each other so as to improve the provision of services to their populations and they may even cooperate internationally with other municipalities in neighbouring countries. In terms of their expenditure, education and health are the largest items, accounting together for 59 per cent of municipal budgets. Local government revenues are derived form local taxation, such as property taxes, taxes on tourism and local taxes on services, from shared taxes such as a share of income tax revenue and from block grants from central government.

Councillors are elected for a fixed term of four years. Authorities with under 10,000 inhabitants have from 3 to 13 members, depending on population, elected at large. In larger municipalities, with over 10,000 inhabitants, a mixed system of district and list systems applies, with up to 30 councillors for the largest authorities. Since 1994, there is only one single round for the district seats, with election therefore by first past the post. These mixed systems are almost entirely party-based. In the smaller authorities many non-party councillors are still elected. County Councils have one councillor per 10,000 voters, with a minimum of 50 members. Executive authority is in the hands of a full-time paid mayor, directly elected by the people for a term of four years. He supervises and runs the administration. The elected Council must establish a finance committee and may establish other committees. There are interesting provisions for local referenda and popular initiatives at local level. Referenda are mandatory for fusions of municipalities or splitting up existing municipalities. A minimum of one-quarter of the elected councillors, a Council committee or a proportion of the voters of the municipality fixed at a level between 10 and 25 per cent by local by-laws can initiate a referendum. Such a proposal is not binding on the Council, which may reject it. However, the outcome of a referendum once held is binding on the Council. A popular initiative may be proposed by 10 per cent of the voters in a municipality and must be debated by the Council within one month, but the Council is not obliged to act upon it.

POLAND

The Solidarnosc-based governments that held office between 1989 and 1993 were enthusiastic about local government reform, as a key part of the wider process of political reform. They were preparing far-reaching new reform measures that have been suspended by the SLD/PSL coalition after. This was in large measure due to PSL opposition to reforms which would have strengthened the intermediate tier at the expense of the smaller rural municipalities which constitute an important power base for the PSL. These intended reforms would have partially reversed the abolition of the District level that resulted from earlier reforms in 1973–5. The 1990 reform did not attack the problem of structure, but concentrated the supervision and coordination of decentralised central government functions in the 49 Voivodships (Counties), under a Voivod

(Préfet) appointed by the Council of Ministers and instructed by the central government. He may appoint local sub-directors. He is subject to a degree of local democratic control by the Voivod Assembly, made up of delegated councillors from the local authorities making up the Voivod.

At the local level, there are now 2,549 municipalities of which the smallest has 858 inhabitants and the largest (Lodz) has 846,514 inhabitants. Of these, by far the largest number, 1,547 in all, are rural municipalities. Warsaw is a special case. It is a so-called Union of Boroughs, bringing together the seven boroughs of the capital under an upper tier federal structure, with, in all, 1,654,491 inhabitants. Amalgamations and splits in existing authorities require a decree of the Council of Ministers, after consolation of the inhabitants of the areas concerned and the local Voivod.

Councils are elected for a fixed term of four years by proportional representation on a list system, with each municipality with under 200,000 inhabitants returning between 15 and 45 councillors depending on size. Larger municipalities elect an additional five councillors per 100,000 population, up to a maximum size of 100 councillors in total. Lodz, the largest municipality, with almost 850,000 inhabitants, has 80 councillors. The Council elects an Executive Committee made up of the mayor, elected by the Council by a two-thirds majority, four deputies who need not be councillors, and 4–7 councillors. This body prepares and implements the decisions of the full Council. It is assisted by the full-time professional municipal secretary. Municipalities may organise local referenda and receive citizens initiatives.

The main functions of local government in Poland are roads, traffic planning, utilities, sewerage, municipal housing, culture, arts and leisure, local social services and central state functions devolved to it. Municipalities may levy local taxes, but they also receive a share of certain national taxes, such as income and corporation tax. They may also raise loans, but only up to a ceiling of 5 per cent of their overall expenditure in any given year.

There remain strict supervisory controls over local government decisions, which must be submitted to the Voivod who may annul the decision within thirty days if he finds it to be unlawful. Repeated violations of legality may lead to the suspension or even dissolution of a municipality and its replacement by a central government Commissioner, though this requires the approval of the Sejm, on a proposal from the Prime Minister. Appeal against such decisions lies to the courts.

The next stage of reform, dealing with the further decentralisation of local government functions, complete separation of municipal self-government functions and devolved central government functions, entrenchment of local government autonomy and a revenue sharing scheme in the Constitution and reform of local government in the large cities, was shelved by the SLD/PSL government, but these issues are real and will eventually require solution.

THE CZECH REPUBLIC

The constitutional provisions (article 101 in particular) relating to local government in the Czech Republic are fairly detailed and firmly entrench the rights and autonomy of local government. In the old Czechoslovak Federation there were over 6,000 municipalities, 71 districts and 7 regions in the Czech lands. The districts and regions were decentralised central government agencies. The regions were then abolished in 1990. The districts were retained, essentially still as decentralised agencies of central government, but with alongside it an elected District Assembly with some limited supervisory and budgetary powers, including sharing out central Government grants between the individual municipalities. The main issues of debate about local government reform in the Czech Republic are the question of decentralisation and the creation of an intermediate or even semi-federal structure, which is recognised in the Constitution, though it has as yet not been implemented. Opinion is divided on this issue. It is favoured by most parties except ODS and in Moravia opinion runs strongly in favour of at least some decentralisation. The Czech Republic has also met the problem found all over the region of disentangling devolved central functions from those of municipal self-government, the continued fragmentation of the municipalities, which is actually stronger in the Czech Republic then elsewhere.

The Constitution lays down that the territory of the Republic shall be divided into so-called higher units of territorial self-administration (regions or lands such as Bohemia, Moravia and Silesia). These authorities are to be established by a special constitutional law, requiring a three-fifths majority. This has not yet happened, due to ODS opposition. In the new situation after the 1996 election, progress can be expected on this issue. The basic unit of local government is the municipality. As already indicated, the districts are not local authorities, but decentralised agencies of central Government. There are as yet no regions, as we have seen. There are now 75 districts plus Prague and 5,678 municipalities, a significant increase on the 4,120 that existed in 1968, but fewer than the

11,051 that existed in 1950. The largest (Prague) has 1,212,010 and the smallest just nine inhabitants; 4,513 municipalities have less than 1,000 inhabitants. Mergers and division of municipalities require the agreement of the municipalities concerned, including possibly a local referendum and also ministerial approval.

Another familiar ambiguity lies in the fact that as agents of central authority, the districts supervise and audit the accounts of the municipalities in their area. In that capacity the district authority can suspend unlawful decisions of the municipalities and investigate irregularities in the financial administration of 'their' municipalities. The districts' main task, though, is to exercise decentralised functions of the central state. Conceptually at least they are intended to be all-purpose bodies in that role, giving them a coordinating role, based on an overview of contiguous and possibly overlapping policy areas, depending on different national ministries that could be in conflict, but this neat structure has been increasingly breached by the creation of numerous *ad hoc* decentralised agencies, often with a different geographical remit than the 'all purpose' districts. The Head of the district office is a central Government appointment.

Municipalities exercise general competences in relation to the provision of local services and many functions delegated to them by the central authorities. Councils are elected for a fixed term of four years and have between 7 and 70 members, depending on their population and size. Councils may establish committees and most larger ones do so. The creation of both a finance committee and an audit committee is mandatory. The Council elects the mayor, who chairs the Council and heads the executive committee (5–13 members). The political executive is assisted by a municipal office and specialised offices established to handle particular functions delegated by the central government. Municipalities may cooperate in the provision of costly services. Prague and some other larger cities such as Brno, Plzen, Olomouc, Ceske Budejovoice and Ostrava have a special status, which varies slightly from one to the other. They have a kind of federal structure, with an umbrella authority for the whole city and sub-divisions, based on identifiable quarters of the city, which exercise certain localised functions. Local referenda may be held, but not on fiscal matters. Local government is financed by local property taxes, fees, licences, revenue from the provision of services, raising loans, shares of certain national taxes and national block grants distributed by the districts. A very real problem has arisen from conflict between the increasingly fragmented and therefore politically, financially and administratively weak local authorities and the powerful pseudo government

of the districts, equipped with considerable powers of control and patronage and the aura of central authority, which dies hard.

SLOVAKIA

The Slovak system of local government had already begun to diverge
from that in the Czech Republic before the end of the federation in 1993.
The Slovak Constitution establishes the principle of local self-government
and the municipalities as the basic building-blocks, though permitting
'higher level sub-divisions' (article 64§3). It also establishes the distinct
Slovak system of direct election of all mayors (article 69§3). Article 71
also lays down the principle of delegation of central state functions to the
municipalities and the corresponding control by the central Government over that part (but only that part) of municipal activities.

There are now 2,821 municipalities in Slovakia. There has been a
slower proliferation of local authorities in Slovakia since 1989 than in the
Czech Republic, and concentration since 1950, when there were 3,359
municipalities, has been very limited. 1,946 municipalities have under
1,000 inhabitants. The largest is Bratislava, the capital, with 444,062 inhabitants, and the smallest is Hovrance with 17 inhabitants. The average
size is 1,875 inhabitants. Bratislava and Kosice have special status. Bratislava has a Lord Mayor and Council for the whole city and in addition 17
city district mayors and councils. Kosiče also has a Lord Mayor and council and 22 district mayors and councils.

The decentralised national administration is organised into 38 districts and under them 121 sub-districts on the basis of between one
and five sub-districts in each district. Districts and sub-districts have
no elected councils and hence are exclusively administrative agencies,
appointed by the Ministry of the Interior and reporting to it. On an even
larger scale than in the Czech Republic, *ad hoc*, single-purpose districts,
organised on a different geographical basis and often reporting directly
to other ministries, have been established for other services such as
the fire service, police and the important forestry administration. Districts also, as elsewhere in the region, exercise supervisory powers
over the elected municipalities and as such are the first level of appeal
against municipal decisions. The Chairman of the District Office, appointed by the Interior Minister, may also coordinate the work of other
ministries' district offices. There is also a complex system of subsidiarity
operating between the district and sub-districts. Some policy areas, such
as agriculture, fisheries, energy, transport, roads, primary health care and

social services, are the direct responsibility of the sub-district, with supervision and appeal functions being exercised by the district. Other functions, such as forest management, mineral resource management or cultural heritage, are the direct responsibility of the district.

Municipalities have a directly elected executive mayor. Mayors are elected for four years, by a first past the post (one round), at the same time as the council. Councils, with between 5 and 60 members, depending on size and population, are elected at large in smaller authorities or by a plurality system in multi-member districts, returning up to 12 councillors. The Council then proceeds to elect an executive of up one-third of the total membership of the Council, which is headed by the mayor. The administration is headed by a chairman of the Public Affairs Office, who is appointed by the Council. Other staff are appointed by the executive. Thus, the Slovak system differs significantly from the Czech model.

In all four countries, tension has arisen between the laudable and in principle correct decision to free local government by radical decentralisation, to create smaller units, closer to the citizen, and to end their entanglement with local agencies of the central Government that was a characteristic legacy of the communist era. This has created new problems. Local authorities must operate within national financial guidelines and within their legal powers. Many smaller local authorities lack the expertise and experience required. Often, therefore, almost by default, the decentralised national agencies have effectively recentralised the system. In Poland and the Czech Republic no strong intermediate democratically elected tier has been able to be established for political reasons. This has inevitably strengthened the Czech districts and the Polish Voivods as the only intermediate authority between weak municipalities and the central Government. In Hungary and Slovakia, too, the Hungarian Commissioners of the Republic and the Slovak Chairman of District Offices have achieved a position of authority going well beyond their formal arm's-length supervisory role. Hence the initial reforms have thrown up new problems, requiring a new round of reform.

9 The Judiciary

We shall focus on the political role of the judiciary and hence on the Constitutional Courts that stand at the apex of the judicial system. Under the old communist system, the judiciary was not only not independent, but it was also part of the ideological machinery of state power and as such was a tool of the authorities. Clearly, political organs of state power and the administration which executed their decisions were not subject to the control of an independent judiciary. However, by the late 1980s the notion of a more independent judiciary was beginning to surface in public debate, in both Hungary and Poland. There were, however, until 1989, strict limitations on how far this debate could achieve practical results, within the confines of the old system, though a Constitutional Court was even actually set up in Poland.

Strong entrenchment of the independence of the judiciary, more independent appointment processes, a real capacity to control both the administration and even the legislator in terms of adherence to the Constitution and the protection of the rights of the citizen, have been major preoccupations in the region since 1989. Establishment of an adequately independent judiciary and above all a Constitutional Court have been seen as important symbolic 'calling cards' in the process of Europeanisation required both for membership of the EU and for the Council of Europe.

Thus all four Visegrad states have established a Constitutional Court, or, in Poland, where it already existed, strengthened its role. All of them have endowed their Constitutional Court with an important arbitration role between the various branches of the government, with a significant capacity to protect the constitutional order against incursions by the executive and to a limited and more variable extent by Parliament. All have sought to guarantee the Court its independence from the current government.

POLAND

The Polish Constitutional Court was established first of any in the region and well before 1989. It was in a certain sense established too early, in that it still retains some of the defects inevitable at the time of its foundation, just after Martial Law was declared. It was Solidarnosc that originally demanded the creation of both a State Court of Impeachment to try senior party officials and a Constitutional Court. After the introduction of Martial Law, the regime favoured the creation of the Impeachment Court as an instrument against corrupt communist office holders from the 1970s. The Constitutional Court, for which the regime certainly had no enthusiasm, was, as it were, smuggled in on the back of the Impeachment Court by progressive reformist lawyers. Thus a constitutional amendment establishing such a Court was passed in 1982, but the implementing law regulating the appointment and functioning of the new Constitutional Court was only adopted in 1985 and entered force in 1986, the delay showing the reluctance of the regime. Even so, the Court operated for three years as part of the communist system and even declared two laws and numerous regulations unconstitutional. It arbitrated important disputes between central and local authorities, though these were not of major political significance. Quite apart from the wider political environment in which the Court operated, its founding legislation imposed further severe restraints upon it. It could not receive individual petitions nor could it examine pre-1982 legislation or examine the conformity of legislation or executive acts with international treaties signed by Poland. At that time, the election of the judges by the Sejm offered no real guarantee of their independence and freedom from pressure from the party, though it was already better than appointment by the government. Most importantly, rulings finding legislation unconstitutional were not (and indeed still are not) final. They must be transmitted to the Sejm, which reviews them and may, within a six-month deadline, overturn them by a two-thirds majority. Clearly, before 1989, this requirement for a qualified parliamentary majority to overturn Court rulings represented no practical protection for the Court, since such a majority could always be mobilised by the government if it decided to do so. Yet even so, before 1989, two Laws and almost 40 executive orders of various types had been quashed by the Court. In regard to the executive orders, the ruling of the Court was final. By this means, the Court was already developing a track-record that was actually obliging the authorities to act in a less arbitrary manner.

As part of the 1989 Round Table package of reforms, the constitutional provisions relating to the Court were significantly amended and its role expanded, though the right of the Sejm to overrule its decisions was not removed. The Court was given a real new power of 'preventative' review of bills before their promulgation, which could be triggered by the President of the Republic. This presidential power to require prior judicial review of a bill came to be exercised by the President on his own authority, without any requirement of a counter-signature by a minister. It was also given the right to issue universally binding rulings on constitutionality, without there being a specific case on the issue before any Court. This type of judicial review can be triggered by a series of state bodies such as the government, the higher courts, a minimum of 15 deputies or senators or trade unions and very frequently the Ombudsman. It may be asked by any court for a ruling on a constitutional matter arising in a case before that court. Courts are still making inadequate use of this procedure, analogous to the article 177 preliminary ruling procedure before the European Court, though its use is growing. There were no such referrals in 1992 and six in 1993.

The method of appointment of the judges was also amended. The 12 judges are elected by the Sejm for a non-renewable term of eight years. Members must have ten years of experience of working within the legal system or as professors of law. At present there are eight professors and four non-professors. Nominations are made by the political groups in the Sejm. There is system of partial renewal every four years. In 1989, judges close to Solidarnosc were appointed and in 1993 the new SLD/PSL coalition elected judges close to them. There is thus a rough balance on the Court. Indeed, when a judge close to Solidarnosc died, that judge was replaced by a nominee close to Solidarnosc, retaining the balance.

Thus at present the two main powers of the Court are to rule on the constitutionality of laws and executive acts. Though the Sejm may overrule judgements finding laws unconstitutional by a two-thirds majority it must do so within six months. The Court has ruled that if the Sejm fails to act within six months, then the law ruled unconstitutional becomes void. As before, decisions on subordinate legislation are final and not subject to reversal by the Sejm. The new Constitution adopted in 1997 eliminates the power of the Sejm to overturn judgements of the Constitutional Court. However, this change will only apply after a two-year transitional period.

Normally cases are heard by a small chamber of five judges rather than by the full Court. The Government or the President of the Republic may appeal decisions made by chambers up to the full plenary Court. There have only been two such appeals, both before 1989, and both failed.

The Court has from the start been deeply involved in political and constitutional conflicts. In 1993, the Court rendered 34 judgements on the constitutionality of laws, 14 decisions on requests for universal interpretations, and 28 abstract rulings. Most came from the Ombudsman. In 14 cases it found that there was a conflict with the constitution. It does not in general deal with issues of 'political opportunity'. However, it has been prepared to take account of some political considerations. It has also been prepared to weigh in the balance the very special and strictly temporary circumstances arising from the transition and the need to balance protection of citizens' social rights against the current budgetary constraints on the state.

The Court has been called on to rule on the legislative power of the Senate, the validity of the procedure by which the so-called 'Little Constitution' of 1992 was adopted, on the constitutionality of presidential dismissals of members of the Broadcasting Commission and on issues related to the independence of the judiciary. In the process, it has developed a body of jurisprudence on separation of powers, natural justice, a limited rather than absolute ban on retroactivity, especially in relation to fiscal matters and the protection of acquired rights. The Court has become in a short time an important and valuable part of the Polish governmental system. Its most urgent priority is that the Sejm should lose the right to overturn its rulings, which may happen in the process of constitutional revision.

SLOVAKIA

The Slovak constitution establishes a Constitutional Court with 'a mandate to protect the integrity of constitutional principles' (article 124). It is composed of ten judges appointed by the President of the Republic for a fixed but renewable term of seven years from a panel of twenty candidates proposed by the Slovak National Council (Parliament). The President and Vice-President of the Court are also appointed by the President of the Republic from among the judges. The President does not require any ministerial counter-signature when making these appointments. He can therefore act independently of the Government of the day. The tenure and independence of the judges is assured by the constitution itself. They may only be removed by the President of the Republic and not by the Government, where a judge has been convicted of a serious offence in a court of law or has been disciplined by the Constitutional Court itself. The judges enjoy the same immunity as MPs.

The constitution defines in considerable detail the powers of the Court and lays down that there is no appeal against its decisions. Nor can Parliament overrule Constitutional Court decisions. The Court is given jurisdiction over conflicts between the various branches and agencies of the central government, constitutional conflicts between laws and the constitution and between delegated legislation or acts of local authorities and the constitution, or between generally binding rules and international treaties that commit Slovakia. The Court may also review challenges to decisions of both central and local authorities that are alleged to violate the fundamental rights and freedoms of any citizen. The President of the Republic, the government or at least one-fifth of the members of the Slovak National council may launch a petition on the grounds that basic rights have been violated. However, unlike in Poland, the Court does not have the power to review bills before their promulgation.

Where the Court finds that a law or other legal rule complained of is in violation of the constitution, it shall first bring the matter to the attention of the body responsible for that act, which shall be obliged to bring it into conformity with the constitution within six months. Thus, the Court does not directly annul the act in question in the first instance. However, if the body concerned, including, where relevant, Parliament, does not act, then the incriminated rule shall automatically be void as a whole or in part (article 132).

The ordinary courts are required to refer matters of constitutional conflict and conflicts between various legal norms to the Constitutional Court. Its ruling is binding not only on the court that made the reference, but also on all other courts.

As elsewhere in the region the Slovak Constitutional Court has played an important political role, being drawn into adjudication of political conflicts of a serious nature such as the procedures for resignation and removal of ministers, and interpretation of the requirements of the electoral law for tabling lists at parliamentary elections. Prime Minister Mečiar has attacked the Court on several occasions. The Court has received 1,618 petitions in its first two years. Only 31 required an interpretation of the constitution. Most sought review of criminal convictions.

THE CZECH REPUBLIC

There was a Constitutional Court in Czechoslovakia, established in 1991, that was responsible for both constitutional arbitration and the protection of basic rights and freedoms, as set out in the 1991 Federal Constitutional Act. President Havel had been active in promoting the creation of a Constitutional Court in the old Federation and then in ensuring that a similar institution was established in the Czech republic after 1993. With some delays over the appointment of the judges, the Court began to operate in the Czech republic in June 1993. Following the German model, the Czech Constitutional Court does not have its seat in Prague with the other political institutions of the Czech republic. Its seat is in Brno.

The constitution declares (article 93) that the Constitutional Court is the 'judicial authority for safeguarding constitutional legality'. The fifteen judges are appointed by the President of the Republic. For these appointments, the President does not require the counter-signature of a government minister, as he does for most of his official acts. Hence, he operates here with an autonomy of the Government of the day, which is important for the independence of the Court. His proposals must be confirmed by the Senate. As long as the Senate has not been established, its powers are exercised by the National Assembly. Judges enjoy immunity, which can only be raised by the Senate.

The Court decides on petitions alleging unconstitutionality of Acts of Parliament, delegated legislation or even individual measures adopted by public authorities, or their compatibility with international treaties ratified by Parliament. The Court is also competent to adjudicate disputes between central and local authorities over competences. It is also the court of impeachment of the President of the Republic. The Court also hears election petitions. It can also receive and hear complaints about violations of human rights and basic freedoms. An interesting and novel power accorded to the Court is to oversee the implementation of the rulings of international tribunals that are binding on the Czech Republic. This would primarily concern the rulings of the International Court of Justice in the Hague and the European Court of Human Rights.

Rulings of the Court are effective immediately and cannot be appealed or reversed by Parliament. They are binding on all courts of law, all public bodies and all persons.

Where constitutional issues are raised in cases before the ordinary courts, the court concerned must refer the issue to the Constitutional Court for a preliminary ruling, which the competent court must apply to the case itself. The President of the Republic may refer bills to the Constitutional Court for a ruling on their constitutionality before he signs them into law.

The Constitutional Court has not been called upon to adjudicate such serious conflicts between the various branches of government – presidency, government and parliament – as has been the case in Poland, Hungary and Slovakia. However, it has been called on to consider some very politically sticky issues relating to the expulsion of the Sudeten German minority after 1945. In 1995 the Court ruled that whilst the so-called Benes Decree that had been the basis of the expulsions was constitutional, there could be compensation in individual cases. The Court has also been required to rule on legislation on the screening of former communist officials.

HUNGARY

Independent judicial control and supervision of the executive in Hungary as elsewhere in the region, with the partial exception of Poland, did not come into existence before 1989, though as an idea it had begun to be raised in developing reformist circles in Hungary from the mid-1980s. In Hungary, the Constitutional Court now shares these functions with the ordinary courts and with the administrative jurisdictions in particular.

The Constitutional Court was established in late 1989 and began functioning in 1990. It is established under article 22A of the constitution, added in 1989 as part of the initial package of reforms. It provides that the detailed organisation and functioning of the Court shall be laid down by legislation. This legislation is one of the twenty areas that require a two-thirds majority in parliament. This would normally require consensus with the opposition, but at present the MSZP/SDS coalition has a two-thirds majority in parliament without recourse to any additional outside support. However, there are at present no intentions to amend this law.

The 15 judges are elected for a term of seven years by the National Assembly. A two-thirds majority is required, which would normally require broad consensus within Parliament, though as indicated above, the current government does have the necessary majority on its own. However, it has been concerned to maintain consensus about such issues. Nominations must be made by a nomination committee composed of one representative per parliamentary group, which ensures that the opposition parties (four out of six groups at present) have a role in the process. The current coalition agreement between the MSZP and the SDS lays down that the two parties shall reach a prior agreement as to whom to support in such elections and of course they can then deliver the necessary two-thirds majority. Judges must be independent of political parties. They may not belong to a party or engage in political activity.

The Court is declared to have the function of reviewing 'the constitutionality of laws and statutes'. It has the power to annul unconstitutional laws. Its rulings are not subject to any appeal nor can they be overruled by Parliament. Naturally, Parliament can, if it finds the required majority, revise the constitution for the future, but not retroactively. Access to the Court does not require a demonstration of an interest by the would-be plaintiff. As the Constitution states, 'anyone' can bring a case before the Court, allowing public authorities, institutions, corporate bodies, organisations and individuals, whether citizens or not, to bring cases before the Court.

The President of the Republic can and does refer bills to the Court. The Court has a wide jurisdiction. It can exercise a concrete judicial review of constitutionality of laws, delegated legislation and even individual decisions, grounded in a specific case. It can also exercise an abstract control prior to entry into force, where a matter is referred to it for example by the President of the Republic. As the European Convention on Human Rights has been incorporated into the Hungarian constitution, the Court can undertake protection of core rights in accordance with general European standards.

The Court has an impressive record of independence. It has variously ruled against the President, finding that his discretion to reject nominees for official posts proposed by the government was quite limited and against the government on appointments in the media contested by the President of the Republic. It ruled certain aspects of the 1990 electoral law unconstitutional. It also annulled a law seeking to introduce prescription for political crimes committed between 1944 and 1989, whilst permitting prosecution of other, non-political crimes committed during the same period, after the President of the Republic had referred the matter to the Court.

In 1991 legislation was adopted giving the ordinary courts a jurisdiction to undertake judicial review over administrative matters.

CONCLUSIONS

Constitutional Courts have become an important and valued feature of the landscape in the new democracies in central Europe and have in the main been success stories. Though young and in the Polish case weaker *vis-à-vis* Parliament than might be desirable, they have shown their independence and their capacity to develop a strong body of constitutional jurisprudence that is making the at times sketchy, contradictory and ill-thought-out constitutional patchworks actually function. They have proved themselves to be valuable arbitrators and shock-absorbers in the inevitable conflicts that have arisen between the various branches of Government. They have also become identified as defenders of the hard-won basic rights of ordinary citizens. The existence and robust independence of these Constitutional Courts is one of the most visible and tangible indications to ordinary citizens that something has changed for the better and that he or she can have a reasonable and durable expectation that justice and the rule of law will apply.

10 Parliaments

Parliament is the cockpit of politics in all four countries, even if some systems, Poland especially, have some presidential features. In Poland, the stronger presidency and the greater fragmentation of the party system has weakened the role of parliament. The Hungarian and Slovak Parliaments are unicameral. The Polish and Czech Parliament are bicameral, though the Czech Senate has never been established and there is debate about the continuing utility of the Senate in Poland.

In all three (later four) countries, parliament became the engine of the transition and more strongly than any other institution tended to exemplify the cautious, gradualist approach to reform, growing as it were out of the existing communist parliaments which were used as the vehicle of reform. All three communist parliaments enacted the reforms in late 1989 and continued to exist and work well into 1990, until replaced by the newly elected parliaments that emerged from the 'foundation elections'. In Poland, the semi-democratic so-called contractual Sejm, elected in 1989 according to the ground-rules established by the Round Table process, sat until 1991. Thus, there was no root-and-branch reform. It is also true to say that the communist parliaments themselves had, when they began in the late 1940s, also shown a degree of continuity with past traditions, even though this was less then in 1989–90. Throughout, the same buildings, terminology and even formal procedures continued to be used.

However, with the exception of Hungary, parliamentary traditions in the region lacked depth. Hungary had a modern bicameral parliament as early as the Ausgleich of 1867 that created the Dual Monarchy, giving Hungary (which then included Slovakia) full control of its internal affairs. In a limited form, this parliamentary tradition continued in Hungary almost until the end of the Second World War and was briefly revived between 1945 and 1947. Poland did not of course exist as a nation-state before 1918, though Polish deputies sat in both the German Reichstag and the Austria Reichsrat. Almost no political activity was possible in the larger Russian part of what was to become independent Poland. There were thus no 'usable' traditions to draw on after 1918. Parliamentary democracy rapidly failed in the first Polish Republic and did not revive after 1945, as the communists rapidly took total control. Czech deputies had played an active part in the Imperial Reichsrat in Vienna before 1918 and the relatively liberal climate of the Habsburg monarchy enabled significant political activity and the formation of a genuine Czech party system. The Czechoslovak National Assembly established the only working parliamentary system in the region until 1939. It revived between 1945 and 1948. This more positive view of Parliament as an institution flickered briefly into life again during the Prague Spring in 1968, when Jozef Smrkovsky, the Speaker of the National Assembly, became one of the leaders of the reform movement. The federalisation of parliament, creating separate Federal, Czech and Slovak parliaments, was one of the few products of the Prague Spring that was not reversed. It played a not unimportant role in raising Slovak political consciousness.

The Hungarian Parliament meets as it has done since 1904 in a majestic neo-Gothic building on the Danube, that more or less consciously imitates the Palace of Westminster. The Czech Parliament meets in a baroque palace in the lesser town in Prague that was the seat of the Senate during the First Republic and the Czech National Council after 1968. It was in this historic building that the Republic was proclaimed in 1918. The Slovak Parliament meets in a former convent in old town Bratislava, where the Slovak Parliament met between 1939 and 1945, though a modern building is being built near the castle. The Polish Parliament's two chambers meet in a former girls' school, with a commanding view of the Vistula that became the seat of the Sejm in the new Polish state after 1918.

ELECTORAL SYSTEMS

Hungary

Hungary's unicameral Parliament of 386 members is elected for a maximum term of four years (1990, 1994,...). It is intended in principle to be a fixed term Parliament, though, as we have seen, in certain very tightly defined circumstances it can be dissolved early. The electoral system is mixed, involving proportional and majoritarian elements. 176 members are elected in single member constituencies (smcs). The various counties and the capital are apportioned a number of smcs on the basis of their population. In each of these 176 smcs, a two ballot system not unlike that in France applies. Candidates require the signatures of at least 750 votes from that smc to be nominated. Voting takes place in two phases. In the first round, voters vote for a candidate in their Single-Member Constituency (SMC) and also cast a vote for a list. Any candidate winning 50 per cent plus one in his smc is elected. In fact very few candidates are elected in the first round (five in 1990 and two in 1994). In the other smcs, a second round is held two weeks later. In the second ballot, all candidates winning at least 15 per cent of the votes cast at the first ballot can remain in contention, but in any event, the top three candidates are entitled to remain in the field, even if one or other of them did not obtain 15 per cent of the vote at the first ballot. In the second ballot, the candidate winning the most votes (plurality) is elected in what are mostly at least three-way contests. Many MPs therefore end up being elected on a minority vote, often with only about 30–35 per cent of the second ballot vote. Nor is there the French tradition of alliances and mutual withdrawals to ensure a straight fight between the best-placed standard-bearers of right and left in each constituency. This means that the leading candidate on the first round almost always wins on the second round, even if he or she does not manage to gain any additional support. Parties do not have any reflex of mobilising against the first-round leader. Thus, in 1990 the MDF led on the first round in 80 seats, won almost all of these and even a number of others, ending up with 114 smc seats out of 176. In 1994, the MSZP led in 158 of the 176 smcs and actually won in 148 of them. The SDS led in 13 and won in 17. The MDF led in 3 and won 4. There was no effort by the other parties such as SDS, FIDESZ and MDF to organise any kind of even temporary cooperation to prevent the MSZP from gaining an absolute majority. This multiplicator effect in the constituency seats is shown clearly in Table 10.1.

Table 10.1   Hungarian election results

| | First ballot | | Second ballot |
	Victory	Lead	Victory
1990			
MDF	3	80	114
SDS	–	63	35
MSZP	–	3	1
KDP	–	5	3
Smallholders	–	11	11
FIDESZ	–	2	2
Others	2	8	10
1994			
MSZP	2	158	148
SDS	–	13	17
MDF	–	3	4
KDNP	–	–	1
Smallholders	–	–	1
FIDESZ	–	–	–
Others	–	1	3

A further 152 seats are chosen in 20 electoral districts to which between 4 and 28 seats are allocated on the basis of population. Budapest, with 28 seats, is the largest district. Voters cast a second list vote. Seats are allocated on the basis of these list votes by using a simple electoral quotient. Party lists polling less than 4 per cent are not allocated any seats . This then, as a consequence, leads to a slight over-representation of the larger parties. In 1990, 3.5 per cent of the votes went unrepresented and in 1994 that rose to 7.37 per cent.

A third national list section of 58 seats is allocated to parties that have tabled lists in at least seven districts. Hitherto unused votes in each district are cumulated and seats allocated to parties winning over 4 per cent of the vote.

Vacancies in the single member constituencies are filled by holding by-elections and in other cases by the next unelected candidate on the list. To be nominated in a single member constituency, a candidate needs 750 signatures from voters in his would-be constituency. A Regional List can only be tabled by parties which put up candidates in at least a quarter of the single member constituencies in that district.

Poland

Poland's first post-communist or so-called Contractual Sejm that sat from 1989 to 1991 and which was indeed the first more or less democratically elected post-communist legislature in the region, was elected by a complex, almost byzantine compromise electoral system agreed in the party/opposition Round Table in early 1989. This system was only semi-democratic in that it did not open all seats in the stronger Lower House (Sejm) to full electoral competition. It assured a majority there to the Communist Party and its small Peasant and Democratic Party allies. Only one-third of Sejm seats were open for competition. On the other hand, the full complement of 100 seats in the newly recreated senate were open to full electoral competition under a majority system in small multi-member districts.

The second Sejm (1991–3) was elected by a system of pure proportional representation that had a very low threshold, too low to provide any guarantee against fragmentation. Thus, 29 parties won at least one seat, including a Polish Friends of Beer Party, that began as a joke, but actually won 16 seats and then split into two. The largest party only won less than 100 seats out of 460.

This second Sejm, dominated by the various parties that derived from the fragmentation of Solidarnosc, reacted by revising the electoral law in a draconian manner, designed to ensure greater governability, but in the end overreacted. The Sejm is elected for a maximum four-year term. Early dissolution by the President against the wish of the Sejm majority is, as we have seen, quite difficult. Local lists in each of the 37 electoral districts require the backing of 5,000 voters. National lists are presented by the political parties. 391 Sejm members are elected in the 37 electoral districts, each of which receives an allocation of seats based on its population. Seats are allocated to parties by the d'hondt divisor method. The seats allocated to each party are then allocated to individual candidates within that party's list in that district on the basis of the rank order of preference votes for each candidate. However, only parties that have won 5 per cent of the national vote and 8 per cent in the case of electoral coalitions of several parties can share in that allocation of seats in any district, even if they have won that share in the district itself. For the national pool 69 seats form a national pool of seats, allocated as a form of 'compensation'. Only parties with 5 per cent of the national vote or coalitions with 7 per cent can share in the distribution of the pool seats.

The fragmentation of the right-wing parties that led to a rather lopsided, unrepresentative Sejm in which two old system parties, SDL and PSL, won almost a two-thirds majority, although they hardly gained a greater share of the vote than in 1991, and in which the total right-wing vote of over 30 per cent elected almost no one. Among right-wing parties, only the Confederation for an Independent Poland (KPN) achieved representation. This of course has created problems for the political, though not legal legitimacy of this Sejm.

The Senate, created as part of the Round Table in 1989, is now in some sense redundant, but will no doubt survive. It has 10 members elected by a first past the post plurality system in 49 provincial constituencies. Each Province elects two members, irrespective of electorate, except Warsaw and Katowice, which each elect three members. Voters cast two or three votes and those elected are the two (or three in Warsaw and Katowice) candidates with the largest number of votes.

The Czech Republic

Under the 1993 Constitution, the Parliament of the Czech Republic is intended to be bicameral, but an electoral law for the Senate was only adopted in 1995 and the first Senate elections were held on 15 and 16 November 1996. In the meantime, the Chamber has cumulated the functions of both houses, with the limitation that during this interim period, a dissolution of the Chamber was not possible.

The Chamber comprises 200 members, elected for a term of four years, in eight electoral districts. Each district has an allocation of seats according to its population. For example, Prague is a district, returning 30 members. Seats are allocated to party lists by a two-count method, using the Hagenbach-Bischof method for the first count and then allocating remainder seats in the second count by the greatest-remainder method. Only parties with 5 per cent of the vote or 7 per cent for two-party coalitions, 9 per cent for three-party coalitions and 11 per cent for four-party coalitions can share in the distribution of seats. There is no national pool of seats. The overall effect of these provisions is to create two thresholds: the first at national level and the second *de facto* threshold in each district, which may be above 5 per cent unless the district returns at least 20 members. The system both offers serious obstacles to fragmentation and advantages the larger parties. Voters may also give up to four preference votes to individual candidates within a list. However, only if 10 per cent of voters for a list use that possibility do these preferences come into play and then a candidate needs over 10 per cent of the preferences for that list to move up. In 1996, several candidates both for ODS and CSSD undertook quite high-profile and in some cases expensive personal campaigns, often using business networks as multipliers. The system was applied in 1990, 1992 and 1996 and was familiar, being also applied in 1946 and in the First Republic.

The Senate was only elected in 1996 for the first time. Initially, it was proposed and included in the Constitution so as to ensure a continuing platform for Federal MPs after the split-up of the old Federation in 1993. However, few parties in the former Czech National Council, now as it were by accident promoted to a sovereign national legislature, were very eager to create a second, rival chamber, with the possible exception of the Moravian Regionalist Party (Czech and Moravian Centre Party, CMUS). ODS was strongly opposed and sought to have the Senate deleted from the Constitution. Strong pressure from other parties and from President Havel eventually led to the creation of the Senate in late 1995. The electoral law finally agreed upon provides for the election of the 81 Senators in single member districts by a two-ballot system. The term of office is six years, but one-third will retire every two years. ODS wanted the first elections on the same day as the Chamber, but this was rejected. President Havel looks to the Senate as a more independent body, with limited powers, but more expertise and moral authority. He would hope to see university professors, scientists, cultural figures and trade unionists, and personalities from smaller parties elected to the Senate.

The Senate elections took place in November 1996. There was a low turnout and the elections did not see, as some supporters of the Senate had hoped, the emergence of independents or breaking of the party mould. As it was, the major parties put a stranglehold on the Senate, to an even greater degree than in the Chamber. ODS won 49.19 per cent and 32 seats; CSSD 31.80 per cent and 25 seats; KDS 10.74 per cent and 13 seats; ODA 5.19 per cent and 7 seats; Czech Communist Party (KŠC) 1.96 per cent and 2 seats; and others 2 seats. The Communists and Republicans were the main losers. This non-proportional electoral system severely disadvantaged them, as they had no allies, though there was some local KSC and CSSD cooperation that mainly helped CSSD. ODS was the big winner and with it the coalition, with 65.12 per cent of the vote and 52 seats. However, CSSD also increased its vote above 30 per cent for the first time, an increase of 5 per cent on its 1996 election result. Perhaps the polarisation and elimination of the two extreme parties was exaggerated by the system, but it may betray a future trend.

Slovakia

Slovakia has a uni-cameral parliament, called the National Council, elected for a term of four years. To table lists, parties must demonstrate that they have at least 10,000 members, or alternatively have returned members at the previous election. This provision caused some problems in the 1994 elections. The government tried to contest that the Democratic Union of Slovakia (DUS) a break-away party from the ruling HZDS met either condition. Members are elected in fairly large electoral districts and seats are distributed at the first count by the Hagenbach-Bischof method and remainder seats in a second round by the largest-remainder method. Voters can express up to four preferences for individual candidates on their chosen list. There is a 5 per cent threshold. The system is virtually identical to the Czech system. At the last HZDS Congress, Prime Minister Mečiar speculated about a possible reform of the electoral system towards a more majoritarian, British-style system.

THE ORGANISATION AND WORKING OF THE PARLIAMENTS

Before 1989–90, the parliaments of central Europe were still living out a formal existence, acting simply as transmission belts or fig-leaves, rubber-stamping decisions taken elsewhere in the ruling bodies of the

Communist Party. While there might formally at least be some other parties in parliament, their freedom of action was strongly circumscribed and there was always a communist majority anyhow. It was only in Poland, especially in committee work, and by the later 1980s in Hungary, that parliaments were able even at the margins to exert any influence. Independents such as the PAX ('Peace') Deputies in Poland (Independent Catholics) in the Polish Sejm of which later Prime Minister Mazowiecki was the most prominent were always only tolerated and were soon shown the limits of that toleration in 1970. The various parliaments were dusty, unsung institutions, meeting rarely, and their internal bodies such as political groups and even committees had little more than a formal existence. As with other institutions, parliaments had to be built or rebuilt in the open sea as it were. This was even more urgent than in other areas, because the parliaments were required to drive the reform process. They became the cockpits of the ongoing 'velvet revolutions' all over the region. This left no time for reflection. Existing structures and mechanisms had to be adapted and used for new purposes, rather than recast from zero. This would perhaps have been ideal, but it was an unavailable luxury in the prevailing circumstances.

Hungary

Hungary has a unicameral Parliament, with 386 members. Earlier bicameral traditions were not revived after 1989. The gradual process of political reform in Hungary led to relatively early stabilisation of parliamentary procedures and party structures. The same six parties are represented in the current 1994–8 legislature as in the 1990–4 legislature. The mixed election system with elements of both majoritarian and proportional systems has led to alternance with stable governing majorities and minimum representation for all political forces with significant local or national support. The mixed origin of deputies also ensured a balance between the articulation of local and national concerns in Parliament. The combination of the constitutional arrangements and the electoral system chosen in 1990 have ensured a stable executive with a working majority in both terms. The system is based on a clear expectation that the government once formed at the outset of the parliamentary term will last through the full four years. Equally, oppositions expect to remain in opposition for the full term. They do not expect to unseat the government along the way through splits, defections, manoeuvres or reversals of alliances. Such possibilities are not programmed into the behaviour of the parties. Thus, the opposition forces in the present parliament

(MDF, FIDESZ, KDNP and possibly but less likely the Smallholders) are looking at how to create an alternative, and are trying to organise a broad alliance for the 1998 elections.

In 1990, the rights of the opposition – then SDS and FIDESZ – were supposed to be safeguarded by the settlement under which some 30 categories of bills would require a two-thirds majority vote in parliament for their passage, which the then centre-right coalition did not possess.

This settlement has now lost most of it value for the opposition for two essential reasons. Firstly and more generally, the categories of 'two-thirds' laws related mainly to constitutional-type issues concerning the organisation of the judiciary, civil rights, the media, local government and implementing general constitutional provisions. These were always a minority and are now mainly in place. In fact, of 438 laws passed during the 1990–4 term, only 10 per cent were two-thirds laws and fewer and fewer will be required. More philosophically, many of the categories would in normal times in most countries be ordinary laws. Some therefore argued, in an almost British way, that this need for consensus over such a wide range of legislation actually fatally confused responsibility between government and opposition parties, making accountability difficult. Secondly, in a more settled political situation as now pertains, the role of parliament and in particular of the opposition is to control the work of the executive, rather than being a co-legislator, and for that other tools are needed. Finally in the specific case of the present legislature, the MSZP/SDS coalition do have the two-thirds majority, without the support of the opposition. Thus, the reform of Parliament's rules adopted in 1994–5 dealt more with how to improve the working of Parliament's control functions and how to ensure the right of the opposition in that context.

There are currently six groups in Parliament. The largest has 206 members and the smallest 20. The Rules require ten members to form a 'Fraction' (group). During the 1990–4 term, the Smallholders 'Fraction' split and the smaller faction fell below ten and lost its Fraction status. On the other hand, the new Faction, the Hungarian Truth and Light (MIEP) Faction, was formed from defecting MDF deputies. This new party then won no seats at all in 1994. The Fractions have their own leaders, executives and a small staff of advisors, experts and secretaries.

There are currently sixteen committees, with either 27, 19 or 13 members. It has been agreed that the opposition should be disproportionately represented on committees. Thus, for example, on the 27-member committees, MSZP has only 12 members, and with SDS (5) the coalition has only 17 seats, whereas under strict proportionality, MSZP should have

14 members and the coalition 19 seats. The largest opposition party, MDF, rates 4 seats. All factions are represented in every committee and each has at least one committee chair. MSZP has seven chairs, SDS 4, MDF 2 and KDNP, Smallholders and FIDESZ one each. In Inquiry Committees there must be an equal number of coalition and opposition deputies, probably with an opposition chairman. Committee structure is negotiated between the six factions. However, 20 per cent of MPs (a minority right) can demand the establishment of an Inquiry Committee. Ministers may not sit on committees. To date, only one Inquiry Committee has been established, though 32 were proposed. Committees often set up sub-committees.

The business of the house is managed by a House Committee on which all six factions are represented. It is chaired by the Speaker, though he and the Vice-President, who are also members, have only a non-voting membership of the committee, which coordinates and manages business.

A Committee of Committee Chairmen has also been instituted to co-ordinate committee work and advise the House Committee on the drawing-up of the agenda of the plenary sessions of Parliament.

Committee work is at the heart of parliamentary work. In fact, the full House (plenary) usually only meets on Mondays from 3 p.m. to 7 p.m. and on Tuesdays 10 a.m. to 7 p.m. and committees on Wednesdays and Thursdays, leaving Fridays free for constituency and other political business. Thus, the plenary meets for at most three days per week and mostly only two days. In all it met on 379 days during the 1990–4 term, but its committees met for 3,144 sittings. The Constitutional and Legal Affairs Committee met 521 times and the Foreign Affairs Committee 161 times. Committees mostly meet about once per week. The committees have a small staff of 2–4 assistants each and a small budget for commissioning outside expert advice.

Parliament has two basic tasks: legislation and adoption of the annual budget, and supervision and control of the executive and its agencies. The initiative for legislation can come from the President of the Republic, though in fact this is very rare, from the government, which is the most frequent initiator, from committees and from individual MPs. Fifty-two per cent of bills were tabled by the government, only 7 per cent by committees and 41 per cent by private members during the 1990–4 term. However, whilst 92 per cent of bills proposed by the government and 79 per cent of committee bills pass, only 38 per cent (still a high proportion by British standards) of private members bills were actually passed.

Turning to the procedure in Parliament, increasingly bills are referred to only one committee, unlike in the past where several committees often dealt with a bill in parallel. Under the most recent rules revision, there is one main or consolidating committee, to which others can give an opinion. This always used to include the Committee on the Constitution and Legal Affairs, but now this committee itself decides which bills it needs to examine. Now, discussion of most bills begins in committee. Not infrequently, interests groups request a hearing before the committee at this stage and also may present written submissions.

Committees are not obliged to hold such hearings, but often find them useful. Experts may be hired to assist in examining specialised bills. The role of committees is to prepare the debate on the floor, but they do not have the right to prevent a bill going to the floor nor to block amendments tabled to a bill. A committee must act on a proposal within thirty days, or eight days where urgency has been decided upon. Where a committee declines to report a bill out on to the floor, then the minority in the committee can appeal to the full house. Each fraction (Parliamentary group) may exercise this right of appeal only five times during each annual session. The committee usually nominates a rapporteur. The committee reports on the suitability of the bill for further consideration on the floor and on each amendment. Now, amendments which obtained less than one-third of the votes in committee are not considered on the floor, unless taken up by a political fraction or at least 20 members. Amendments had become too numerous, with between 30 and 50 per cent of them coming from the coalition parties, even on government bills.

Finance bills and appropriations bills are important cases for Parliament to exert a detailed control over the executive. However, as in Britain, only the government may propose financial measures, but on the other hand the urgency procedure cannot be applied to such measures. There must therefore be full debate in the Finance Committee and in plenary. All the different 'sectoral' committees examine those parts of the budget that pertain to their areas of policy and submit an opinion to the Finance Committee, which undertakes the necessary arbitration between competing demands and submits a consolidated bill to the plenary.

Parliamentary control is also exercised through a whole battery of other instruments outside the legislative and budgetary procedures. The 1994 rules revision sought above all to extend and guarantee the rights of the opposition parties to trigger various control procedures, if necessary against the wishes of the majority. As we have already seen, this applies to the creation of parliamentary inquiry committees. The procedures put in place for the revision of the constitution and the increased representation of the opposition parties in parliamentary committees are additional examples of this important trend. Indeed, the new rules were arrived at by a consensus between at least four of the six parliamentary groups at the start of the 1994 legislature, though on some issues the Smallholders wanted a recognition of the rights of each opposition party acting individually, rather than a collective right for the opposition acting together. The new rules were finally adopted in plenary by 272 votes against 18, with 11 abstentions.

The range of parliamentary instruments for controlling the executive is quite extensive. At the highest level is the parliamentary nuclear weapon of the censure motion. However, the constructive no-confidence motion is unlikely to succeed and is rarely used. None have been passed and none were even tabled during the 1990–4 term.

Parliament can, as we have seen, establish inquiry committees and this is now, since the 1994 reform, a minority right that can be triggered by 20 per cent of MPs (hence at least 78) and an opposition MP would be chairman. However, in the current legislature, such a committee would require the cooperation of most of the opposition groups in order to attain the necessary number of signatures.

The Finance Committee also undertakes an *ex post* control of government spending on the basis of the independent Audit Commission's reports.

The Constitution itself and a very large number of Acts of Parliament require the government and semi-independent agencies and bodies to report to Parliament annually or more frequently. The bodies required to report cover a very wide area, for example Regional Development Agencies, the Gaming and Betting Board, the National Bank, the Academy of Sciences, and the Chief Prosecutor are all required to report. These reports are considered in committee, rarely in plenary (only four occasions in the 1990–4 term), but may lead to hearings with officials, ministers or representatives of the body concerned and motions calling for action.

Under the new rules, the committees have a right to call ministers and officials before them to enable them to examine some aspect of Government policy in detail.

The opposition (78 MPs) can require a general political debate in plenary on any issue of their own choosing. Otherwise, apart from these set-piece parliamentary occasions, members can raise specific and topical political issues, in short, impromptu 'before the agenda debates' held at the opening of business each sitting day, before the House proceeds to its agenda for that day and again in adjournment debates at the end of the sitting, when more local or constituency matters can be raised with Ministers.

Any member can table an interpellation to the Prime Minister or to other Ministers. Actually, the Prime Minister himself is not obliged to reply personally and rarely does so, mostly transferring the question to another Minister for reply. Indeed, he only did so on three occasions in the 1990–4 legislature. Seventy-five per cent of the interpellations tabled in that legislature came from opposition MPs. The main topics were privatisation, agriculture and land reform, water supply, coal mining and the improvement of the telephone system. The House may vote not to accept the answer, which leads to a discussion in committee and report. This happened in 44 cases in the last term.

Members may ask questions of the Prime Minister and other Ministers (740 in 1990–4 of which 58 per cent came from opposition MPs). There is now a question time once per sitting week.

The Czech Republic

According to the Constitution, the Parliament of the Czech Republic should be bicameral, but between 1992 and November 1996 there was no Senate, and during this long provisional period the lower house exercised the functions of both houses at once. During the period when the Senate did not exist, the Chamber of Deputies could not be dissolved before the normal end of its four-year term. The Chamber of Deputies has 200 members, elected for a term of four years by proportional representation. The Senate has 81 members, elected in single member constituencies by a two-ballot system. The National Council of the Czech Republic, elected in June 1992 as a regional parliament within the federation, became the Chamber of Deputies of the new sovereign Czech Republic on 1st January 1993. The first elections in the independent Czech Republic took place in June 1996.

The Chamber is managed by a Presidium, with a President (ODS in the first term, and now Miloš Zeman, President of CSSD) and four Vice-Presidents, all from the government parties in the first term (1992–6). On the other hand, the Organisation Committee which is responsible for the rules of the house has 30 members drawn from all the political groups in the House. A so-called Political Bureau made up of the President, Vice-Presidents and Chairs of the political groups deals with the organisation of debates, preparation of the agenda and political decisions relating to the role of Parliament as an institution. There are 12 standing committees. In the 1992–6 term, all were chaired by coalition party MPs.

The ODS alone had seven committee chairs. In the new legislature elected in June 1996, opposition MPs now hold a number of chairs, including the Budgets Committee, now chaired by a CSSD MP. Membership of committees however corresponds to the strength of the various parties in the House. Committee members are then nominated by the party groups to fill the quota for each group. Only the Organisation Committee must contain representatives from all political groups. In practice all committees do so.

In the 1992–6 term there were ten groups. Now there are only six, all formed by parties that had tabled lists at the election. There are now no groups that are alliances of parties or independents, as there were in the previous term. Groups have their own organisation, which is, though, quite similar, with a President and a small Executive Committee, which prepares the meetings of the full group that are held before parliamentary sessions. For example, the ODS group Executive has eight members and meets at least once a week. The full group meets at least weekly, and daily during parliamentary sessions. The Executive appoints one of the ODS MPs in the responsible committee as the group spokesperson on each bill. He sets up a small working group of interested ODS MPs to prepare the deliberations of the full group on the matter. Where the committee chair is from the ODS, he or she will be the spokesperson. The ODS group has three secretaries and one political advisor. Five ODS MPs sit on the party's National Executive Committee and six sit on the larger Party Council. The structure of the smaller groups is less elaborate. In the last term, the CSSD group had only one staff member. Unlike in the Left Block (LB) or the KSCM (Communist Party of Bohemia and Morovia), the chair of the group is not chair of the party in the CSSD. Only one party vice-chair is an MP. This situation may change in the much larger CSSD group in the 1996–2000 term. All party group offices in Parliament are small and individual MPs have no offices.

Party discipline both in committees and in the plenary is quite tight, though it is far from being absolute, even within the coalition, except on important matters. Coalition coordination is ensured through the Coordination Committee and by the appointment of a single coalition whip for major bills. Coalition groups actually voted together to a level of at least 60 per cent cohesion in 79 per cent of all votes. The most united group has been the Republicans,with a steady 95 per cent unity, followed by ODS with over 90 per cent. Even the least united, CSSD and CMUS, consistently showed at least 85 per cent cohesion. Nevertheless, it remains fair to say that they were all, at least in the last legislature, more fluid and tentative than is usual in western legislatures, though that is now changing. In the 1996 Legislature there are only six party groups and no independents, which will tend to increase cohesion.

The main functions of Parliament are to legislate and control the Executive. The main source of legislative proposals is the government. Under the Czech Constitution, the President of the Republic no longer has the right to table bills. Deputies may table bills, but very few non-government bills can expect to pass. In 1995, the government proposed 81 measures to Parliament. Once a bill has been received by the President of the Chamber, he refers it for a first reading on the floor of the house. It may be rejected already at this stage, which must be concluded within sixty days. The bill is then, if passed at this stage, referred to a single committee or to main committee and other committees to give an opinion to the main committee by the Organisation Committee. The committees hear ministers or other sponsors of the bill, who explain its purpose and respond to amendments. The bill is then reported back to the plenary for a second reading. Here again, the bill may be rejected, amended or again referred back to committee. The third and final reading must take place not less than twenty-four hours after the second reading. Ministers and also the President of the Republic may take part in the sittings of both the plenary and committees of both houses of Parliament.

The bill then goes to the Senate for consideration and follows a similar path of plenary and committee debate. It can propose amendments that the Chamber is required to consider, but may reject by an absolute majority. This is thus only a suspensive veto, which can, though, provide a breathing space, enabling ill-considered measures or bills adopted by a small majority or with few deputies present to be re-examined. No amendments may be tabled at this reconsideration stage. The bill then goes to the President for signature. He may veto a bill, but that veto can be overridden by an absolute majority in the house. The Constitution provides that Parliament may decide to submit legislation to a referendum.

Interpellations to the government, often on matters of detailed or local interest, are a major part of the supervisory work of Parliament. After the minister's answer, there is a vote on the acceptance of the minister's reply, a weak but useful sanction.

Slovakia

Like the Czech Parliament, the Slovak Parliament grew out of the old Slovak National Council that existed within the Czechoslovak Federation and outlived it to become the Parliament of the new Slovak state. The Slovak National Council was elected in 1992 and could, as did its Czech counterpart, have sat until 1996. However, internal developments in Slovakia led to an earlier general election in September 1994, creating a new post-independence Parliament much earlier than in the Czech Republic. There have now therefore been three free elections in Slovakia (1990, 1992, 1994). The Slovak party system, though, remains volatile and changing. It has not found the kind of stability that has been developing in Hungary and the Czech Republic.

The Parliament with 150 members is small and indeed the smallest lower house in the region. Political groups only need five members and can be created through dissidence and floor-crossing. There are currently eight political groupings in Parliament. Two of them – the Left Electoral alliance (three parties) and the Hungarian group (three parties) – are alliances of parties. Two other parties – the Democratic Union (DUS) and the Workers Party – (ASW/ZRS) were new entrants at the 1994 election. The previous legislature was characterised by splits, floor-crossing, formation and break-up of alliances. The DUS for example was a break-away from the Movement for a Democratic Slovakia (HZDS) of Prime Minister Mečiar. Turnover of MPs has been very high: 50 per cent in 1992 and 41 per cent again in 1994. A democratic and parliamentary culture remains fragile and elusive in Slovakia.

Despite the apparent authoritarianism of the Prime Minister and the not unimportant powers of the President of the Republic, Parliament and especially its committees remains a significant player in the political system. Parliament, especially given the weak discipline, even in the coalition parties, has been able to exercise real power in certain situations, though it has done so erratically and unpredictably.

Parliament has, argue many commentators, significant levers of power in its hands. As we have seen, it can censure and remove the President of the Republic. It can amend the Constitution by the relatively low qualified majority of three-fifths. It can create and abolish Ministries and Agencies and has done so in some cases without the consent of the government. It is of course the budgetary authority. It can and does exercise a power of censure against individual ministers that would not be politically feasible in a more structured parliamentary system even if the power formally existed. In the reverse model, as it were, Parliament has also prevented the Prime Minister from removing ministers whom he wished to dismiss. Party discipline has been so weak that MPs have even sometimes voted against ministers from their own party. There is evidence that parties are now moving to tighten discipline and prevent floor-crossing, by monitoring the activity and votes of their MPs, through the newly created Conference of Party Chairmen in Parliament and through more rigorous candidate selection.

Parliament and its individual members and committees are also equipped with considerable powers of inquiry and interpellation, not only directed at ministers, but also at state agencies and senior officials. There is also a rather unique provision for so-called 'MP Inquiries', initiated by MPs or under mandates given to MPs by the government to act as investigatory advisors to a Ministry, in what is in effect an executive capacity, whilst remaining in Parliament. Such activities are not constitutionally incompatible.

The Constitution itself, the Act on Legislative Procedures and Parliament's own internal rules place parliamentary committees in a key position. Article 92 of the Constitution provides that Parliament 'establishes committees as bodies for proposing legislation and oversight'. Committees can propose bills and may, in the exercise of their oversight functions, summon ministers and members of official bodies before them. In one interesting example, the privatisation committee was established in October 1993, despite the negative vote of the main government party (HZDS). Committee members are nominated by the full house and this is not a mere formality, as the majority has often refused to accept troublesome nominees from the opposition and has filled the opposition quota with other opposition deputies. Committee chairs normally have come only from the government side, unlike Poland and Hungary. This may be changing. The Legislative Committee examines all bills and receives an opinion on them from the relevant specialist committee.

Legislation emanates from the government, committees of Parliament and individual MPs (article 87 of the Constitution). However, the President of the Republic may also submit measures and proposals. A relatively large number of bills are submitted by individual MPs (27 per cent). Many such bills pass, despite opposition from the Government and its Legislative Council, to which all bills are referred for an opinion. Bills are only sent to the floor if a committee actually votes them out by a majority, otherwise they die. Individual members may propose amendments on the floor, but these tend to fail. Once passed, a bill goes to the President of the Republic for signature. He can refer it back, but cannot veto it. Referral back only obliges Parliament to readopt the bill by a simple majority. During the 1990–2 legislature, 150 Acts were adopted, 808 interpellations debated and 335 questions were asked. In 1993–4, 109 Acts were passed. The number of Acts originating in private members bills increased significantly after independence.

The Constitution provides for the instrument of the referendum. This is obligatory for joining or cession from a Union with other states, which would certainly apply to EU membership. Matters relating to taxation or fundamental rights and freedoms may not be put to a referendum. A referendum is called by the President of the Republic, either where Parliament so decides (MPs or the government can make the initial proposal) or on a petition from at least 350,000 voters. However, a referendum may not be held within the last 90 days of the legislative term of office. The referendum vote is only valid if the turnout has exceeded 50 per cent of the vote. Proposals adopted by referendum must be promulgated by Parliament. However, after three years Parliament is free to amend such measures without a further referendum, but only by a three-fifths majority.

Poland

The Polish Parliament was initially the only bicameral Parliament in the region, though it has been joined since November 1996 by the Czech Parliament. As we have seen, there was a certain tradition of bicameralism in pre-communist Poland, but the origin of bicameralism in post-communist Poland lay in the transition deal of 1990. Many observers now doubt therefore whether the Senate has any functional or political utility, especially since its powers have been reduced significantly under the so-called Little Constitution of 1992 to that of no more than suspensive veto. The Sejm is and will remain the dominant Chamber, though both are directly elected by the people.

The Sejm

The Sejm has 460 members and the Senate 100. There are since the 1993 elections six political Clubs (party groups). The largest (SLD) had 167 members and the smallest (KPN) has 16. A minimum of 15 members is needed to form a Club. However, three members may form a Group, thereby obtaining some though not all of the procedural and material advantages accruing to the Clubs, which alone are represented in the Sejm's managing body, the Council of Elders. Thus, the four German minority members from Silesia have taken advantage of this provision and formed a Group. (There are now five Clubs.)

The presiding officer of the Sejm is the Marshal of the Sejm (Speaker), elected at the opening of each legislature by elimination ballot. He is assisted by a number of Vice-Marshals, who collectively form the Presidium. This body organises the work of the house, fixing its sittings calendar and coordinating the work of the various committees, runs the secretariat and handles relations with the Senate. In conjunction with the Rules of Procedure Committee, the Presidium interprets standing orders. The Council of Elders (the Presidium plus the Club Chairs) is simply required to give its opinion on the agenda, though in practice it decides on the agenda and the organisation of debates. It is here that the opposition takes part in consensus building.

There are 24 standing committees in the Sejm, covering all areas of policy. These committees are composed proportionately by the Presidium, after consulting the Council of Elders. In practice, a proportional allocation of seats is given to each Club which then nominates its candidates. A limited number of seats on some, but not all, committees is reserved for Groups and non-attached members. Posts of Committee Chairs and Vice-Chairs are also distributed proportionately among the Clubs. Every Club has at least one committee chair. Even important committees such as Foreign Affairs, Internal Affairs (dealing with internal security and police matters) and Budgets are chaired by opposition MPs. Several committees have also established sub-committees. The Sejm can also establish temporary *ad hoc* committees. Currently, there are such committees on the Labour Code, on the Concordat with the Vatican and of course on the Constitutional revision. The Sejm appoints and can, with the consent of the Senate, recall the members of the Supreme Chamber of Control, which acts an Audit Court, reporting to the Sejm on the legality and regularity of state expenditure.

Bills can be introduced by the government, the President of the Republic, Sejm committees, the Senate or by 15 Sejm deputies. Measures with financial consequences can only be tabled by the government. If the Presidium has doubts about the constitutionality or legality of a bill, it is then first examined by the Legislative Committee. Otherwise, they proceed on their way through three readings. Most bills in fact have their first reading in committee, but bills dealing with the constitution, finance bills, electoral law measures, local government organisation and other important bills have their first reading on the floor of the Sejm. Normally, the first reading may not take place earlier than seven days after a bill has been tabled. In urgent cases, this requirement can be dispensed with. Sponsors of bills or their spokesmen may be heard to explain their proposal. The Sejm may at this stage vote to reject the bill, otherwise it goes to a lead committee and possibly one or more other committees for the detailed committee stage. Committees then establish a timetable for examination of the bill. Sub-committees may be established and hearing with experts may be held. Sponsors may be asked to clarify or amend their bills. A rapporteur is appointed in the lead committee. The lead committee then recommends to the Sejm approval, rejection or amendment of the initial bill. At the second reading in the full house, the bill is considered on the basis of the committee report and any additional amendments. Where there are new amendments, the bill may be referred back to the committee. Then the bill, with or without a second committee referral, goes for a vote on the third reading.

The bill then goes to the Senate for consideration. It may table amendments within a deadline of 30 days. These amendments are then reconsidered in the Sejm committee and again on the floor of the Sejm, on the basis of the committee's report. The Senate rapporteur can attend to explain the Senate's amendments before the Sejm. These amendments are then voted on and accepted or rejected. However, a Senate motion to reject a bill can only be overridden by an absolute majority of the Sejm, otherwise the rejection stands. When a bill has passed both houses, it goes to the President of the Republic for his signature. A presidential veto can only be overridden by a two-thirds majority vote in the Sejm.

The annual budget must be tabled in adequate time by the government so as to permit proper parliamentary examination. The Sejm must decide within 30 days whether it intends to propose amendments and if so moves to consider these in detail. Should the Sejm fail to approve a budget within three months, then the President of the Republic may dissolve the Sejm. The Budget Committee coordinates preparation of the budget after receiving amendments from the spending committees.

Motions of no-confidence require 46 signatures to be tabled, and nominations for Prime Minister in the various possible phases of the complex appointment procedure require 40 signatures. At present only one opposition party (the UW) can muster adequate support alone without agreement with other parties.

Committees play a central part in the supervision of the executive. They may require written and oral evidence from government departments and state bodies and may compel the attendance of designated ministers and officials. Committees may address motions calling for action to state bodies. At every sitting there is a one-hour period for interpellations and up to two hours for questions. Interpellations may be tabled by any individual member to ministers, state bodies and the National Bank of Poland. Initial answers are given in writing and they are then debated within 21 days of tabling. If the answer is deemed unsatisfactory, supplementaries can be put for up to ten minutes. A vote may then be taken on whether to accept the answer and close the matter or not. This is, as it were, the heavy artillery. Questions deal with lesser and more detailed issues. They must be tabled at least 12 hours before the sitting and there is no debate on the replies given.

Party discipline is weak in all the various ex-Solidarnosc parties even in the various components of the SLD. Efforts are being made to tighten discipline, especially in the UW. It has been by no means unknown for significant minorities in the governing parties to oppose proposals put forward by the government or to support opposition bills.

At an average sitting of the Sejm, such for example as that of 28–30 June 1995, about 15 bills are finally passed into law and between 7 and 10 more are considered at various stages of their passage, involving dealing with presidential vetoes, Senate amendments and referrals to committee.

A referendum can be held 'in cases of particular interest to the state' (Little Constitution, §19). It may be initiated only by the Sejm, acting by an absolute majority or alternatively by the President of the Republic, but then only with the consent of the Senate.

The Senate

The Senate is a smaller and more intimate body. It has only one hundred members, elected on the same day as the Sejm. An early dissolution of the Sejm therefore also means the dissolution of the Senate as well. The Senators represent the 49 Provinces (Voivods) and the capital city.

The Senate cannot censure the government and takes no part in the procedure of Government formation. Nor does it have any absolute veto power over legislation. It is therefore basically a revising chamber, with some other residual powers. It considers bills passed by the Sejm and may propose amendments within a strict deadline of 30 days. If it does not, the bill is considered passed. As in the Sejm, the committee stage is important. The committee responsible considers the Sejm bill and makes a recommendation to the full Senate, either for approval, rejection or amendment of the bill. The Senate also plays a part in the initiation of referenda, the appointment of judges and the revision of the Constitution, as we have seen.

The Senate may also initiate bills, as has been mentioned. These then go to the Sejm for consideration, and if passed there, return to the Senate and remain subject to amendment by the Senate in the normal way. The 1989–91 Senate proposed 27 bills and of these 17 passed into law. Some were important, dealing with local government, industrial injuries compensation, the Senate's electoral procedure and collective bargaining. In the 1991–93 Senate term, nine bills only were proposed and four were passed. Draft senate bills are tabled in committee by individual members and then proceed to a vote in the full house if approved in committee.

There are 13 standing committees in the Senate and several *ad hoc* committees have also been created, such as that on the Europe Agreement set up in 1992. Committees in the Senate are small, averaging about 12 members and ranging from 9 to 23 members. Committees may decide to hold joint sittings with their Sejm counterpart, but this facility is very rarely used. As we have seen, ten Senators sit on the special Constitutional Committee, with 46 Sejm deputies. Senate committees are more inclined than their Sejm equivalents to hold hearings with experts and representatives of interest groups. These hearings are used to prepare deeper plenary debates on some important general problem, outside the legislative routine. Recent examples include debates on the situation of Poles abroad, Poland's eastern policy, agricultural reform and local government, all issues in which the Senate has shown close and sustained interest.

The new Constitution adopted in 1997 has weakened the powers of the Senate. This is a logical development, as the special historical circumstances which gave rise to the Senate and made it necessary for it to have significant powers are now long over.

11 The Party Systems

The party systems in the four Visegrad states are still young, fragile and unstable. They are still developing, though they have reached different stages of development. Some, such as Hungary and the Czech Republic, show sign of stabilisation. This is less obvious in Poland and the Slovak Republic. There has been only one normal election (excluding the first transition elections in 1989–90) in Hungary (1994), three in Poland (1991, 1993 and 1997) and one each in the independent Czech Republic (1996) and Slovakia (1994). This is still a very narrow basis for party systems to develop to maturity and stability. This will take time. However, the transformation of the former communist parties is virtually complete in Hungary and Poland, is far advanced in Slovakia, where the new post-communist parties have been returned to power, but has not started in the Czech Republic, where the KSCM remains unreconstructed and actually lost support in 1996. The centre-right part of the political spectrum remains chaotic in Hungary and above all in Poland and Slovakia, but not in the Czech Republic. Even here, the battle for domination of the centre-right between conservatives and christian democrats is not fully over, though it now seems that christian democracy cannot become the major political force on the right there. Religion, politically important in Poland and Slovakia, far less in Hungary, is marginal as a political force in the Czech Republic. Nationalism, especially in Slovakia, has created unexpected kinks in the party spectrum. The less nationalist groups of both left and right, SDL, KDU and the Hungarian parties have cooperated against the nationalist-populists (HZDS, SNS, WP). As a result, the Slovak party spectrum has not yet fully settled down. Will the nationalist/internationalist cleavage or the traditional left/right cleavage prevail?

The historical development of the various party systems in the region in the inter-war period and in the short semi-democratic interlude between the end of the Second World War and the full communist takeover (almost non-existent in Poland) was also rather different. Czechoslovakia had the most lively democratic party system. Yet, in the event, the very late and almost overnight progress of the Velvet Revolution in 1989 meant that the 'old' parties had no chance of re-emerging in any significant sense. Now, after a false start, the Social democrats (CSSD) have become firmly established as the main opposition party, marginalising the unreconstructed KSCM. Poland had no deep-rooted democratic party system to return to and so followed a new model, with Solidarnosc moving from its trade union role into that of an umbrella political movement, then in all but name a political party, before splitting in several parties in 1990. Hungary had a lively though short-lived party system between 1945 and 1947, building in part on its earlier semi-democratic traditions. The very gradual process of transition in that country led directly to a party-driven reform process, rather than one driven by a mass movement as in Poland or Czechoslovakia. It also offered relatively more favourable conditions for old parties (KDNP and Smallholders) to re-emerge on the right of the political spectrum.

More broadly, some patterns are emerging though not uniformly and not consistently. The umbrella mass-movement phase is clearly over everywhere. OF, VPN and Solidarnosc no longer exist. The pro/anti the former system cleavage is also fast disappearing as a salient dimension. Most obviously, it does not exist any more in Hungary. The formation of the MSZP/SDS coalition in 1994 between the reformed communists of Guyla Horn and the SDS, the most radical anti-communist party of the former opposition, is a potent symbol that this phase is indeed over. Nor does it exist in the Czech Republic, where the government and opposition are all either former anti-system parties or new parties. In Poland, though, both parties in the SDL/PSL coalition admitted that the main reason for that coalition rather than another is essentially historical: it was a coalition between parties coming from the old system stable. Both might have been comfortable with other allies, but for the moment could not make other alliances. Therefore a Polish version of the Hungarian coalition involving the SDL and the UW might be more logical, but in Poland its time has not yet come. On the other hand, events do seem to have moved significantly since the formation of that coalition in 1993. The failure of the right and the former Solidarnosc groups to organise anti-communist coalition around Walesa in the second round of the 1995 presidential election suggested that this cleavage was indeed now finally losing its saliency. However, at the 1997 election, it was still evident as the AWS and the SDL were the main opponents. Everywhere in the region the centre-right is grappling with the need to realign and consolidate, even in the Czech Republic where it has been the most successful in managing the process. Forms of democratic 'alternance' have become possible everywhere, though they have not actually occurred in the Czech Republic yet. Viable alternative coalitions are in fact available everywhere.

THE CZECH REPUBLIC

The Czechoslovak party system was well developed between the World Wars. The state was governed by an almost permanent core coalition of five moderate system imminent parties, to which German and Slovak parties were occasionally added, at least in the middle years of the Republic from about 1926 to 1936. After 1989, this former party system could not be even partially revived. Following the 1990 election, the dominant party in the Czech Republic was the OF (Civic Forum), until it split apart. Unlike the Slovak Republic, no coalition partner was arithmetically necessary. However, for reasons of symmetry with Slovakia, similar coalitions were formed at the Federal level (OF/VPN (Public Against Violence) Christian Democrats) and in the two Republics. Thus, in the 1990–2 legislature, only the communists and Moravian autonomists formed a disparate opposition. Later, unlike in most other former communist states, the Czech Social Democrats have been able to re-emerge and now represent by far the largest opposition party to the centre-right coalition led by Vaclav Klaus, with 26 per cent of the vote in 1996. The old KSC, now the Czech and Moravian communists (KSCM), remains unreconstructed and cannot now expect to make the comeback achieved by the Hungarian MSZP, the Polish SDL or the Slovak SDL.

The Civic Forum (OF) was always a very broad church, from radical market liberals such as Vaclav Klaus, to value conservatives, social liberals, and even new leftists. Its loose movement structure and its visceral unwillingness to become a party organisation probably inevitably condemned it to a relatively early split. Very early, two identifiable wings emerged in OF: a social liberal wing around Havel and Dienstbier and free market wing around Klaus and Dlouhy. A much smaller social democratic tendency also developed. The Klaus wing forced the pace, pushing for rapid change towards becoming a conservative, market liberal party. This provoked the split in OF, which by the 1992 elections had spawned three separate parties: ODS (Civic Democratic party) of Vaclav Klaus, the ODA (Civic Democratic Alliance) of Vladimir Dlouhy, and the Civic Movement, later Free Democrats SD of Jiri Dienstbier.

A relatively stable and intelligible political spectrum has developed, though as in all emerging party systems there is a continual ongoing process of realignment, especially between the smaller groups in Parliament that continually split and reformed in new configurations during the first legislature. Nevertheless, these realignments have been at the margins and are in any case now entering an end phase. The broad contours of the party system remain, after the 1996 election, as they were laid down in 1992.

On a left–right continuum, the four original coalition parties, the ODS, ODA, and the two (now one) Christian Democratic parties, form a solid centre-right block. To their right are the Republicans. The Moravian Autonomists that won seats in 1992, but none in 1996, are close to the political centre. The LSNS leaned more to the coalition than did the SD with whom it merged in 1996. The new merged party won no seats in 1996. The three parties of the centre-left in the 1992 legislature, now reduced to two, form a cluster on the centre-left. The CSSD straddles the centre and the space to the immediate left of centre. The Left Block (LB) that held seats in the 1992 legislature, but won none in 1996, stood to the immediate left of the CSSD, and the unreconstructed KSCM constitutes the far left of the Czech political spectrum.

This impressionistic placement is borne out by analysis of the voting records of the parties in the 1992–6 legislature. The four coalition parties form a cluster. Within that cluster, ODS is most distant from the left and ODA, with the Christian Democrats slightly nearer. LSNS voting behaviour placed it very near to the coalition. The Moravian Centre Alliance's voting behaviour placed it equidistant from the coalition and the left, hence dead in the centre. The three left-wing parties formed an obvious cluster, but one that was more spread than the coalition cluster. The CSSD is closest to the coalition cluster, followed closely by LB and with the KSCM lying isolated. The voting behaviour of the Republicans distances them from all other parties.

The Left

The Communists (KSCM)

This orthodox communist party is one of the rare parties in central and eastern Europe still to retain the old communist label. It came in second to OF in the 1990 election with a solid 13.24 per cent, which gave it a firm basis for survival. In the 1990–2 term, it haltingly began the classic process of renewal, running at the 1992 election as part of wider Left Block coalition. However, the conservatives in the party soon regained control and reversed the process of modernisation and renewal. The Left Block coalition then split. Most of the old KSC membership stayed with the KSCM and a new separate KSCM group was formed in Parliament with ten members. Thus after the 1993 Congress, there were three parties derivative in large part from the old KSC – the 'successor' KSCM, the

Left Block and the small Democratic Left. The whole Left Block gained 14.3 per cent in 1992, and the KSCM alone gained only 10.8 per cent in 1996 and failed in its declared goal of distancing the CSSD again as it had done in 1992. Nor can it even expect to position itself, as it had hoped, as a 'rebalancing' left pole of the opposition, acting as a 'conscience' and pressure on the CSSD. It campaigned in 1996 as the champion of the losers in the reform process, as Czech nationalists opposed the German pressures both in regard to EU membership and on the issue of the Sudeten area; opposed to NATO membership and to the Maastricht Treaty, though not to the EU membership as such. Its campaign was almost entirely negative. It distanced itself not only from the CSSD, but also from the neighbouring reform communists such as the Hungarian MSZP and the Polish SLD.

Its membership and electorate is aging and are mostly over fifty years old. It is composed of old cadres of the KSC and its associated groups, and those particularly in the public sector and large privatised firms who are or feel themselves to be losers from the economic and political reform process. It still retains a strong presence in local government, with 12 per cent of the vote at the last municipal elections in 1994, though heavily concentrated in certain areas such as northern Moravia. The party now seems unlikely to be able to make the changes that would be needed to ensure itself a continued meaningful role in Czech political life, despite the opportunity that the CSSD's clear move into the centre might have offered it.

The Left Block (LB)

Originally, the Left Block was, as we have seen, a broad electoral coalition that included the KSCM. After the KSCM left the coalition, the LB retained 24 of the coalition's original 35 deputies and moved to consolidate into a party in December 1993. It held its first congress in February 1995, adopting a new programme at that time. The LB has about 3,000 members, mostly in Prague, northern Moravia, east and west Bohemia. Its electorate is mostly younger voters in the 20–50 age bracket, mainly intellectuals and teachers. Leadership is in the hands of a steering committee, with a chair and four vice-chairs. The LB has applied for admission to the Socialist International, but has not yet been accepted.

The party clearly seeks to position itself to the left of the CSSD, but to the right of the KSCM, as a respectable, democratic left , exerting pressure on the CSSD more effectively than the unreconstructed KSCM can hope to do. No doubt, had the LB gained seats in Parliament in 1996 it would have worked with CSSD, but at a critical distance from it. For example, it supports Czech EU membership, but opposes NATO membership. It has a more cautious approach to privatisation, preferring a mixed economy with a significant state sector being retained. It is above all opposed to creating private monopolies. It places great emphasis on social policy and the need to moderate the impact of the market reforms and opposes privatisation in health care provision, cuts in welfare and education budgets. Its future must now be in doubt. It was squeezed by the CSSD at the 1996 elections, winning only 2 per cent. Without a platform in Parliament it may lose its electorate to the CSSD and possibly also to the KSCM.

The Social Democrats (CSSD)

The CSSD is now, since the 1996 election, the main opposition pole, around which an alternative to the ODS-led coalition could be formed. It is the most dynamic and attractive opposition party, with a new leadership that showed consistently improving opinion-poll figures during the 1992–6 term. It won only 4 per cent and no seats in 1990, and a modest increase to 6.5 per cent and sixteen seats in 1992, still well behind the Left Block coalition and even the KSCM. Polls gave it between 12 per cent and 21 per cent always well above its 1992 result, though the 1994 local government elections were, at 11 per cent, below its poll ratings. However, they did represent a solid advance on 1992. In 1996 it won 26.4 per cent and 61 seats, a massive gain, compared even with its best opinion-poll results. It clearly gained significantly during the campaign itself. The CSSD itself soon assumed the position of the main opposition party to Klaus, blocking and permitting any breakthrough by the KSCM. This rather bold strategy paid off handsomely in 1996. Its vote was even higher in the senate elections and in polls since the 1996 election. The Czech political scene is now therefore quite different from that in Hungary, Poland or Slovakia, where post-communist parties, rather than social democrats, constitute the dominant force on the left.

The CSSD was founded in 1878, back in the Austro-Hungarian Empire, and was represented in the Reichsrat in Vienna and then became the largest party in the new Czechoslovak Parliament in 1920. It was a major player in the coalition politics of the First Republic. Following the communist takeover in 1948, the party was forcibly merged with the KSC by undemocratic means and continued in exile, remaining a member of the International. As the Velvet Revolution unfolded, exiles and internal sympathisers met on 19 November 1989 to re-establish the party and held a congress in March 1990. The new party operated only in the Czech part of the country and therefore remained unaffected by the split in 1993. Initially, it had severe internal factional disputes, some internal corruption and made inappropriate leadership choices, bringing in too many exiles without adequate understanding of the situation in the country. It was only after a leadership change, when Miloš Zeman became leader in February 1993, that the party began to flourish. It is a long-standing member of the SI and an observer member of the Party of European Socialists (PES). The CSSD sees itself as being on the right of the European socialist spectrum.

The party has 13,000 members, but just to put forward a full slate of candidates in all municipalities would require 40,000 members! It is organised throughout the Czech republic in about 700 local branches, with from 5 to 50 members. The basic unit is the 89 slightly larger district branches that group a number of local branches. The party has recently established 15 regional executives. There is usually a district office, with at least one full or part-time party official. The National Executive operates a quota system (20 per cent women and 10 per cent youth). It has an Inner Board responsible for day-to-day management and a Chair (Miloš Zeman) and five vice-chairs. It employs a small national staff of four full-timers. The CSSD has a small executive and a full-time secretary. Its parliamentary group works closely with the extra-parliamentary party and has established several joint working parties. Parliamentary candidates are selected at the regional level. Chairman Zeman told the party's 27th Congress in May 1995 that the most important organisational task was to strengthen the regional and local organisation and to achieve the right balance between local and central party bodies.

The CSSD is strongest in northern Moravia and then northern Bohemia. It is weakest in Prague. It won 34.5 per cent to 27.5 per cent for ODS in northern Moravia, but only 19 per cent to 44 per cent for ODS in Prague. Among its members, only 25 per cent are women, though the CSSD has more women voters then men. Only 22 per cent of its members belonged to the old KSC. Its draws its support from employees, workers and pensioners, though it is more a party of the middle intelligentsia than of the working class. The party had sought unsuccessfully to constitute a common front of the democratic opposition parties under the banner of a'realistic block' (CSSD, LSNS, SD, the Moravians and the LB). It remains open to forms of cooperation with individuals, groups and smaller parties, though after its electoral victory in 1996 it may achieve a hegemonic position on the left, with the status of the largest party in Parliament and the bar of 35 per cent of the vote clearly being within its reach if it were to mop up the electorate of these smaller parties on the left and in the centre.

The party has made improved social legislation, more progressive labour law, expenditure on education and training, opposition to the privatisation of health care and pensions its main priority issues. It has supported privatisation, but has been critical of the manner in which it has been carried out by the ODS-led coalition. CSSD argued that privatisation has not actually been carried out in accordance with proper market principles, as uncontrolled private monopolies have been established, and market-distorting, 'clientalist' subsidies have prevented the necessary restructuring that the disciplines of the market would require, storing up even greater problems and job losses in the future. At the same time, the CSSD argues that the necessary social measures to deal with the consequences of restructuring have not been put in place.

In foreign policy its divergences with the Klaus government are fairly limited. CSSD strongly supports EU and NATO membership. At times it seems more pro-EU than Mr Klaus, who often sounds like a Eurosceptic. CSSD believes in a social Europe and supports greater political integration. Despite a joint commission with the German SPD on bilateral relations, the CSSD has taken a tough line on the Sudeten issue, but responsibly did not campaign on the question in 1996.

The strategic goal of the party is first to achieve dominance of the left of the Czech political spectrum, so as to marginalise the KSCM and hence remove any residual fears about the CSSD as a potential government party. With its 26.4 per cent in 1996, the party virtually seems to have attained this goal. It can now turn to its second goal of using that position as a springboard to force a change of government, without any reliance on KSCM support, which the CSSD rejects. CSSD leader Miloš Zeman has become the *de facto* leader of the opposition and the alternative Prime Minister to Vaclav Klaus. He is now President of the National Assembly, one of the top three personalities in the state. With President Havel and ex-Prime Minister Klaus, he is one of the most charismatic Czech political leaders.

The Centre

The Free Democrats (SD) and the LSNS

The SD of Jiri Dienstbier, a centre-left derivative of OF and the much older LSNS, a derivative of the National Socialists, was first founded in the nineteenth century, merged in late 1995 with the aim of creating a broad

Liberal party and capable of obtaining more than 5 per cent of the vote, ensuring the continued representation of liberal ideas in Parliament. However, the alliance did not have time to 'take' and was often uncomfortable. Despite the charisma of Jiri Dienstbier, the centre was squeezed by CSSD and failed to cross the 5 per cent hurdle at the 1996 elections.

The SD, formerly the Civic Movement (OH) led by Jiri Dienstbier, Foreign Minister after the Velvet Revolution, narrowly missed gaining parliamentary representation in 1992 with 4.8 per cent of the vote. Its poll ratings during the 1992–6 term varied, but always hovered around the 4 per cent mark. Faced with difficult strategic choices, it sought to unify diverse groups under the liberal label. One minority wing wanted to work with CSSD. The majority prepared the ground for the creation of a genuine liberal party, which became the SD and joined the Liberal International in September 1994.

SD continued to defend the moral and ethical dimension in politics that had been so central in OF. It sought a middle way between ODS and CSSD, regarding itself as a movement, an oppositional party, a party of ideas. It strongly supports Czech membership of the EU as part of its goal of opening up Czech society. It adopts a cautious approach to privatisation and argues for an 'ecology of people'. It strongly supports decentralisation and active local government. Jiri Dienstbier has been elected to the Prague city council. Its main support is in Prague among liberal intellectuals and academics.

LSNS changed its name from the National Socialist Party (nothing to do with Nazis) to Liberal National Socialist Party at its 1993 congress. It is the continuation of the historic National Socialist Party, founded in 1897, which was a moderate social democratic party during the First Republic. It was the party of President Benes and the second oldest Czech party. It was in reality a centre party and key player in coalition politics between the wars. During the communist period, it remained a satellite party within the National Front controlled by the communists, thus retaining important property in central Prague and its own newspaper. In 1989 it tried to re-establish itself and refused to merge into OF. It failed to gain any seats at the first election in 1990. It therefore formed a purely tactical alliance with the Greens and Farmers Party under the label of LSU (Social and Liberal Union) to contest the 1992 elections. It won 6 per cent and 15 seats. It soon split over such issues as nuclear energy and the attitude to be adopted towards the ODS-led coalition. Part of LSU was shifting to the left, which was unacceptable to the old NS elements. A new leadership, a new programme and a new name relaunched the party, which leant more to the right and initially opted to go it alone without allies. This made the later alliance with the SD more difficult to understand.

At the time of the merger, the LSNS had 10,000 members, well down on its 17,000 members in 1993 (it had 600,000 members before 1948), organised at district and regional level. It owned a valuable building in central Prague, that enabled it to borrow money, and three newspapers. It was deliberately centrist or even right-leaning. It actually voted for the ODS government's programme, adopting a stance of constructive criticism. It brought a small business dimension to the alliance. The merger was not a success, no seats were won in 1996.

The Czech and Moravian Centre Union (CMUS)

The CMUS was formed out of three parties that ran as a coalition in 1992, including the Czech and Moravian Centre Union and the Agricultural Party. They have now merged into a single party and between them have 15,000 members. At the 1992 election, the CMUS won 5.9 per cent of the vote and 14 seats. Later, it was joined by two former Republican MPs. Its poll ratings remained under 2 per cent and it failed to win representation in 1996, despite close to 15 per cent of the vote in parts of Moravia. Its members and voters are middle class, from smaller towns and villages in Moravia. It is a regionalist/autonomist party, supporting decentralisation, the creation of regional political institutions and a Senate. It is pragmatic and centrist. Its headquarters are in Brno and not in Prague.

The Right

The Christian Democrats

The Christian Democrats are close to the centre, though value conservative. There were actually two Christian Democratic parties: the traditional KDU–CSL and the much smaller KDS, formed after 1989, which has now merged into ODS. Were it not for the fact that CSL–KDU has been and remains a member of the ODS-led coalition, there might be some justification for classifying this party (but not KDS) as belonging to the centre, rather than the right.

(a) KDU–CSL   The Peoples Party (CSL) was originally founded in 1919. It was a major player in the coalition politics of the First Republic. It was a 'block party' during the communist period. After 1989, it linked up with the newly founded small Christian Democratic Union (KDU) as

the KDU–CSL. The old CSL remained the core of the new merged party, but it derived some legitimacy from the merger, distancing itself from the past. It now has 2,500 local branches, especially in southern Moravia, and 84 district parties, each with a chair, an executive and paid officials. There are Bohemian and Moravian regional coordinating bodies. The party's National Executive has 70 members, including all KDU–CSL ministers and MPs as *ex officio* members. The other members are chosen by the district parties. An Inner Board of 15 members runs the party on a daily basis. It has a very large membership for the modern Czech Republic – 75,000, of whom more than half joined after 1989. It has a strong basis in local government, with over 1,000 mayors. It is strongly Catholic, though it does include a small minority of Protestants and even non-believers among its electorate. It developed a strong network in the Church and Catholic organisations, though the conservative Church hierarchy has not always supported the party. Its main strength lies in southern Moravia. It is weakest in industrial northern Bohemia. It has 120 full-time officials, 80 out in the districts and 40 in the party HQs in Prague and Brno. It is a full member of both EUCD and EDU.

KDU–CSL considers itself to be a mainstream European Christian Democratic party, taking the German CDU or the Austrian ÖVP as its models, and is committed to the social market economy. Though most of its voters are Catholics and it finds it difficult to break out of its electoral ghetto, it argues that its values should have appeal to society as a whole. Its approach is decentralist, whereas its ODS partner in government is centralist. It favours regional government and a Senate. Its main areas of policy concern are agriculture, education and culture, social policy and health care. It strongly supports both EU and NATO membership. It obtained 8.42 per cent in 1990, 6.3 per cent in 1992 and 8.4 per cent in 1996. It has the advantage of a stable core electorate, but with little potential for growth. It has been in government since 1990 and is now a key player, as a bridge between ODS and CSSD, whose external support or at least 'toleration' is necessary for the government now.

(b) KDS The small and strongly catholic Christian Democratic Party (KDS) was formed after 1989 by those who felt that the CSL was irredeemably compromised by its past history as a block party. The KDS stands to the right of the KDU–CSL and ran in alliance with the ODS in 1992. It won an excellent deal, with 10 MPs elected on the ODS list and ministers in the coalition. It could never have hoped to gain seats alone; in June 1995 it merged with ODS.

Civic Democratic Party (ODS)

The ODS, led by Prime Minister Vaclav Klaus, has been the dominant party in the Czech Republic since 1992. It made the running in the split-up of former Czechoslovakia. ODS is a secular market-liberal conservative party that models itself on the British Conservative Party. Indeed, Vaclav Klaus openly models himself on Margaret Thatcher. Reality is, as we shall see, rather more complex. The ODS (with its small KDS ally) became the largest party in 1992, with 29.7 per cent of the vote and 76 (66 ODS) in the 200-members Assembly, and the leading force in the four (now three) party centre-right coalition that was then formed and continued after the 1996 elections, despite retaining only 99 seats in Parliament. The party was formed out of the split in OF, provoked by ODS leaders such as Klaus (who was then Finance Minister in the OF/CSL–KDU coalition) as a response to what they saw as the too slow pace of privatisation and market reforms, which they sought to radically accelerate. The ODS programme declares that 'ODS is a conservative party and a right-wing party'. It is based on individualism and individual initiative. In 1996, it ran a campaign for 'a market economy without adjectives', i.e. an unqualified market economy, not a social market economy. The party has 22,000 members.

The party has a President (Vaclav Klaus) and four Vice-Presidents, elected by the Congress. The National Executive has eighteen members elected by the eight party regions. Five MPs are *ex-officio* members of the Executive. The parliamentary party has a small executive, with a Chair and two Vice-Chairs. The full parliamentary group meets at least weekly and Klaus attends monthly. Party spokesmen organise working groups and caucuses of the ODS members of the relevant committees on each bill that comes before Parliament. The parliamentary group (club) has a small office and a staff of three.

The main electoral base of ODS is in the cities, especially the larger cities such as Prague, where it won 44 per cent in 1996. ODS is weakest in rural areas and areas of industrial decline, such as northern Moravia. It has a strong following among people with higher education, among university graduates, entrepreneurs and workers in smaller private companies.

The party believes firmly in private, individual initiative as the motor of both the economy and society and opposes all forms of corporatism. It seeks to apply these principles beyond the purely economic sphere to such matters as health care, education and even culture. Its aim is to open the economy to competition. It is a value conservative party, though not specifically Christian, and indeed, as in Britain there are potential contradictions between its value conservative principles and its espousal of individualism as the most fundamental principle of economic and social activity. Here it should be remembered that religion has played a much less important political role in what is essentially a very secular society than in Hungary, Poland or Slovakia. Indeed, 50 per cent of Czechs recognise no religious affiliation or practice at all. ODS seeks to reduce the role of the state, imposing rigorous controls on public expenditure, through the elimination of subsidies. However, its specific policies have often been divorced from the purity of its market rhetoric. To the frustration of its ODA coalition partner, it has often adopted a more populist and clientelist policy, removing subsidies only slowly, if at all; delaying restructuring and opposing deregulation of the rented housing market. The limits of this pragmatic approach were shown in the 1997 economic crisis, caused among other things by too slow restructuring. ODS is centralist in its approach to government, again like the British Conservatives. It has opposed both the creation of a Senate, which would provide some regional representation, and any form of devolved regional government, though both are mandated by the constitution. Now, after the 1996 elections, ODS is forced to compromise on both these issues, since its coalition partners and CSSD want progress here. ODS supports both EU and NATO membership, though Mr Klaus opposes political union and the social dimension, believing that the EU should become more market-orientated. ODS proved remarkably successful at holding its vote at the 1996 election after four years in power, but the arrogance of Vaclav Klaus, who ran a hardball purely ODS campaign, rather than a coalition campaign, alienated his partners who sought to tie ODS to a much more detailed coalition agreement this time even before the election result made it necessary to deal with CSSD as well. ODS is having a much less free hand than in the last parliamentary term. This arrogance was instrumental in Klaus' fall in 1997.

Civic Democratic Alliance (ODA)

ODA was also formed out of the debris of OF. It is often hard to see why it should be a separate party to ODS. Logic would dictate the creation of one single, large conservative party. Policy differences with ODS are minimal. It is perhaps largely a matter, as so often in the region, of history, style and personalities. ODA for example has opposed the much harder line towards former communists in public life adopted by ODS and there have been clashes of personality between Industry Minister

Dlouhy (ODA) and ODA Chairman Jan Kalvoda and Klaus. ODA is often perceived as being more centrist than ODS, which may actually be incorrect. Its leading minister Vladimir Dlouhy is the most popular politician in the Czech Republic, according to the polls. It won only 5.9 per cent, well behind ODS, in 1992, but its polls ratings placed it consistently higher and in 1996 it stabilised. It has been part of the centre-right coalition since 1992.

ODA has 2,500 members, mostly in Prague (500) and southern Moravia. Most of its voters are in these same areas. It has a loose decentralised structure, with local ODA Clubs, with a minimum of five members. There may be several Clubs in larger towns. In Prague for example there are 20. The Party has a Chair, Mr Jan Kalvoda, and five Vice-Chairmen, including Dlouhy. It has councillors in 270 municipalities. There are nine regional party organisations. Like all other parties, it is mainly financed by state subsidies, but it is beginning to get some contributions from business.

Ideological differences with ODS are minimal, though there were differences on issues such as the split-up of the country that was even more openly favoured by ODA. There was also disagreement on restitution of Church and other property sequestered by the communists. ODA favoured regional government and a Senate. ODS did not. ODA is more decentralising and less totally market-orientated, especially in regard to culture and education, where it sees a continuing role for the state, at least through provision of tax incentives to private initiative. On some deregulatory issues, on the other hand, ODA is more purist than ODS. As a smaller party it can perhaps be less populist and less clientelist on matters such as housing. It is very pro-European and does not share Klaus's Euroscepticism. Its voters are hard to classify. Some argue that they are more centrist, more open to other alliances, but this is not clear. Some also argue that the existence of two conservative parties with different styles actually maximises the overall conservative vote.

The Republicans (RSC)

This party is clearly on the far, populist and nationalist right. It is openly racist. It espouses all the populist anti-parliamentary causes of the classic far right such the French Front National or Haider's FPÖ in Austria. It won a worrying 6.0 per cent in 1992, but suffered continual internal splits and bad press during the 1992–6 term. It seemed in difficulties and its poll results lay under the 5 per cent threshold for much of the period. It was isolated, ineffective and fragmented in Parliament. It is to a large extent a one-man band, the creation of its leader Mr Sladek. It draws above average support among the unemployed, alienated youth, especially in northern Bohemia. In 1996 it increased its vote, but not dramatically, to 8 per cent.

SLOVAKIA

The party system in Slovakia has not yet fully stabilised and may not do so for some time. It is characterised by splits, new party formation, temporary election alliances and 'renversement d'alliances' in the course of the legislature, the collapse of coalitions and the consequent destabilisation of governments. Since the early break-up of Public against Violence (VPN), the Slovakia equivalent of Civic Forum (OF), the party system has revolved around the dominant and turbulent figure in Slovak politics, Vladimir Mečiar. Parties have defined themselves in relation to Mečiar: for him or against him.

Furthermore, the Slovak party system has always been different from that in the Czech lands, even going back between the wars. These differences re-emerged after 1989. The Slovak party system was affected far more than the Czech party system, by a double transition: out of communism and out of Czechoslovakia. Very soon after the Velvet Revolution the national question moved centre-stage, upstaging all other issues, causing the split in VPN. Unlike the Czech Republic, the new fronts did not form around issues related to the pace of market reform, but rather around positions on the national question. The poles of realignment were for or against Slovak independence. Thus the initial VPN–Christian Democrat (KDH) coalition led by Mr Mečiar dislocated over this issue and was replaced until the 1992 elections by a Christian Democrat-led coalition that was less nationalist in outlook. This coalition was effectively defeated at the 1992 election and was replaced by a government led again by Mr Mečiar and dominated by his nationalist Movement for a Democratic Slovakia (HZDS) and the Slovak National Party (SNS). Opposition to the autocratic style of Mr Mečiar and its more extreme nationalist tendencies led to the defection of HZDS moderates around Foreign Minister Moravčik, who formed a new party, the Democratic Union (DUS). Moravčik then organised the defeat of Mečiar in Parliament and replaced him in the spring of 1994 at the head of a coalition of the main opposition parties, the SDL, KDH, his own DUS and an even smaller splinter party from the HZDS, with the external support of the Hungarian parties. This coalition lost the 1994 elections and Mečiar returned at the head of a new nationalist-populist coalition of his own HZDS, SNS and the new leftist Slovak Workers party (AWS).This polarised balance between pro-Mečiar groupings and the anti-Mečiar, less nationalist, groupings remains in a state of flux, as new conflicts have appeared within the new coalition between HZDS and its partners. Party discipline and cohesion remained weak and unstable and continuing defections and cross-voting remained frequent. For example, a bill forbidding the privatisation of the second Bratislava TV station was passed by a majority including Workers Party and SNS and opposition votes.

The Left

The Party of the Democratic Left (SDL)

The SDL is a typical former communist party . Its leaders seek to demonstrate that it is indeed a 'new' party, with new members, but its core is still the reformist wing of the old communist party, as even its own literature admits. It held its founding congress in December 1991. It brings together both former communist party members and non-party people, mostly intellectuals. Most recent estimates suggest that its membership is about 40,000. SDL has a strong local organisation throughout Slovakia, with party branches in about two-thirds of town and villages, based on the reformist parts of the old party structure. It also retains a network of affiliated organisations for youth (NDL), women (ZDLZ) and workers (ZRS). This later split to form a new party. It has three types of party organisation: local, regional and national. At the national level, the congress is the highest decision-making body. SDL has a Board, which is, as it were, the party's parliament, and Executive, and within the Executive a day-to-day management committee. The party Chair is the young and charismatic Peter Weiss, assisted by a female and a male Vice-Chair.

The party is adamant that it is not purely the continuation of the old communist party, an accusation often made against it from the right. It claims to be a modern social democratic party, with close links to the SPÖ and SPD on which it seeks to model itself, and to the SI, of which it is not yet a full member. It adhered to the Stockholm Declaration of Principles of the SI as early as its first party congress in 1991. With its full integration into the western socialist movement in mind, it has cooperated with the Slovak Social Democratic Party (SDSS), which is a full SI member, from 1992 and went into the 1994 elections in an electoral coalition with the SDSS and some smaller groupings, though without merging the parties.

It is electorally strongest in the eastern part of Slovakia and in the smaller towns. It is fairly weak in Bratislava. SDL voters are more likely to be women than men, aged between 35 and 55, non-religious, with only secondary school education.

SDL has had to protect itself against attacks on its two weakest flanks, namely that it is a continuation of the old communist party and secondly that it is not sufficiently Slovak or nationalist. Like all Slovak parties it has been unable to resist the rising tide of nationalism entirely. Initially, the party conceived of its reaction to the growing nationalist trend in terms of a more traditional defence of Slovak interests within the Czechoslovak framework by, for example, opposing the extreme market liberalisation measures proposed by Vaclav Klaus. This was clearly an inadequate reaction in the longer term. It has been ambiguous and undecided in its approach. It did not come out for full Slovak independence and then it first opposed and later supported Havel's proposals for a referendum on the national question. Eventually, however, it voted for both the Slovak Declaration of Sovereignty on 17 June 1992 and the new Slovak Constitution of 3 September 1992.

SDL supports 'the development of a social and ecological market economy' (party programme). It has a moderate and prudent approach to privatisation, placing emphasis on control of private monopolies and social rights. Whilst it accepts the political changes of 1990 and 1993, it has opposed the authoritarian tendencies of Mečiar. It fully supports the integration of Slovakia into the international community. It favours Slovak EU membership and was in power when the application was made. It is less clear on NATO membership, which it does not oppose, though it calls for a referendum on the issue. It has taken a pragmatic and conciliatory line in relations with Hungary, both on the Gabčikovo/Nagymaros dispute and on the position of the Hungarian minority in Slovakia, though here it has not been able to advance too far beyond nationalist Slovak public opinion. It has sought to promote a negotiated settlement with Hungary on both issues and to that end was prepared to make some concessions. It promoted dialogue both on a party-to-party basis with the MSZP, which prefigured the positive governmental contacts between Horn and Moravčik, leading to the Framework Treaty signed in Paris in 1995, and on the agreements with the Hungarian minority parties.

The Social Democrats (SDSS)

The SDSS is a small party with an influence beyond its size. It is an old party, with roots back before communism, and hence is a full member of the SI. It was led briefly by Alexsander Dubček before his untimely death in a car accident in 1992. It has a strategic value to the SDL as an entry card to the wider international social democratic scene.It was not represented in Parliament in either 1990 or 1992. In 1994, it ran as part of an electoral coalition (the Clover Leaf), with SDL, the Greens and Agricultural Workers. This list did poorly, with 10.4 per cent of the vote and 18 seats, but SDSS candidates were elected on this list. SDSS has only about 5,000 members. Its electorate overlaps with the SDL sources of voters: eastern Slovakia, Bratislava and Kosiče. It has more male electorate, aged 35–55, coming from medium-sized towns (20,000–50,000 inhabitants). Its voters are better educated and non-religious. The coalition in 1994 had a common platform, but each party retained its own programme as well and ran on its own priority issues. For SDSS, these were social issues, education and health policy. The party supports EU and NATO membership and is pragmatic on relations with Hungary.

The Greens

The Green Party was founded in 1990 and was represented in the Slovak National Council in the first term (1990–2), with six seats, but not in the 1992–4 term. Greens returned to Parliament after the 1994 election as part of the Clover Leaf electoral coalition. It is a moderate pragmatic party, seeking to promote environmental concerns in concert both with NGOs and economic interests. The party is aware that there is a paradox: an active green policy is needed to clear up the mess left by forty years of uncontrolled industrialisation, and yet due to the need to catch up with the west economically, their message of limited and sustainable growth falls on stony ground. Indeed, interest in and support for environmental issues has actually fallen. Like all Slovak parties, the Greens could not directly oppose the Gabčikovo project, though they have sought the most environmentally friendly solutions and a compromise with Hungary and the Hungarian minority.

The Slovak Workers Party (ASW)

The ASW is a new entrant to the political scene. It was only founded in 1994 around the former trade union wing of SDL (ZRS) that split from the parent party and made a dramatic entry into Parliament with 7.3 per cent of the vote and 13 seats. It immediately joined in a coalition with HZDS and SNS. It has occupied the political space left by the move of SDL towards the centre. It is nationalist and populist, but opposes modernisation and privatisation. It is equivocal towards Slovak membership of the EU and NATO which it openly opposed in the 1997 Referendum though belonging to a coalition that formally supports both. Relations within the coalition have been stormy over both distribution of patronage and privatisation. It is the same old problem of Mečiar's authoritarianism.

The Populist Right

Though for consistency, a right–left classification has been applied to Slovakia as well, it is misleading in the Slovak case. A more accurate alignment would be between internationalist modernisers and nationalist populists. The SDL, its SDSS and Green allies, the KDU and the small splinter parties from HZDS are modernisers and HZDS, SNS and ASW are populists. Seen from that standpoint, both the Moravčik coalition and the present coalition are logical, though they cross the left–right divide.

Movement for a Democratic Slovakia (HZDS)

The HZDS was founded by Vladimir Meciar in 1991 after the break-up of VPN caused by the ever more open conflict between the more and less nationalist elements in VPN. It is a very broad church, and despite, or perhaps because of, Mečiar's dominance has been prone to splits and severe factional infighting. It covers a broad range from old communists, often recycled as business men or managers, through populists, nationalists and technocrats without any political history. It is held together by populist nationalism and the iron grip of Mečiar himself, who has printed his own personal stamp on HZDS. He is its founder and its main electoral asset. It rapidly moved to adopt a nationalist position, in direct confrontation with the Czechs, and soon achieved a near hegemonic position in Slovakia. This made compromise with the Czechs all but impossible.

HZDS draws its main support from older voters, over 55, voters with only elementary education, workers in state enterprises which remain numerous in Slovakia, and the unemployed. It draws support from Protestants. It receives majority support from farmers and farm-workers. In 1992, it won a near absolute majority in Parliament, with 37.3 per cent and 74 out of 150 seats. In 1994, it won only slightly less support, with 35.0 per cent and 60 seats. HZDS is called a 'movement'. Its organisation and structure has until now been very loose. At the most recent congress in 1996 of the movement, Mečiar announced that he intended to build a stronger local party organisation that would have roots in all the towns and villages of the country. A more formal membership base and greater internal discipline would be developed, hence moving away from its original 'movement' structure towards a more classical party structure. Despite the hopes of the anti-Mečiar coalition formed in 1994, but defeated at the 1994 election, HZDS has shown itself to be a survivor and has entrenched its hegemonic position in Slovakia and remained indifferent to both internal and international criticism of its policies and political culture. With parties to its right and left and an essential pragmatism, HZDS has always had more strategic choices than other parties. It has adopted a statist, populist neo-socialist economic policy, slowing down privatisation and the development of the market economy as far as possible.

The Slovak National Party (SNS)

The SNS was established in March 1990, but it had links back into the 1930s which had obviously been interrupted after the Second World War. It decided, perhaps rather bravely, to remain outside the VPN umbrella at the 1990 elections and achieved a surprisingly good result, perhaps because it was perceived as the most, or only, 'authentically Slovak' party in the field. As such, it was initially the only party in Slovakia to openly support the idea of Slovak independence. It remained in opposition until 1992. By then public opinion had radicalised and its views had become virtually mainstream. It therefore joined Mečiar's HZDS in a nationalist coalition that took Slovakia to independence. It regards itself as economically to the right of HZDS, being more free market in its approach and more value conservative in cultural, ethical and educational matters than HZDS. As such, it has always given its first priority to achieving a strong position in education, culture and media policy, rather than seeking economic ministries in the coalition distribution of portfolios. Its nationalism has made SNS strongly supportive of the Gabčikovo project and opposed to the Framework Treaty with Hungary, let alone any increase in the collective rights of the Hungarian minority. SNS favours tax cuts and less state interference, especially for small business. It supports a gradualist approach to privatisation, which it sees as a tool, rather than an end in itself. It wants to increase competition by creating new private businesses and breaking up the new private monopolies that often replaced the old state monopolies, which has brought it into conflict with HZDS. SNS did surprisingly well in 1990 with 13.9 per cent, falling to 7.9 per cent in 1992 and again to 5.3 per cent in 1994. It then returned to power as the most junior partner in the tripartite nationalist coalition with HZDS and ASW. It could be that the monopoly of the nationalist issue that stood it in such good stead in 1990 has disappeared and with it the longer term *raison d'être* of the SNS.

The Christian Democrats (KDH)

Christian democratic clubs began to form in December 1989 through the church network. These formed the nucleus of the KDH which then formally set up in February 1990. At the first elections, it formed an alliance with the old 'bloc' Peoples Party that had maintained a shadowy existence throughout the communist period as part of the National Front. Though it did less well than the polls predicted, it nevertheless established itself as the second largest party, with 16.7 per cent in the House of Nations (the upper house of the Federal parliament) and 19 per cent in the Slovak National Council. It regained this position in 1994 after falling back to third place in 1992, behind both HZDS and SDL.

The KDH is, along with SDL, the only structured and organised mass party in Slovakia, with a full network of active local branches, based initially on the parish organisation of the Catholic Church. It has about 26,000 members. It holds the support of some 35 per cent of regular church-goers, almost exclusively Catholics, and has almost no support (1 per cent) among non-church-goers. Its support is also mostly among older and women voters. At the same time, Mr Carnagursky, the party leader and prime minister after the first fall of Mečiar, is close to the new Slovak entrepreneurial circles. The party has also received significant support from the Slovak Catholic hierarchy.

KDH identifies with the centre-right and the mainstream of European Christian Democracy, modelling itself in particular on the German CDU and the Austrian ÖVP. Like them, it belongs to the EUCD and the EDU. It declares that it believes in 'spiritual principles derived from the bible'. It supports the social market economy and acceleration of privatisation and creation of small business, but balanced by a policy of social justice, social consensus and fairness. KDH is strongly in favour of EU membership, accelerated European integration, closer relations with the west and NATO membership.

The Christian Democrats sought to resist excessive Slovak nationalism and were among the last to be reconciled to the inevitability of the split. KDH sought to develop democracy and transform the previously sterile relations between Czechs and Slovaks, in the hope that the common state could be preserved. Therefore, KDH proposed 'a treaty between the Slovak Republic and the Czech Republic as the basis of a common state' and as 'the guarantee of the equity and partnership between the two Republics'. This approach was overwhelmed by the wave of Slovak nationalism after 1992. Within independent Slovakia, it has been the main pole of the anti-Mečiar opposition.

The Hungarian Parties

The Hungarian minority represents about 567,200 people (10.8 per cent of the Slovak population) on the basis of an official declaration of minority status, though a larger number (608,000) declare Hungarian as their mother tongue. They live concentrated in a narrow strip along the north bank of the Danube and to the east along the Slovak/Hungarian border. In this region, they constitute 60 per cent of the population. They tend to live in smaller towns and villages with below 5,000 inhabitants. Hungarians represent a majority in 13 towns and exceed 10,000 inhabitants in five major cities (Komarno, Bratislava, Dunaska Streda, Nove Zamky and Kosice). Throughout the communist period, the minority was not allowed to establish any political parties. Even its right to establish cultural bodies was quite limited. It was allowed to establish one single cultural organisation, the CSMADOK, (Czechoslovak Hungarian Cultural Association) though it did gain some legally entrenched cultural rights.

Since 1989, there have been four political parties in the Hungarian community, though two of them have operated together in electoral coalitions in 1990, 1992 and 1994. The smallest, the Independent Hungarian Initiative (formed as early as November 1989), later the Hungarian Citizens Party, worked together with VPN and was therefore in government in Slovakia between 1990 and 1992. After the collapse of VPN, it fought the 1992 and 1994 elections on its own, winning 2.3 per cent of the vote each time and no seats. It defines itself as a liberal party and has observer status in the Liberal International. Coexistence, a broad platform for minorities, though actually mainly Hungarian was formed in February 1990. It is the strongest of the Hungarian parties. It is a broad-based and centrist party, claiming both conservative and liberal traditions. The Hungarian Christian Democratic Movement (MKDM) was also founded in 1990. It is affiliated to EDU and EUCD. It is a classic Christian Democratic party. It is the second largest Hungarian party and has worked with Coexistence at all three elections. The fourth and most recent party is the Hungarian People's Party, a more rightist Christian party, founded in December 1991. It also joined the coalition in 1992 and 1994. Together, the Hungarian parties win about 10 per cent of the vote. It would therefore seem that few Hungarians vote for any other parties. They collectively supported the short-lived Moravčik in 1994. That support, though vital in parliamentary terms, actually hurt the Slovak partners in the subsequent election. In return for their support, an eight-point platform of minority rights was agreed and largely implemented.

The political goals of the Hungarian parties are local autonomy, but within the Slovak state. They are not separatist. They demand language and education rights and facilities in those areas where the Hungarian minority represents at least 20 per cent of the population. They want to see Hungarian local government districts, but this is fiercely opposed by the Slovaks. They rejected the 1992 Slovak Constitution as offering inadequate minority rights. The Hungarian parties were strongly opposed to the Gabčikovo dam project and are the only Slovak parties to do so. They support market reforms and call for a land reform.

HUNGARY

Hungary represents a different case from Poland and Czechoslovakia and hence also from the Czech Republic and Slovakia. Hungary was the earliest of the central European states to enter a transition phase, with the possible exception of Slovenia. This was already evident by the time of the first round of elections in 1990, where Hungary stood out. The transition had been long and gradual, since the mid-1980s, well before the collapse of communism either in Hungary or its neighbours. The umbrella opposition movement stage exemplified by OF, VPN and Solidarnosc was bypassed in Hungary, though the Gabčikovo/Nagymaros dam issue and the Danube Circle that organised opposition to it did provide some elements of mobilisation around a 'liberation myth' in much the same way as Charter 77 and later OF and VPN and Solidarnosc. By 1989, however, this phase had already given way to party building.

The opposition was represented in the Round Table talks and in the 1990 elections by three parties, all of which shared in that liberation myth: the Hungarian Democratic Forum (MDF), the Free Democrats (SDS) and the Young Democrats (FIDESZ). Initially these three groups appeared merely to represent different and at times overlapping strands and personalities within the opposition movement; by the time of the 1990 election they had become more starkly differentiated and taken on clearer profiles. Thus, unlike the other central European states, electoral competition was already real in Hungary in 1990, because it was between different strands of the opposition, rather than a legitimising plebiscite between the opposition and the party of the old system. Traditional cleavages in Hungarian political life re-emerged and found their identification and articulation within the different strands of the former opposition. Two historically well-known blocs developed: the traditional, more nationalist and value conservative bloc led by MDF, with its Christian Democratic and Smallholder allies, and the urban, modernising, internationalist, intellectual bloc represented by SDS and FIDESZ. The young dynamic entrepreneurs were represented more by FIDESZ, which at that time was closer to its liberal cousin SDS than to MDF. At that time, MDF, paradoxically, appeared closer to the old regime reformers and therefore more institutionally and economically prudent and gradualist.

After the first election, at which six main parties won parliamentary representation, a three-'camp' political system emerged. On the left, there was the reformed communist party, now called the Hungarian Socialist Party (MSZP), and some smaller parties outside Parliament, such as the Workers Party (Munkaspart), of 'unreconstructed' communists, and the Social Democrats (SD). Together, these socialist parties represented about 20 per cent of the vote. In the centre, SDS and FIDESZ and some smaller parties outside Parliament formed a liberal camp. On the right, MDF, the Christian Democrats (KDNP) and the Smallholders Party (FKGP) formed a conservative camp.

After the second election in 1994, only the same six parties were returned to Parliament, though with radically changed levels of support. The former three-camp system polarised into a two-camp structure: the centre-left (MSZP and SDS) governing coalition, and the centre-right opposition (FIDESZ, MDF, KDNP, and possibly the increasingly maverick populist FKGP).

The coalition remained stable throughout the 1994–98 term. The party spectrum altered little on the surface, though as in the 1990–4 term, important changes were taking place below the surface. There was no significant recovery of MDF. The Populist-Nationalist Smallholders party emerged as the main opposition party, with 25 per cent in the polls and certainly the most aggressive and vocal. This party, as in the period between 1945 and 1947, won support outside its rural core areas. It stands on an anti-communist and an anti-western, anti-modernist position, for 'God, Home and Family', as its leader Mr Torgyan puts it. The success of the Smallholders has placed great strains on the moderate right and centre and above all on their alliance. The key issue for MDF, KDNP and FIDESZ is what should be their relationship with the Smallholders. This has led to a split in MDF. Its liberal elements, including former Foreign and Finance Ministers, left the party after the election of the nationalist Sandor Lezsak as Chairman. They formed a new party, the Democratic Peoples Party (DPP). Both DPP and FIDESZ aspire to create a liberal centre and reject any alliance with the Smallholders. MDF is trying to steer a middle course between this emerging liberal grouping and the Smallholders. These developments have undermined the effectiveness of the opposition and led to fears about polarisation that would leave no alternative to the present coalition other than the Smallholders.

The Left

The Workers Party (Munkaspart)

The Munkaspart is the heir of the unreconstructed part of the old communist party that rejects the modernisation and 'socialdemocratisation' of the MSZP. Munkaspart maintains that it is carrying on the old communist party after the 14th Congress at which the reform of the old party was agreed. It retains a degree of support among pensioners and workers in the remaining large state enterprises, who see themselves as victims of the economic reforms. It won 3.7 per cent in 1990 and 3.2 per cent in 1994 and hence no seats at either election. Its results were average or above average in Budapest. Its best results were in the south and east and the north and east and worst in western Hungary. Its best constituency result in 1994 was 9.49 per cent.

The Hungarian Socialist Party (MSZP)

With the liquidation of the old communist party (MSZMP) at its 14th Congress in 1989, a new reformist party, the MSZP, led by Imre Poszgay and Premier Nemeth and later Guyla Horn, the present Prime Minister, emerged from the ruins. The new party then declared itself to be 'a leftist socialist party, advocating democratic socialism, the rule of law and the market economy, rejecting democratic centralism and dictatorship' (founding principles). It was clearly defeated at the 1990 elections in its bid to retain control of the reform process that it had itself set in train and consigned to opposition and apparent permanent isolation. It won only 10.9 per cent of the vote and 33 seats. Benefiting from the substantial political and economic mismanagement of the centre-right coalition that created large groups in society that felt themselves to be the losers in the transition process, and the increasingly bitter divisions between the two liberal parties, and from the excellent image of Mr Horn, the party's new leader, MSZP rose steadily in the polls throughout 1993–4 to enter the election as the front runner. The only real question seemed to be whether it could win absolute majority. With 32.99 per cent it won 209 seats, an absolute majority.

Its strength is fairly evenly distributed across the country. In June 1994 it rarely won less than 20 per cent anywhere, even in its weakest areas in western Hungary. In eastern Hungary, especially in Protestant rural areas, its vote was often at the high 40 per cent mark. The party has several internal currents. The central, majority current of modernisers is dominated by party leader Guyla Horn. The more openly social democratic current is associated with the first MSZP finance minister Bekesi. The traditional old guard is to be found in the trade unions. There have been tensions on regional and trade union lines, but unity remains strong. Only one MSZP MP voted against the 1995 austerity budget.

Building on its core constituency among the heavy-industry working class and pensioners (48 per cent of the total MSZP vote in 1994), the party has sought to move into the centre and build bridges to civil society and to other political parties as an independent political force. It was this strategy that enabled it to break out of its isolation, win a majority and establish a coalition with SDS. It has avoided the trap of becoming simply the party of former *apparatchiks* and losers from the reform process. The typical MSZP voter is a middle-aged, male, urban intellectual, with higher education. Its voting base in all groups has become more balanced and its geographical spread more even.

The MSZP claims to stand on the principles of the 1989 Stockholm Declaration of the Socialist International. It became an observer in the SI in 1992 and a full member, with strong SPD and SPÖ support in 1994. It is therefore seeking to present itself as a modern, open social democratic party, incorporating, as its programme states, 'advocates of the popular national left wing, social liberals, christian socialists and other left-wingers'.

It has about 45,000 members (1994 figures), organised in 2,800 local branches, 392 districts and 20 regions. The supreme organ is the Congress, which elects a 23-member Presidium. The party's parliament is the 118-member National Board, with delegates from regional organisations and the parliamentary party. It maintains 16 specialised network organisations (Women, Youth, Teachers, Pensioners, Farmers...).

The party accepts the transition to the market economy, but approaches privatisation with great caution and considers that the private sector should be only part of a mixed economy. Its key aims are to promote economic growth, reduce unemployment, to establish genuine social partnership and to strengthen social security and social provision such as family allowances. It firmly supports the process of political democratisation, especially with regard to the media and the role of Parliament.

In foreign policy, it supported the EU application made by the former government, and NATO membership, though here its support is more ambiguous. It would wish to see if other alternative security arrangements can be made. The bottom-line reality is that MSZP did support NATO membership once it was on offer. It did, though, argue for a referendum on both EU and NATO membership and in government supported a yes vote in November 1997. It favours improving economic and political relations with its near neighbours, such as Slovakia, Romania and Serbia, and resolving the delicate and controversial issue of the collective rights (if any) to be accorded to the Hungarian minorities in these countries. Foreign policy was mostly consensual during the last parliamentary term and was not an issue in the coalition negotiations with SDS.

The Social Democrats (SD)

The Social Democratic Party was a historical party that had parliamentary representation in Hungary throughout the 1930s, but was forcibly merged with the communists in 1949. Attempts promoted by the Socialist International (SI) to revive the party, which had continued to lead a shadowy existence in exile, were a failure. The exile leadership and the new internal leadership disagreed about strategy. There were also splits, personality clashes and financial irregularities. The party's efforts to find an electoral base by building out from its traditions failed. There was no political space for it between the reform communists of MSZP and SDS. It registered only 3.7 per cent in 1990 and even less (3.5 per cent) in 1994. Party membership is about 2,000.

The Liberal Centre

The Alliance of Free Democrats (SDS)

Like the other opposition parties, the SDS grew out of the ferment of intellectual opposition that developed in Hungary from the early 1970s.

Each came to represent a particular strand or sensibility within the opposition movement, some rooted in the nineteenth-century and early-twentieth-century Hungarian political cleavages. The first intellectual opposition group grew around the Review Beselö. It was an urban, cosmopolitan movement among intellectuals, often Jewish intellectuals, such as Janos Kis, who naturally gravitated together to found SDS in November 1988, as soon as it became legal to found political parties. SDS took an active part in the 1989 Round Table and led the successful campaign for a referendum opposing the direct election of the President of the Republic before the parliamentary elections, thereby foiling the strategy of the reform communists. After losing the elections, SDS made a pact with MDF providing for an SDS leader to be elected President, for a limited number of types of Acts of Parliament of a constitutional character (some 20 in all) to be subject to the requirement of a two-thirds majority in Parliament and introducing the constructive no-confidence system to stabilise governments. SDS was thereby at least partially 'co-opted' into the majority, which was probably to its ultimate disadvantage.

SDS was culturally and politically the most anti-communist current within the former opposition. It is a slightly left-of-centre Social-Liberal party. It has a strong, but minority, internal Social Democratic tendency, which tried to promote the idea of SDS membership of the SI. In the end the party opted for membership of the Liberal International, though the Social Democrats within SDS retain links with the SI. SDS has always been close to the cultural and environmental opposition. It is an urban, west Hungarian party; with an outward-looking, European, modernising outlook, committed to a dynamic market economy.

It was defeated by MDF in the 1990 election. For the first part of the 1990–4 term, it was the main opposition party. It was then seen as the likely core of an alternative coalition, with FIDESZ. It was then overtaken first by FIDESZ and then by MSZP. By the time of the 1994 election, its only realistic ambition could be to prevent MSZP from winning an absolute majority and exercising a strong liberal moderating influence on MSZP. It won 24.7 per cent in 1990, but fell to 19.7 per cent in 1994.

It faced a serious strategic dilemma after the 1994 election. It was not arithmetically necessary to the MSZP, which had an absolute majority alone. However, it could help create a coalition with a two-thirds majority and could legitimise the new government. It would give the coalition over 50 per cent of the popular vote. It would reassure opinion at home and abroad. Seventy per cent of all voters and 91 per cent of its own voters wanted such a coalition. Yet, for many in the party, there were concerns about how much real moderating leverage the party would have; there were fears at becoming a powerless fig-leaf, with few future strategic options, especially if the government became unpopular. For many, too, going into coalition with MSZP, led by Horn, was psychologically very difficult. Many had been persecuted after 1956 and Horn had played a key role in the repression at that time. There was a not surprising distrust of MSZP for many in SDS. However, SDS had to face hard reality: it was losing ground and had to halt the slide; it was going nowhere fast. To refuse the challenge of entering government simply to retain its political virginity as an anti-communist protest party, mired in the past, would have reduced its credibility and in the now more pragmatic Hungary have left it without any clear role. It could not even count on being seen as the main opposition to an MSZP one-party government. The leadership therefore favoured a coalition, with a detailed coalition agreement as a means of stabilising the party and with the additional aim of strengthening the positive, modernising tendencies in MSZP.

SDS is, as we have seen, slightly left of centre, urban and progressive on social and cultural issues. Its main support is found in Budapest and western Hungary, towards the Austrian border. Its voters are younger, well-educated people; writers, teachers, creative artists, intellectuals and environmentalists. In 1990 it won 27.1 per cent in Budapest and led in 20 out of 32 constituencies in the first round. In 1994 it won 20.8 per cent in Budapest, 25.6 per cent in Vös, 22.2 per cent in Györ-Moson-Sopron County and 22.9 per cent in Komaron, its best County result. The spread of its vote was flatter than in 1990. It has 35,018 members (1994 figures).

The party strongly supports a social market economy, with reduced state intervention and increased competition. It places great emphasis on building Hungarian democracy and supporting civil society and civil rights and on media and cultural pluralism. It is internationalist and favourable to EU and NATO membership.

Young Democrats (FIDESZ)

FIDESZ began life as the Federation of Democratic Youth in 1988, during the last twilight years of communist rule. Its leader, Viktor Orban, was the most charismatic leader and orator in the opposition. Its constituency was very similar to that of SDS, but with more emphasis on youth, as untainted by connections with the old regime. Its voters come from west Hungary. They are well educated, urban and strongly anti-communist. When it became a political party, it adopted a rule that its members should be under 35, as a deliberate form of political renewal. This rule has now been relaxed. It was active in the demonstrations against the Nagymaros dam and in the movement to rehabilitate Imre Nagy. These were two emblematic causes of the opposition in the 1980s. FIDESZ seemed a dynamic, new and fresh party, a master of street events and creative use of the media. It was always strongly committed to free enterprise and to reducing the tutelage of the state over economic life. It won 8.9 per cent in 1990, mostly in Budapest and the Györ region in western Hungary.

During the 1990–4 term, it was front runner in the polls during 1992 and 1993, but the bubble burst as quickly as it had arisen when a financial scandal over a building that the party owned, tarnished its pristine image. It was also beset by internal conflicts over future strategy. By the time of the 1994 election, it was diverging from its former SDS ally and moving to the right. It was not seen as a possible partner for MSZP. It still tried a half-hearted second round alliance with SDS. However, no strong liberal bloc arose. Actually, FIDESZ did not have a bad election, achieving 8.02 per cent, close to its 1990 result, but compared with earlier expectations this result was disaster. The whole green/alternative wing of the party was wiped out. Orban came close to resignation. The rightward trend continued, the leftwing of the party has been marginalised and FIDESZ has now joined an opposition platform with MDF.

The party's strongest support came in Fejer, with 10.1 per cent, Györ, with 8.11 per cent and Veszprem, 8.02 per cent. Viktor Orban achieved its best first-round constituency result with 21.3 per cent. The party has 14,000 members.

The Right

The MDF was and is a broad church. It has been called a coalition within a coalition. It was formed from the more nationalist and value conservative elements in the old pre-1989 opposition. It was founded in September 1988 by 350 intellectuals, including well-known writers such as Sandor Csoori and Istvan Csurka. It called for the creation of a democratic Hungary. At its second Congress in October 1989, it elected Joszef Antall as its leader. MDF soon established a broad network of 430 sections and 25,000 members.

It was always cautious and pragmatic, working much more closely with the reform communists than SDS or FIDESZ were willing to do. Thus, for example, it did not support the SDS referendum initiative against the early direct election of the President. It supported a gradualist approach, working with the MSZP reformers rather than against them during the Round Table. MDF was rewarded by receiving significant MSZP votes in the second-round run-offs in the 1990 election, enabling it to defeat the more radical opposition parties SDS and FIDESZ. It benefited mightily from the 'multiplier effect' of the constituency system with a fragmented party spectrum. With only 20.7 per cent of the vote, it came out on top with 164 seats, though not with an absolute majority. It became the obvious core of the centre-right coalition.

MDF sees itself as a centre-right Volkspartei, like the German CDU, the Austrian ÖVP or Non-confessional Scandinavian conservative parties. It belongs to both EUCD and EDU, both of which held meetings in Budapest as early as 1990, and now with observer status in the European Peoples Party. However, it remains broader than these models. The internal tendencies inherited from the historic phase coexisted uneasily. There were broad populist/nationalist, christian democratic and national liberal currents within MDF. It contained traditional nationalists, Catholics, Protestants, economic liberals. These diverse groups were federalised by the demands of exercising power and by the leadership of Antall. Even he was unable to prevent destructive splits, especially by his Vice-Chair Istvan Csurka, who eventually left to form a rightist nationalist party. The party could not defend its economic record at the 1994 election, nor defend itself against charges of authoritarianism, especially in the cultural field and in seeking to control the media. By 1994 its old tactic of running a 'red scare' campaign against MSZP no longer worked.

MDF suffered from splits to both left and right. As indicated, the most serious split came from the populist right in the MDF, led by its then Vice-Chair, Istvan Csurka. In the summer of 1992, he published an article in the press which reopened the old wounds of the nineteenth-century Kulturkampf in Hungary. He argued that there was a Jewish leftist conspiracy against national values. That might have been bad enough, but he went on to attack Antall for weakness towards this issue and demanded his resignation and called for a radical nationalist course by the party. At the 1993 Congress, an uneasy compromise was cobbled together, involving a balanced Executive. It was only a truce. Later in the year, Csurka left MDF and took a block of MPs with him and founded a new party that failed totally in 1994. The split seriously hurt MDF. For cosmetic balance, a smaller liberal faction was then also forced out. By the time of the 1994 election, the coalition majority had been reduced to just four by endemic splits in MDF and the Smallholders.

MDF has 30,800 members (1994 figures). In 1994, it fell to 11.74 per cent and retained only 37 seats, a loss of 127, though this was even a recovery from some of the direr poll results before the election. It held its position (with 14.9 per cent) better in Budapest than elsewhere, actually coming second in several constituencies, with over 20 per cent of the vote. Its best result was 27.3 per cent. Outside the capital, it did its best in the smaller towns. It draws its support disproportionately from older voters and from the better-educated middle class.

The Christian Democratic Party (KDNP)

The KDNP was refounded as the successor to the Democratic Peoples Party that had existed between 1945 and 1949. It sees itself as being in the mainstream of European Christian Democracy. It promotes conservative, Christian values in cultural and social life, social market principles and the integration of Hungary into the west (EU and NATO). It did best in rural Catholic Hungary. Its electorate is typically older, church-going and female. In 1990, it scored 6.5 per cent, but only 5.7 per cent in Budapest. Its strongholds are in north-west and north-east Hungary and its weakest areas are in the protestant south-east. It was a loyal and unassuming partner in the Antall coalition and was rewarded by a modest increase in its vote to 7.03 per cent in 1994.

The Independent Smallholders Party (FKGP)

The FKGP has a long and checkered history. It was founded in the inter-war period and revived after 1945. It gained 57 per cent of the vote and an absolute majority at the 1945 election, due to being the furthest right of the parties that were permitted by the Soviet Armistice Commission. It even won a majority in the Budapest city council!

It was revived as early as 1988 by some of its former leaders. It became popular in the countryside by raising the issue of restitution of collectivised land to the peasantry. It did well in rural Hungary, though less well than polls had predicted, with 11.73 per cent of the national vote. The FKGP entered the MDF-led centre-right coalition. It is a survival from the inter-war tradition of peasant parties that existed all over the region and has no international links. During the 1990–4 term, the party was beset by a series of byzantine personality conflicts, internal battles and splits. It even organised anti-government protests, despite itself being a coalition partner. Its parliamentary group split when the party leader sought to leave the coalition. MPs loyal to the coalition then sought to remove the party leader and there were for a period two rival parliamentary groups, which later reunited. Despite these problems, the party virtually held its own, with 8.82 per cent in 1994. Its electorate is rural and conservative, but the party has a well-developed structure in the countryside and still counts 64,000 members (1994 figures), making it the largest party in Hungary in sheer membership terms. Since the 1994 election, it has not joined the common opposition front with MDF, KDNP and FIDESZ, but has veered in an increasingly populist direction, arguing for a presidential regime and extensive use of referenda. It has soared in the polls and has at times been the largest party in the opposition.

The Hungarian Truth and Light Party (MIEP)

This break-away right-wing nationalist and populist party was formed by former MDF Vice-Chair Istvan Csurka in 1993 when his position inside MDF finally became untenable. It espoused a nationalist-populist anti-intellectual tone, based on the ideas of Csurka. It won a mere 1.58 per cent of the vote at the 1994 election and no seats in parliament, condemning it to political irrelevance, but it did win over 5 per cent in some Budapest constituencies and 3.55 per cent in the capital as a whole, its best County result.

POLAND

The Polish political spectrum is the most divided, unstable and confusing of all the central European states. The process of splitting and recombination is still far from complete and the final form of the party spectrum remains open. The first semi-democratic election was conducted without political parties. The freely elected Senate was (and is) elected under a first-past-the-post system (two seats and two votes). This required the opposition to run two candidates and no more in each senatorial district. Local civic committees, run by Solidarnosc, gave candidates the all-important 'investiture' of the trade union and of Lech Walesa personally. In the Sejm (lower house), Solidarnosc won all the seats that were open to it under the Round Table Agreement. Seats in the Government section were apportioned between the Communists (PZPR) and their Peasant Party (PSL) and Democratic Party (DS) allies.

The seeds of the conflict within Solidarnosc between a liberal faction and Walesa were already sown at this election. The Government under Mazowiecki and the parliamentary group under Geremek were controlled by future opponents of Walesa. The future clash between the governmental and parliamentary wing of the movement on the one hand

and the extra-parliamentary wing associated with Walesa on the other was already in gestation. It broke out openly at the 1990 presidential election, with Walesa defeating his Solidarnosc Prime Minister Mazowiecki.

The second democratic election produced a severely fragmented Sejm, with 30 parties, some of them very small, eleven winning just one single seat; many and at least five larger ones could claim some affiliation with Solidarnosc. There were, too, some new parties and some survivors from the old system. The largest party only won 12.31 per cent of the vote. Arithmetically (political considerations apart) no less than a minimum of five parties was required to reach a majority. Given that the second largest party – the Communists – and the fifth largest – the far right nationalist KPN – had to be excluded from the calculations, any realistic majority coalition needed the support of eight parties.

The 1993 election was conducted under a new electoral system, with a 5 per cent threshold and using the d'hondt divisor method of attribution of seats between party lists. It did, as intended, reduce fragmentation, but it also ensured that the two old regime parties (SLD and PSL) with just 36 per cent of the vote between them won 66 per cent of the seats in the Sejm, not just an absolute majority, but almost a constitutional majority. Parties in the right of the political spectrum were so divided that 33 per cent of the total vote was 'wasted', electing nobody. This left only (apart from KPN) a centrist opposition in a seven-party Parliament.

The main parties can be classified according to three broad methods. Firstly they can be classified according to their origins: (i) ex-Solidarnosc the left-wing Labour Union (UP), the Centrist Union of Freedom (UW), the Christian right-wing parties Centre Agreement (PC) the Christian National Union (ZChN); (ii) old regime parties (SLD, PSL, SD); (iii) parties rooted in the pre-war period (PPS); (iv) new parties (KPN, Union of Real Politics, UPR). There are actually over 200 parties in Poland!

The second method of classification relates to the economic programmes of the parties. Thirdly, an important cleavage is their constitutional ideas (presidential or parliamentary regime). On the centre-right, another important division arose out of support for or opposition to Lech Walesa in the 1995 presidential election.

Following the defeat of the ex-Solidarnosc parties at the 1993 election, mainly due to their divisions, a lesson perhaps reinforced by the narrow victory of Aleksander Kwasniewski in the 1995 presidential election, a degree of recombination has begun to take place. The extra-parliamentary parties on the right then formed two(!) coalitions; The Pact for

Poland brings together the Centre Alliance, the People's Agreement and the Christian National Union. This bloc was essentially christian-conservative and pro-Walesa. The November 11th Coalition brings together the UPR, the Conservative Party, the Christian Democratic Party and the Christian People's Party (former Rural Solidarnosc). This second bloc was more radically free market and libertarian and considerably less pro-Walesa, if not indeed directly anti-Walesa in some cases. At the same time, the liberal/centrist ex-Solidarnosc grouping around Mazowiecki and Geremek, now led by former 'big bang' finance minister Leszek Balcerowicz, has merged with the Liberal Democratic Congress to form the Union of Freedom (UW). Thus, there is now the beginning of an effective realignment and consolidation of the party system, which remains far from complete. Political parties in Poland have been programmatically weak. The ex-Solidarnosc parties have also been organisationally weak and lack local grass-roots structures. Only the SLD and PSL, as old regime parties, have, as elsewhere in the region, retained and built on a surviving network inherited from the pre-1989 period, which enabled them to go into political hibernation between 1989 and 1993 and then revive. As we shall see the Solidarnosc parties came together in 1997, bypassing those earlier efforts at coalition building.

The Left

The parties of the left can impressionistically be placed on the following left–right continuum: SdRP–Solidarnosc–UP–PPS.

The Alliance of the Democratic Left (SLD)

The SLD is an alliance of left-wing groups, in which the Social Democracy of the Polish Republic (SdRP), the successor to the Communist Party, the United Polish Workers Party (PZPR), is the dominant core component. The SLD also includes the Organisation of Polish Trade Unions (OPZZ) (the former 'official' trade union), youth and women's organisations and one wing of the historic socialist party (PPS).

The main component of SLD, the SdRP, is the best structured and organised party in Poland, with 60,000 members organised in Voivod (County) and local branch organisations. The party is a member of the SI. Of the 200 SLD Deputies and Senators, the SdRP has 128 parliamentarians and the trade unions 60.

The SdRP seeks to present itself as a 'new' modern social democratic party in the European mould. It seeks discreetly to put some distance between its present face and its past as the reformist wing of the PZPR. It accepts the democratic political reforms and in general terms it also accepts the economic reforms of the 1989–93 period. In the constitutional field, it favours a parliamentary system. It considers that the powers of the presidency should not be increased, rather they should be reduced. They proposed eliminating the so-called 'presidential ministers' and making overriding of presidential vetoes on legislation by parliament easier. They also wished to see a parliamentary 'reading' of the text of the constitution, rather than an extensive presidential 'reading' as Walesa attempted. They were broadly successful in these goals.

In foreign policy, the SdRP fully supports EU membership and indeed was in government when the application was made, but regards adequate completion of Poland's internal preparation as an important precondition, so as to ensure that the immediate deregulatory shock of membership is not too great. The party supports participation in the Partnership for Peace (PfP) under NATO auspices and in due course full NATO membership without conditions. On both these issues, the SdRP is often accused of being insufficiently nationalist by its PSL coalition partner.

On ethical issues such as abortion, religious education in schools, the role of the church in politics and ratification of the Concordat with the Vatican, the SdRP takes as resolutely a lay standpoint as is realistic in Catholic Poland. It has sought to avoid excessively militant confrontation with the Catholic Church, whilst emphasising its clearly secular outlook, which is in any case becoming more popular in modern Poland. This standpoint places it closer to the opposition UW than to PSL, its coalition partner.

SLD's economic policy is favourable towards privatisation, though coupled with adequate social measures and government intervention to cushion restructuring and assist sectors of the economy facing particular difficulties. It would still favour controls on the inflow of foreign capital and a jump change in the exchange rate to discourage such inflows and make imports more expensive.

The SLD is frequently critical of PSL, its conservative coalition partner, and sees it as a brake on reform in many areas. However, this coalition has historic logic: both partners are survivors from the old system. UW and UP are both closer to SLD in policy and even value terms than PSL, but neither were (or are) ready to work with SLD for historical reasons. SLD could therefore find no other partners in 1993. Despite continuing internal difficulties, the coalition survives. This may, though, be the last hurrah for the ex-communist anti-communist cleavage in Poland.

The SLD won 11.98 per cent in 1991 and 20.41 per cent in 1993. It claims not to be a class party, seeking broader support across the board. Undoubtedly, it still gains most of its support from the working class and from losers from the reform process.

The Union of Labour (UP)

The UP is a small, secular, left-leaning, ex-Solidarnosc group, led by Mr Bugaj, a long-standing Solidarnosc activist. It supports decentralisation of the state and stronger local and regional government. UP favours an interventionist, growth-orientated economic policy and an active social policy to promote the process of industrial regeneration, using foreign capital for that purpose, but under strict control. It believes in a competitive exchange rate, set to encourage Polish exports. It has opposed privatisation in its present form. In many ways, therefore, it is programmatically to the left of the SLD, but due to its Solidarnosc origins is clearly strongly anti-communist. Perhaps for that reason, it gave serious consideration to joining the coalition with SLD in 1993, but finally decided against this, though it often votes with the coalition and might be prepared to provide it with the necessary additional support to pass the new constitution if brought to the floor of the Sejm during this parliamentary term. UP won 7.28 per cent of the vote and 41 seats in 1993, compared with only 2.05 per cent in 1991. It won no seats in 1997.

The Polish Socialist Party (PPS)

The venerable Social Democratic Party, later the PPS, founded in 1892, was important in the early democratic period of the First Republic. In 1946 it was forcibly merged with the communists to form the United Polish Workers Party (PZPR), the new name for the merged party completely controlled by the communists. It remained in the Socialist International. Some of its former supporters were active in the opposition during the 1980s. However, it was unable to re-establish itself as a significant force after 1989. It did not take part in the elections of 1989 and in 1991 called on its supporters to vote for the UP. At its 26th Congress in November 1992 it rejected cooperation with the SdRP and elected P. Ikonowicz as leader and affirmed its independence. It has 2,000 members. In 1993, three PPS deputies were elected on other tickets and form a PPS group in the Sejm.

Solidarnosc

Solidarnosc was represented in both chambers in 1991–3. It failed to win seats in the Sejm in 1993, gaining only 4.9 per cent, but continues to be represented in the Senate. It favours mass populist privatisation, controlled inflow of foreign private capital, a balanced industrial policy during the transition, more protectionism and a balanced trade policy between the EU and former COMECON countries. It supports decentralisation and stronger local government. On the constitution, it has made radical proposals for a system of tripartite corporatist social partnership, with the trade unions having a strong role and with a clear Christian foundation to political life. It stands very close to the Church, which has openly supported its proposals on the constitution. The parliamentary wing has been ready to disagree with the trade union wing and resists attempts to give it instructions. Its greatest strength is in southern Poland (Silesia and Krakow) and Gdansk. It became the core of the AWS in 1997, and should now be placed on the right.

The Centre

The Union of Freedom (UW)

This is the broad, liberal, modernising, internationalist wing of Solidarnosc that formed around figures like Mazowiecki, Geremek, Kuron and Balcerowicz, its current leader. It emerged by a very short head as the largest party in the very fragmented first fully freely elected Sejm in 1993, with 12.31 per cent of the vote and 62 seats. Together with the Liberal Democratic Congress, its close political cousin, with 7.48 per cent and 37 seats, it formed the core of a series of Solidarnosc-based coalition governments in the 1991–3 legislature, including the longest (15 months), led by Hanna Suchoka, who came from its ranks. In opposition after the 1993 elections, it merged with the Liberal Democratic Congress (KLD) that failed to win any seats in 1993, with only 3.99 per cent compared with 7.48 per cent in 1991, to form the Union of Freedom (UW). Had both parties gained representation in 1993, they could have expected to form a significant liberal bloc of about 130 deputies out of 460. The old Democratic Union, the core of the new party, won 10.59 per cent in 1993, down on its 12.31 per cent in 1991.

The UW has about 20,000 members, but has a very weak regional and local structure. It is a Warsaw and big-city-based leadership party, not a mass membership party. Its new leader Balcerowicz regards creating an effective party organisation as one of his priority tasks, especially in terms of building up its local government roots and its links to the modernising middle class that needs to be developed as its natural constituency. More policy work and a more professional party management style is also needed, he argues. These conclusions are borne out by the fact that the party's 1995 presidential candidate Jacek Kuron, though well known and personally popular and respected, scored under 10 per cent in the first round and was unable to reach the second round. Had he done so, he might well have been elected against Kwasniewski.

The party is closely – perhaps too closely – identified with the 'big-bang' economic transition and hence with its down-side, as well as with its positive aspects. It also has an urban, intellectual image. For conservatives, it is seen as 'Jewish', despite the fact that there are sadly almost no jews in Poland any more.

It has strongly supported rapid privatisation, economic deregulation and opening of markets as part of a wider goal of building a functioning market economy and active and democratic civil society. It favours a hands-off approach, with indirect state intervention only, via the tax system. It is a low-taxation party. It has strongly promoted decentralisation and strengthening of local government. Indeed, it includes important municipal leaders such as Martin Swieciki, Mayor of Warsaw, within its ranks. On constitutional matters it is pragmatic, leaning slightly towards a parliamentary model. It proposes a mixed parliamentary/presidential system. It would retain, but not expand, the powers of the president, but also expand the role of both the prime minister and parliament.

The party has internal problems in the ideological and ethical areas, as it contains both strong Catholics such as Mazowiecki and liberal secularists such as Kuron. It contains both pro-Walesa people (the former KLD group) and anti-Walesa people such as Mazowiecki. It is simultaneously criticised for being too left and too right. It also finds it difficult to define its attitude to the Church, creating ambiguities about the party's image. And it needs to find a means of establishing a dialogue with the working class, with which it has few links, and to expand its base beyond the public sector and liberal intelligentsia with which it is so closely identified.

It is by far the most pro-European party in Poland. It believes that EU membership is a vital and urgent part of the modernisation strategy and would make the democratic transition irreversible. It therefore actively promotes the European idea in Poland and argues for the acceleration of the necessary internal measures to prepare Poland for early membership. It, almost alone, wants to open a wider public debate on this issue now, so as to broaden public knowledge and awareness and thereby strengthen support for membership, which it recognises is shallow. As from 1997 UW was in government again.

The Right

The right is suicidally fragmented, chaotic and riven with political and personality divisions, which in effect 'gave' the 1993 election and the 1995 presidential election to the left. Only one party of the right, the Confederation for an Independent Poland (KPN), won seats at the 1993 election and then only a toe-hold. Due to its divisions, the right is chronically under-represented in the present Sejm and ensured the defeat of Walesa in 1995. In tune with its historical traditions, the Polish right is unrepentantly factious and beset with posturing and ego trips, more over personality clashes and rival leadership claims than over policy differences, though these undeniably do exist. In 1993 this obdurate fractiousness meant that roughly one-third of the vote went to almost a dozen fairly significant parties of the right, but almost no one was elected, apart from the 19 KPN deputies. Some of these parties, such as the Christian National Union, with 6.37 per cent, and the Citizens Centre Alliance, with 4.42 per cent in 1993, had been represented in the 1991–3 Sejm.

The restructuring of the Polish right, as it moves into the post-Solidarnosc and post-Walesa era, is now one of the central issues in Polish politics. The urgency of the matter was reinforced by the debacle for the right of the 1995 presidential election. It could neither agree on a single right-wing anti-Walesa candidate who might have got into the second round, nor support Walesa in the second round in a unified way. Now, the next parliamentary elections are coming up fast. In order to make some sense of the right wing of the Polish political spectrum, we shall look at the two rightist parliamentary groupings, the KPN and the Non-Party Bloc for Reform, the PSL, and the two broad extra-parliamentary alliances rather than the plethora of individual and often minuscule parties on the right. We shall include the PSL, because despite its origins as a block party and its current alliance with the SLD, it is in reality a value conservative party, akin to the FKGP in Hungary, and is a reminder of the venerable tradition of pre-war peasant parties in Poland. Its future is crucially linked to the whole question of restructuring of the Polish right, to which it will logically belong if it survives. For the moment, historical memory is too strong. However, eventually, two broad blocs must emerge, along Hungarian lines: SLD + UP + UW on the centre-left and PSL + the two centre-right coalitions + KPN on the right.

The Peasant Party (PSL)

The PSL, in Polish called the Polish People's Party, has a venerable pre-war history. Its first leader Vincenty Witos was one of the key figures in the first democratic phase of the First Republic. The PSL was an important player in the distinctively central European International of peasant parties in the inter-war period. Its later leader Mikolajcyk was Prime Minister in the government in exile during the Second World War. Like all peasant parties in central Europe, the PSL was seen by Stalin as a dangerous potential rival. It alone of all the 'bourgeois' parties had a mass following. It was ruthlessly destabilised and its independence destroyed. It was kept as a block party, a symbol – important in Poland – of the alliance between workers and peasants, a key element in the communist ideology. After 1990, an alliance under the name PSL was formed from a merger between the old block party, a second new PSL, drawing on the inter-war traditions. This 'new' PSL alliance broke down before the 1991 elections. A rival Peasant Accord was formed from most of the 'historic PSL' elements and former rural Solidarnosc. This new Peasant Accord (PL) was close to Walesa and won 5.46 per cent in 1991, running close to the PSL's 8.67 per cent, but in 1993, PL only won 2.37 per cent and no seats in the Sejm.

The PSL has strong roots in the countryside and a well-developed organisation. It retains 200,000 members, more than in 1989, and is one of the few parties to actually increase its membership, making it the largest Polish party in terms of its membership. It won 8.67 per cent in 1993 and nearly doubled its support to 15.4 per cent in 1993. It is the second largest party in the Sejm.

The party is often criticised for being merely a single-issue pressure group, a corporatist party. In presenting itself to foreign audiences, it underlines that though its name is more usually rendered in English as Polish Peasant Party, its name in Polish means Polish People's Party. It therefore argues that historically it was actually a broader rural party, defending the whole gamut of rural interests, but that during the communist period it had been forced into a purely sectoral role. The PSL underlines its long traditions and continuity. Indeed, it celebrated its hundredth anniversary in 1995. Its deepest roots are in the countryside, though it does also have some limited support in smaller towns.

It sees almost all the other parties as anti-agriculture. The PSL does not just regard itself as the spokesman of agriculture, but for all rural issues: processing industries, alternative rural jobs, rural housing and infrastructure. It seeks to 'educate' the other parties on rural issues, since it needs allies if it is to promote gradual and socially acceptable change in Polish agriculture, as its moderate wing seeks to do. The PSL sees itself as centre/centre-right in the political spectrum, with a clear Christian Democrat current inside the party, which may, some in the party argue, be where its longer-term future lies.

It supports privatisation, but not voucher privatisation. It favours a strategic use of the exchange rate (in effect a devaluation of the zloty) and restriction of privileges for foreign capital. It would seek to retain a significant state sector in strategic industries. In some ways, therefore, it appears less market-orientated than its SLD partner. On constitutional matters, it opposes strengthening the role of the president, but supports decentralisation.

EU membership is a problem for the party and there are internal divisions on this issue. Many PSL MPs opposed the Europe Agreement of 1991. Overall, the PSL can accept EU membership as inevitable, though it is likely that many in the party will remain opposed in order to defend Polish agriculture. The PSL supports NATO membership.

The Confederation for an Independent Poland (KPN)

The KPN was established clandestinely in 1979 and then led a shadowy illegal and even semi-legal existence until 1989. It is strongly nationalist, traditionalist, anti-communist and slavophile. It has supported gradual privatisation, moderate government intervention, slow devaluation, and reciprocal protection in relations with the EU. It wants the rapid adoption of a new constitution, with a clear distribution of powers between a stronger president, parliament and government. The KPN sees itself as a moderate party of the centre-right, close to the Church. The KPN accepts NATO membership, despite regarding NATO as redundant at the present time. It sees itself as eurosceptical, comparing itself to Phillipe de Villiers, rather than outright opposed to the EU membership in principle. Its president Mr Moculski makes frequent comparisons with General de Gaulle. It won 7.50 per cent in 1991 and 5.8 per cent in 1993. Its voters are young and urban, with secondary education. It claims 35,000 members and 300 local offices. Its long-term strategic goal is to create a broad alliance on the right. The KPN is difficult to classify on a left–right scale. Its nationalism and anti-communism places it clearly to the right.

It takes a centrist position on relations with the Church. On the other hand, it tends to reject unbridled market liberalism.

The Pact for Poland

The Pact, formed in June 1994, is a broad pro-Walesa, Christian Democratic, traditionalist alliance of five parties. Its main components are the Centre Alliance (PC) and the Christian National Union (ZChN). Its member parties were pro-Walesa, pro-privatisation and pro the reform process, close to the Church on social and cultural matters. It supported Walesa's position on the constitution in favour of a strong presidency. The member parties all support EU membership. The individual parties remain independent and the Chair of the Pact rotates between them, and their divergences on economic policy still remain. The Pact fared well in the 1994 local government elections, its first electoral test, reducing communist and PSL influence in rural Poland for the first time.

The 11th November Agreement

This second rightist coalition links five other smaller right-wing parties. They are even more traditionalist, but are even less ready to accept Church authority. They are libertarians, total free marketeers. For example, the Union for Real Politics (UPR) supports the total privatisation of education and health care provision. The UPR claims 25,000 members (which seems exaggerated). It is prepared to join NATO, but not on any terms. The UPR and its partners are very eurosceptical and anti-Maastricht. The Agreement did less well than the Pact for Poland in the June 1994 local elections and achieved no success at the 1995 presidential election.

The Non-Party Bloc for Reform (BBWR)

The BBWR is not a genuine party. It was formed after the 1991 elections and won 5.4 per cent in 1993. Originally, it was intended as a non-party pro-Walesa platform, a counterweight to the anti-Walesa ex-Solidarnosc groups. It favours a mixed parliamentary/presidential system, rapid EU membership and full privatisation. It is now no longer as close to Walesa, and split in January 1995. It would now seem to have no strategic future.

These various groups were still deeply split and going nowhere. The loss of the 1995 presidential election by Lech Walesa at last galvanised the fragmented and quarrelsome Polish right into trying to overcome at least some of its divisions. In the winter of 1995–6, former Prime Minister Jan Olszewski established a new populist-nationalist party (Movement for the Reconstrution of Poland, ROP) to the right of Solidarnosc and less linked to the Church. He built on the dynamism coming out of his respectable 7 per cent score in the presidential election. He developed a strong standing in the polls and with between 11 and 14 per cent of voting intentions soon challenged Solidarnosc, which registered only about 15 per cent. A nationalist-populist 20-point programme was adopted on 3 May 1996.

Solidarnosc felt the squeeze and led its leader Marian Krzaklewski to redouble his hitherto unsuccessful efforts to unite as much as possible of the right, shore up his position as the dominant leader on the right and stop the haemorrhage of support to the ROP. Its earlier efforts in that direction, through its alternative draft constitution and an initiative referendum on privatisation, had failed. Now, under pressure from ROP, Solidarnosc succeeded in putting together an electoral alliance (Solidarnosc Electoral Alliance, AWS), bringing together at first some 25 parties and groups, later growing to 36, as AWS became a magnet on the right. Apart from Solidarnosc itself, the only significant groups within AWS were the Centre Concentration (PC), the Christian National Union (ZChN), the Liberal Conservative Party (SKL), itself a merger, and the Confederation for an Independent Poland (KPN), the only right-wing party represented in the 1993–7 Sejm. The AWS is a very broad church, running from Christian Democrats and Christian Populists, value conservatives to market liberals. AWS soon took off strongly in the polls, reaching 26 per cent by June 1996, with only 13 per cent for ROP that now rapidly lost momentum and with it its opportunity to control the right of the political spectrum. Now, with its new-found dominance AWS did not wish to encumber itself with premature alliance that would limit its freedom of action and create internal strains. It rejected direct cooperation with ROP to its right and UW to its left. Another complicating factor was the strains within the governing coalition. In may ways, PSL was ideologically closer to AWS than to its then coalition partner, SLD. Only the past kept SLD together. Throughout this pre-election period, ideas of an AWS/PSL coalition were constantly canvassed, and indeed PSL had taken part in a right of centre coalition in 1992.

Thus, going into the election, the Polish party scene had already become considerably simplified. On the left only SLD and the Union of Labour (UP) could win seats in the next Sejm. In the centre only UW survived. To the right, only PSL, AWS and ROP were likely to win seats.

At most, six parties would be represented in the next parliament. These were also the only parties with any serious structure or record of political activity. There were, though, still several possible coalition options, depending on the distribution of the seats: a left coalition of SLD + UP; a centre-left coalition on the Hungarian model of SLD + UW; a centre-right coalition of AWS + UW; or a right coalition of AWS + ROP + SDL. In this last case, all three parties were likely to be needed to reach a majority, as the polls stood in the pre-election period. The choice before the electorate had become much simplified: they had to choose between SLD and AWS as the leader of the next coalition. As the coalition permutations indicate, UW was in a key position: it could lean left or right. It faced difficult choices.

As we have seen, UW is quite a broad church. It has always had difficulty in unifying its many strong and charismatic personalities and determining a clear identity, as between its right-leaning wing under Mazowiecki, a group that condemned the leadership for not excluding cooperation with SLD. Others in the leadership did not want to exclude such cooperation and had indeed worked with SLD on the constitution, taxation issues, Europe or abortion. One member of the UW executive even accepted a post of Deputy Minister in an SLD ministry. Strains were considerable and six deputies left to join AWS. Party leader Balcerowicz, the former 'big bang' Finance Minister, sought to steer a middle course.

As it was, the election result spared UW from agonising choices. The strength of AWS and its position as by far the largest party made it impossible for UW to ally with SLD. AWS led with 33.8 per cent (201 seats). SLD won 27.1 per cent, up 5 per cent on 1993, but with 164 seats (−5). UW won 13.4 per cent and 60 seats (−14). For PSL, the election was a disaster with only 7.31 per cent and 27 seats (−105). ROP only just over the 5 per cent ceiling with 5.56 per cent won only 6 seats. The German Minority won 4 seats (−2). AWS won an absolute majority in the Senate. There were now only five parties and only three of any size in both Sejm and Senate, as UP had been eliminated. The political spectrum was settling down, with a recognisable right and left block. Coalition possibilities were limited. A Grand Coalition of SLD + AWS was arithmetically possible, but politically impossible. The only other possibilities were a centre-left SLD + UW Coalition, but it was just short of a majority. It could expect to find no other allies, though PSL might have given some support. This would have been a weak and unstable option, though it may have been the west's dream ticket of modernisers. Equally, a three-party conservative coalition of AWS + ROP + PSL would be unstable, with a narrow majority, and would face severe internal contradictions. Almost by elimination, only a centre-right AWS + UW coalition remained. After some posturing and pressure on UW to agree to a non-party government, an AWS + UW coalition was formed with Jerzy Buzek (AWS) and Mr Balcerowicz (UW) as Deputy Prime Minister and Minister of Finance, though privatisation policy was to be in the hands of an AWS Minister.

12 Other Political Actors

It is axiomatic that in a democratic society there will be a multiplicity of competing and cooperating political actors in addition to political parties, acting independently of each other and of the political parties, promoting their own interests in a kind of political market place. Alliances between such interest groups among themselves and with political parties and the political institutions, shift and reform constantly in that market-place of political influence. On the other hand, in the totalitarian phase of communist rule it was both theoretically and practically impossible for independent interests to exist. No interests, let alone organisations, could exist outside the control of the hegemonic party. To the extent that independent organisations or even parties appeared to exist for reasons of tactics or external image, these were in reality fronts, controlled directly or indirectly by the Communist Party, the state bureaucracy or even the security apparatus. However, by the last phase of communist rule, from the early 1980s, the situation had become considerably less black and white, as sporadic and precarious, though undeniably independent, forms of civil society began to emerge, seeking to carve out 'party free' areas. As we have seen, this was very much the approach of the Danube Circle, the Chartists and above all Solidarnosc and KOR. Hence the idea and even a certain limited experience of an independent civil society was by no means totally unknown in the Visegrad countries by the time of the fall of communism in 1989.

Clearly, the extent and purpose of such civil society was very different from that found in normal democratic societies. In pre-1989 central Europe, civil society organisations were the opposition; they were the only alternative sources of popular expression; they were complementary to each other. After 1989, they had to redefine their purposes. They now had to become fragmentary social forces, representing part of society and certain interests in society, rather than aspiring to articulate the concerns of society as a whole. This latter task now fell to the revitalised political institutions that had of course been either absent or dysfunctional during the communist period.

These changes, though necessary and legitimate were difficult for the broad-based civil society organisations. How, for example, was Solidarnosc now simply to become reduced to a mere trade union, representing a mere sectional interest? In a strange paradox – yet another – it was perhaps easier for some of the surviving former communist organisations, such as the old official trade unions, to make this transition and recycle themselves. They had clearly become sectional minorities under siege, yet they had retained a large part of their membership, organisation and resources. They were also more popular than the old communist parties and so easily became a focus for the militant discontent of losers from the reform process. On the other hand, other interests such as entrepreneurs, consumers, environmentalists, or professional groups such as lawyers or teachers, had to organise from the ground up and develop a new culture of interest representation. Another and key related area was the creation of an independent media. Before 1989, it had been axiomatic that the press and media were under state control and were indeed instruments of state policy and control. In a democratic society, the media are in principle both independent and pluralist, though reality may often lag behind this ideal. In the new post-communist societies, the development of pluralist media, with the related problems of ownership and control, is an imperative requirement for a functioning civil society.

The trade unions are finding the process of adaptation difficult and ambiguous. In particular, the whole area of relations between themselves and political parties is a minefield, fraught with difficulties for them. Too-close exclusive links with any one single party is a discredited formula from the past. Furthermore, as unions in western countries have long discovered, such exclusive links are counterproductive in a pluralist society, the more so in societies like those of central Europe, where the party system remains unstable. One can all too easily bet on the wrong horse, as it were. Even so, those unions that represent a certain degree of continuity with the old 'official' unions, such as the Hungarian MSzOSz or OPZZ in Poland, do retain close links with the MSZP and the SLD respectively. In fact, the SLD is an alliance in which the OPZZ is a constituent group, with 60 MPs out of the 167-strong SLD group in the Sejm. One of the SLD Vice-Chairs is from the OPZZ stable. There is also a strong trade union wing in the MSZP, which has opposed the modernisation of the party. On the other hand, in the Czech and Slovak Republics, the unions have diversified their political links. Thus, in 1992 sixteen union leaders stood as candidates in the elections in the Czech Republic. There were 6 CSSD, 2 KDU–CSL, 1 ODS, 1 ODA and 4 from smaller parties. There were none, it is worth noting, from the KSCM (communists). In Slovakia, several union leaders stood on the HZDS ticket, and others on the Electoral Alliance List (Social democrats, Greens and Agricultural Workers Union) in 1994.

Employers' organisations have tended not to operate through links with the larger established parties. Rather they have either not sought links with parties at all or they have supported new entrepreneurs' parties that were often very small. In Poland, the initially satirical Friends of Beer Party split and one wing became a serious pro-business party. The Polish Congress of Liberal Democrats that later merged with UW was a party of private business interests. In Hungary, the small Republican Party aims to become a party of business interests, but has so far not achieved a significant following. In Slovakia, both HZDS and KDH have been 'colonised' by private entrepreneurs.

How have the various interest groups evolved? How have those that already existed under communism – mainly the trade unions – actually adapted to the new political environment? How has government reacted to the development of more independent interest groups in society? Nor should the wider external context be ignored. External aid donors such as the EU's PHARE programme, the EBRD, the G-24 programmes and the various EU and national democracy programmes have all sought to work with interest groups and NGOs on the ground. They have acted as an important catalyst for the creation of new NGOs where they did not already exist. Responsiveness to the requirements of these international aid donors has become an important criteria that NGOs and interest groups must factor into their structures and activities.

In Poland, the old communist unions (OPZZ) have distanced themselves from the former communist union, claiming not to be its direct successor, though retaining its assets, which are considerable in terms of buildings and a nation-wide organisational network. OPZZ was also able to retain a large part of the membership of the former communist unions and its social activities. Thus, OPZZ still has over 4 million members, against only 1.7 million for Solidarnosc. A 'purist', more industrially militant and less political union has split off from Solidarnosc under the name Solidarnosc 80, with about 500,000 members. Specialised industrial unions, such as the mine workers (25,000 members), train drivers, and air traffic controllers, remain small and politically independent, but can because of their control of strategic industrial sectors exercise considerable industrial muscle.

The trade union scene had already begun to change in Hungary as early as 1988. In that year, the League of Independent Trade Unions was set up. Later, in 1989, a new grass-roots Workers Council movement emerged. The official union SZOT (Socialist Confederation of Trade Unions) embarked on a slow process of transformation, in the course of which several of its component unions left. The principal 19 industrial unions were then reorganised into four independent federations (civil service; public service; manufacturing; chemical industry). The SZOT was then renamed the Hungarian Socialist Trade Union Organisation (MSzOSz), with a new reformist leadership that remained politically close to the reformist MSZP.

In Czechoslovakia, the 6,000 strike committees that blossomed during the Velvet Revolution in 1989–90 sought to wrest control over the old official trade union from its existing leadership and indeed took it over at the Congress held on 2 March 1990. It then replaced the old union, which was dissolved, by a much looser body, the Czech Trade Union Confederation (CSKOS), that affiliated to the ICFTU international. In fact, this new body was a minimalist umbrella organisation, without strong control over the component unions that were affiliated to it. It actually showed an unexpected continuity with the old structures, retaining as much as 40 per cent of the old shop-stewards and most of the old organisational structure. It continued to organise 50.8 per cent of all workers, against an insignificant 5.2 per cent organised by newer independent trade unions and 44 per cent of workers who remain unorganised. The dominance of CSKOS remains total in manufacturing, where it organises over 70 per cent of all workers in the sector. Union membership is lowest in the newly privatised sector of the economy. CSKOS is politically and industrially centrist. It has a small rightist rival in the KUK (Confederation of Cultural Workers), comprising 22 unions, with in total 150,000 members. In practice, it has worked well with CSKOS. On the other political wing, there remains an even smaller unreconstructed Trade Union Association, with about 50,000 members. There are, as in Poland, some small but militant and potentially neuralgic sectoral unions, such as train drivers and bus drivers, who have a track record of effective, non-political militancy.

Other types of interest groups have also begun to appear. These cover employers and business groups in the emerging private sector, such as the Hungarian Association of Entrepreneurs (VOSZ) set up in 1990. The Polish Medical Council, the Association of Hungarian Judges, the Polish National Notary Council are all recent examples of new professional associations that have already plugged into the international networks of their professions. Pluralistic youth movements, such as the Scouts, the YMCA and the traditional Sokol youth movement in the Czech Republic, as well as political and religious youth movements, have reappeared, replacing the old monolithic communist youth movement.

In all four countries, the Church, mainly the Catholic Church, played a major role in opposition to the communist system. Often it was the only semi-protected space within which opposition movements could operate. As a practical matter, it had its network of priests, nuns and lay workers as well as buildings, and in Poland even a Catholic University in Lublin and its own press that was less censored than other newspapers. These networks were vital to the opposition. Thus priests were active in both Solidarnosc and Charter 77. The Church leadership seemed to follow a kind of twin-track strategy. On the one hand, it appeared to seek forms of accommodation with the regimes in place, enabling the Church to avoid outright confrontation and retain its legal existence and infrastructure in being. This was often seen by its critics as a dangerous form of moral compromise and opportunism and even complicity, as for example when the Polish Church recommended moderation after the declaration of martial law in December 1981. The second track was the deeper one of providing aid and comfort to all those of whatever conviction who sought to oppose the system. The churches thus played a major role in the collapse of communism, though they took a much lower profile in Hungary and especially Czechoslovakia than in Poland. In Hungary and Czechoslovakia they did not become the natural umbrella for civil society, as in Poland. In Hungary, it was only radical Catholic groups such as Regnum Mariarum that were in any sense dissidents, since the official hierarchy preferred compromise with the regime.

The collapse of communism has seen the influence of the churches wane, especially in the social and political spheres, particularly in Poland. Even so, the Catholic Episcopal Conference and its secretary Bishop Pironek remain a political force, which intervenes actively in Polish politics, but now with less uniform success, through pronouncements, active support for various candidates for office and through its direct involvement in the Constitutional Commission. Thus, the Church strongly supported Walesa's re-election in 1995 and was instrumental in his comeback to the point of ensuring him a place in the second round, though it could not achieve his re-election. The Church has also taken up strong positions on abortion, on education policy and on the ratification of the Concordat, which the SLD government opposed.

Governments in the region have sought to return to some form of corporatist tripartism. This has been the case even in the Czech Republic, the most free market of the four countries. Governments have felt the need to manage the transition in a consensual way, coopting all the main interests into the process, after an initial period in which the trade unions and other socio-economic actors were weak and marginal. Unions have not been a major brake on economic reform. Even in the Czech Republic, they have not emerged as a direct opponent of the free market Premier Vaclav Klaus. They have mostly accepted restructuring. However, after 1993 there were some indications that the ODS government in Prague was seeking to adopt a less pragmatic course, though in practice that has hit severe limits. It seemed, in the debate on the new Labour Code, to ally itself more than before with the position of the entrepreneurs. Even so, unemployment remains very low and restructuring gradual. In the new situation after the 1996 election, the government can be expected to seek even more consensus.

Tripartism was already formally institutionalised in the old Czechoslovakia through the Council for Economic and Social Accord, which then led to the general agreement of 28 January 1991 covering wages policy, labour law, and employment policy. In Hungary the Interest Reconciliation Council was established under the Employment Act of 1991. It is directed by the Ministry of Labour, though it has an independent secretariat. This Council has sought to strengthen links with parliament through the responsible committees. It deals with labour law, labour market policy and training policy and sets guidelines for wage negotiation rounds. The new MSZP/SDS government has sought to place tripartism and hence the Council at the centre of its economic policy. It is using the Council as a forum for developing consensus among actors on broad and comprehensive economic and social policy. Tripartism has been much more difficult and restrictive in Poland, though the government did seek to reach an accommodation with the trade unions in 1991 before the unions became more militant and ready and able to take selective strike action. At the end of 1992, the government sought to negotiate an Enterprise Pact which would have traded off wage moderation against an active labour market policy and influence over the privatisation process for employees. Before the pact could be put to the Sejm, the government fell.

Finally, the international dimension, with its need to generate cooperation between international bodies such as the IMF, EBRD and the EU's PHARE programme, governments and local NGOs did much to revitalise the civil society sector, which international bodies often imposed as an interlocutor. These external funding bodies actually exerted a significant influence on the domestic politics of the central European states and encouraged both the emergence of local NGOs and the totally new concept of cross-border cooperation.

In the communist system, control over the media, both print and broadcast, was absolute and the media was part of the control system of the power structure. This should now be a thing of the past, but old habits die very hard, especially in Slovakia. The new post-1989 power holders expressed good intentions towards the idea of a free and independent media and indeed all the various constitutions contain effective provisions to that effect. In Slovakia, especially in Hungary before 1994 and in Poland, nationalists often sought to criticise free media and bring them under tighter control. Private radio and television stations have been established in Hungary, the Czech Republic and Poland, representing a partial source of pluralism. Otherwise, the ongoing conflicts over control of the media and the power of appointment of directors of the state broadcasting bodies have been frequently referred to the Constitutional Courts for adjudication.

13 Foreign Policy

Foreign policy has been at the heart of political debate in all the countries of the region. How could it be otherwise? Their emergence, survival and development as states in the inter-war period had always depended on their relations with their powerful eastern and western neighbours and the balance of power within the region. Their fate had been decided after 1945 on the basis of the then prevailing geopolitical situation. Nowhere, not even in Czechoslovakia, could communism have triumphed purely internally. Its success was Moscow-driven. All attempts at reform or revolution succeeded, as in 1989–90, or failed, as in 1953 (Berlin), 1956 (Poland and Hungary), 1968 (Czechoslovakia) or 1981 (Poland), because of the attitude of Moscow.

Indeed, even after 1990, at least until the defeat of the conservative communist coup in Moscow in 1991 and the final withdrawal of Soviet forces from the region, there could be no absolute guarantee that there would not be a backlash in the USSR and an attempt to re-establish Soviet hegemony in the USSR's 'near abroad' security zone and extend it back into central Europe. After all, each of the Visegrad countries had a common border with the USSR and at that time had Soviet troops in their territory. Foreign policy, in terms of securing the democratic gains of 1989 and making them permanent through the dismantling of the Warsaw Pact and COMECON, reorientating trade westwards, and securing western support and membership in western organisations – IMF, Council of Europe, NATO, EC – was a matter of vital concern to all the new democratic governments in the region in 1990.

This chapter will look at the foreign policy concerns of the four Visegrad countries and how foreign policy is made. Their foreign policy agendas have been closely linked to their transformation process and their distinct national histories. Indeed, the foreign policy agenda should not be dissociated from the domestic reform agenda. They have been dialectically related. 'Return to Europe', in the OF slogan of 1990, encapsulated the foreign policy agendas of the new democratic governments and was closely linked with the other key priorities of constitutional change and market transformation. It is for example no accident that the most ardent Polish modernisers in UW are also the most ardent promoters of Polish EU membership. They regard the virtuous circle Europe–democratisation–market economy as a package, as a tryptic, in which each element mutually underpins the others.

Escape from eastern dependency and support for the reform process have been constraints giving urgency to membership in western organisations. But more specifically, policy objectives have gone through various phases with different priorities and levels of ambition.

There was an early euphoric period during the heady winter of 1989–90 when, briefly, in the aftermath of the fall of the communist regimes, everything seemed possible. At that moment, unrealistic and perhaps unjustified hopes of almost immediate integration into the EC and NATO were entertained, though a more attentive reading between the lines of western statements might have signalled a warning that little encouragement was going to be given to those hopes.

At that time the EC was in the upper trajectory of a long period of renewed dynamism that lasted from 1985 to 1992, which was being driven by the internal market project and which was intended to lead almost automatically into economic and monetary union. This project was considered to be the absolute priority, requiring concentration of all political energies and no distraction. Of course, seen in that light, the events of the winter of 1989–90 were a massive and unwelcome distraction, coming at the wrong time. For EC decision-makers, the key priority was deepening internal integration. For US policy-makers, the key priority was their relationship with Gorbachev's Soviet Union. Requests for NATO membership were equally unwelcome, as they could undermine Gorbachev and later Yeltsin. For both, the demands of central Europe came very clearly in second place and their immediate reaction was to seek to cool the ardour of the new central European governments, by offering alternative responses that did not include early EC or NATO membership

This western reaction brought the central European down to earth with a bump and they were thereafter faced with difficult and unpalatable choices. Western reaction was the political equivalent of a harassed air-traffic controller's holding pattern at an airport. Various forms of holding ante-chamber strategies were brought into play. These were many and varied: Council of Europe observer status and then promotion to full membership; the PHARE Programme, offering aid without membership; upgrading of so-called 'first generation' agreements into Europe Agreements; the creation of the North Atlantic Cooperation Council moving on to the Partnership for Peace by NATO. In parallel, various proposals for regional cooperation between the states of central Europe themselves leading to forms of open-ended pre-accession strategies were set in vain. The aim was clear to offer constant amelioration of the substance of cooperation, but without any firm commitment to early membership either of the EC or NATO. There was always progress and movement so as to keep the central Europeans on side, but it never amounted to exactly what the central European wanted the most. This situation persisted certainly up to the demise of the USSR in December 1991 and reasserted its importance as Yeltsin came under increasing pressure from a pincer movement of old communists and Russian nationalists.

Suggestions of regional cooperation were historically revolutionary. Relations between the states of the region had been more often bad than good. During the communist period, any form of regional cooperation purely within central Europe alone (that is without the USSR) was obviously heresy and taboo. Here, too, attitudes and strategies evolved very quickly or were overtaken by events. The first attempts at regional cooperation in the Pentagonale (later Hexagonale and then the Central European Initiative) involving Italy, Hungary, Yugoslavia and Austria (later Czechoslovakia and Poland came in) were part of the strategy of surmounting the bloc structure that was still extant when the process began in 1988. As history accelerated and that goal was rapidly achieved, the focus shifted to the need for a platform for structured dialogue between central Europeans and west European regional counterparts such as Italy and Austria, and the need for a kind of central European 'Trade Union' seeking to present the collective case of the region to the west. Out of this last need a central European core group, the Visegrad three, later four, came into being. The western agenda was different and quite rightly raised suspicions among the central Europeans. It sought, as we have seen, to create a holding area. In this period, a series of loosely interlinked and overlapping regional cooperation groupings came into existence in the central European corridor running from the Baltic to the Black Sea, in which no less than 200 million people live. The Visegrad states form a pivotal part of this chain.

THE CENTRAL EUROPEAN INITIATIVE (CEI)

Initially, the Central European Initiative (CEI) was called the Pentagonale, because it had five members, and then the Hexagonale when its membership rose to six. In 1991, it was renamed the more permanent Central European Initiative. It was launched in 1988 by the then Italian Foreign Minister, the dynamic Socialist from Venice, Gianni de Michelis, the first Socialist and Northern Italian to hold that office for a very long time. It was an attempt to diversify Italian foreign policy, by carving out a regional role as the communist system began to fall apart. It was aimed at transcending the blocs and developing forms of economic and technical cooperation with central Europe in key areas such as transport and telecommunications to be piloted by Italy and Austria, the CEI's 'western' members. At the time of the first Ministerial meeting on 10 and 11 November 1989, only Poland and Hungary had made any progress towards the transition towards democracy and the geopolitical situation remained very unclear.

At first, therefore, the process was cautious and low-key, taking into account that the CEI contained members from all three security groupings within the CSCE system (NATO, Warsaw Pact and Neutral and Non-aligned). The initial design built on pre-existing cross-border regional cooperation arrangements such as the Alpa-Adria Arbeitsgemeinschaft. This was then extended and given, as it were, a political superstructure.

As indicated, the Pentagonale was founded at a Ministerial meeting held in Budapest on 10–11 November 1989. Its founders, Austria, Italy, Hungary and Yugoslavia, were rapidly joined by Czechoslovakia in March 1990. Poland joined at the Dubrovnik Ministerial meeting on 26–27 July 1991. Three ex-Yugoslav Republics – Slovenia, Croatia and Bosnia-Herzogovina – were admitted at the 1993 Summit. Since the 1992 Klagenfurt meeting in March 1992, four non-member states (Romania, Bulgaria, Ukraine and Belarus) have been given the right to participate in CEI working groups in which they have an interest and to be involved in contact group meetings in the margins of formal CEI Ministerial meetings.

The CEI structure remains deliberately very informal and loose, though quite complex in those areas where cooperation is at its most intense. There is annual rotating presidency and permanent national coordinators who together form the basic infrastructure. There is no permanent secretariat. There are annual Summits at Prime Ministerial level and two Foreign Ministers meetings per year. The national coordinators (senior diplomats) form a preparatory network for the Summit and Ministerial level meetings and oversee the work of the various working groups. Each working group (13 at present) is run by a national coordinator. These groups cover specific areas of cooperation such as Transport and communications (Italy), Environment (Austria), Telecommunications (Austria). The heavy positions are held mainly by Italy and Austria. The CEI is not involved in economic integration as such. It has developed transnational cooperation projects. Over 200 of these have been considered, with coordinated financing from PHARE and

EBRD (which has a group for contact with the CEI) and national resources. Since 1990, there has been a parliamentary dimension, with the Chairmen of the Foreign Affairs Committees of CEI parliaments 'shadowing' the Foreign Ministers and small delegations shadowing the Summits. The CEI 'social partners' also meet periodically. The CEI has of course declined in importance as the Visegrad group took shape and as the immediate transition phase ended, not least because the Czech Republic under Vaclav Klaus has opposed strengthening regional cooperation, seeing it as a diversion from the main priority of joining the EU. The CEI can though play a role in terms of technical cooperation and linking the various forms of regional cooperation.

THE VISEGRAD GROUP

The Visegrad Group can be seen as the inner core of the CEI. Whilst its origins were closely intertwined with the CEI, it has subsequently developed in a rather different direction from the CEI, responding to changing objectives. It originated in the chaotic period and heroic period in 1990. It sought to develop greater strength through unity and cooperation in the delicate and sensitive process of reducing dependence on Moscow through disengagement from the Warsaw Pact and COMECON. The 'second front' as it were related to developing relations with the western organisations such as EC and NATO. It began with an initial Polish proposal back in 1989 and a Czechoslovak Memorandum from March 1990 that was aimed more at gaining admission to the CEI. The real impetus came from the Warsaw Pact Summit held in Moscow in June 1990. Here CEI states were active in pushing for rapid dismantling of both the Warsaw Pact and COMECON. At the same time, the 'Visegrad Three' (Poland, Hungary, Czechoslovakia) began to push for a closer relationship with NATO and the EC. At this stage, they concluded that they could best promote their case by acting together, rather than singly and competitively. As President Walesa put it, 'We are mutually dependent on each other'. This predisposition was not to last, as we shall see.

A decision to cooperate had been taken pragmatically, on political grounds. Only afterwards was it decided to underpin it with a historical and organisational basis, countering the frankly more obvious and recent conflicts between the three partners. There were references to

President Masaryk's ideas of cooperation, to contacts between dissidents, though these had actually been sparse. There were also proposals for forms of practical 'low politics' cooperation. The formal foundation of the Visegrad Group came with the adoption of the Solemn Declaration and the Declaration on Cooperation at the first Summit held on 15 February 1991 at Visegrad on the Danube between Hungary and Czechoslovakia, the site of a medieval royal summit in 1335. A second Summit was then held in Krakow on 6 October 1991. Numerous ministerial and deputy ministerial level meetings have been held, including finance ministers. A Council of Ambassadors has been set up to ensure coordination, and several official level working groups have been established in such areas as transport, energy and communications.

The Visegrad group has been at its most successful at the political level. It cooperated well in the process of dismantling the Warsaw Pact and COMECON. It worked well in the process of negotiating the Europe Agreement, with periodic trilateral side meetings in Brussels in the margins of the official negotiations. During the fortunately abortive Soviet Coup in August 1991, the Group deployed an impressive crisis management capacity, with a high-level expert group meeting on 20 August. A Summit was called but became unnecessary as the Coup collapsed. A system of defence coordination and a deputy ministers' committee in migration was set up. Numerous practical projects are under way.

The Visegrad achieved what was to be almost its last major success in terms of what had become its most important remaining purpose, namely achieving a coordinated approach to the EC. It agreed a joint memorandum that was submitted to the first formal meeting with EC Foreign Ministers in Luxembourg on 5 October 1992 and to EC Heads of State and Government in London on 28 October 1992. It was the beginning of what came to be called 'structure political dialogue'. Economic cooperation has not been highly developed, though there is agreement on the creation of a Central European Free Trade Area.

The break-up of Czechoslovakia and the arrival in power of Vaclav Klaus in the new Czech Republic after 1993, conflicts over the Gabčiko-vo-Nagymaros dam project and the rights of the Hungarian minority in Slovakia between Hungary and the new fourth Visegrad partner, Slovakia, have slowed down the momentum of cooperation. Indeed, Klaus has at times appeared actively opposed to the idea. No doubt, with the accession process now being on track, the main goal of the Group has in any case been achieved.

THE COUNCIL OF EUROPE

Membership of the Council of Europe was the first stage on the road to acceptance by western Europe. It posed fewer problems than either EC or NATO membership. However, it did involve an examination and approval of the democratic credentials of the new applicants first by the Parliamentary Assembly and then by the Committee of Ministers, and as had been shown in the 1960s and 1970s, suspension or expulsion was a real sanction in the event of later backsliding. It therefore represented an important and visible rite of passage for the new ECE democracies. Any European state can become a member of the Council of Europe, provided that it accepts certain basic democratic principles such as the rule of law and guarantees of fundamental rights and freedoms. When communism collapsed, the first and easiest step 'back to Europe' for the new democracies was to join the Council of Europe. Membership gave them a democratic seal of approval. Their applications were vetted by the appropriate committee of the Parliamentary Assembly, which would conduct an investigation and then adopt a draft opinion for the plenary Assembly. This opinion, once adopted, would go to the Committee of Ministers, which almost always follows the recommendation of the Assembly in such matters. The Committee of Ministers acts by consensus. The opinions often laid down requirements in relation to the European Convention on Human Rights, the independence of the judiciary and minority rights. In the meantime, applicants usually enjoyed some form of guest or observer status. Council of Europe membership also had an important socialising effect on parliamentarians and political parties which began to take part in inter-parliamentary contacts and transnational party cooperation in the political groups of the Assembly and in the various party internationals.

Hungary was admitted in November 1990 as the first central European member. Polish membership was delayed until 1991, because at this stage the Polish Parliament was still the so-called Contractual Sejm that was only partially elected. Czechoslovakia was also admitted in 1991, without the issues of the Hungarian minority in Slovakia nor the vexed question of the position of the former Sudeten expellees being raised as an obstacle. The split of Czechoslovakia in 1993 meant that this membership hardly became effective and new membership had to be agreed for the two new states. This was not treated as a formality. Now both the issue of minority rights (Hungarians in Slovakia and Slovaks in the Czech Republic) and the Sudeten issue were investigated. A Liechtenstein veto on the Czech Republic over property rights of the Royal House was abandoned. Hungary was subjected to strong western pressure not to veto Slovakia and hence hold up the Czech application that was being treated in parallel. Hungary did withdraw its opposition.

The Council of Europe has recently introduced a generalised monitoring system to examine how far commitments made at the time of admission have in fact been met.

NATO

All four states are seeking NATO membership, though with differing degrees of urgency and enthusiasm. Slovakia has at times appeared less than committed, preferring to develop relations with Russia, with whom 70 agreements have been signed. All belong to the North Atlantic Cooperation Council (NACC) which brings together NATO members and central and eastern European countries. They are also members of the Partnership for Peace. These arrangements do not of course provide the coveted automatic 'trip-wire' guarantee of the North Atlantic Treaty. This would require unanimous agreement of all fifteen existing NATO members and, most difficult, ratification by a two-thirds majority in the United States Senate. For some central Europeans, like Poland, it may well be that NATO membership is more important than EU membership, especially if Russia becomes even more nationalist.

Hungary, Poland and the Czech Republic only were invited to join NATO in the first wave by the Madrid Summit held in July 1997. Slovakia was not invited to join in the first wave essentially for political reasons. There was broad political support for NATO membership in all three countries that were invited to join, despite some concerns about the cost of modernisation of their armed forces that would be required. In Hungary, in line with the MSZP position, a referendum was held on 11 November 1997, which approved membership by a strong majority. The whole political, economic and intellectual establishment favoured a 'Yes' vote. Only the small left-wing Munkaspart (Workers Party) and the even smaller far right MIEP (Hungarian Truth and Light Party) campaigned openly against membership.

The situation in Slovakia was more complicated. Despite the signature and ratification of the basic treaty with Hungary, Slovakia remained relatively isolated on the international scene and continued to be criticised for its record on minority rights and press freedom. It appeared unlikely that Slovakia would be proposed for the first wave of either EU or NATO membership. Prime Minister Mečiar sought to take domestic political advantage of this sense of isolation that favoured the nationalist current in public opinion that he was best able to represent. He organised a referendum on NATO in June 1997. He did little to campaign for a 'Yes' vote, thought he was publicly committed to that position. His two coalition partners campaigned for a 'No' vote. Only the opposition parties voted wholeheartedly for a 'Yes' vote. In the event, due to linkages with other domestic political issues, the referendum was invalid, due to the very low turnout. It is, however, quite likely that Mečiar privately actually hoped for a 'No' vote.

THE EUROPEAN UNION

The USSR had, from 1957, opposed the process of European integration, regarding it as a European economic arm of NATO. Hence it rejected relations with the EEC and imposed this position on COMECON members in Central Europe. However, as early as 1965 for Poland and 1968 for Hungary, the growing economic importance of the EEC and especially the development of the Common Agricultural Policy (CAP) obliged them to seek some informal trade and later fisheries arrangements with the EEC. So as to save their political face, these arrangement were concluded through the respective representations to the GATT in Geneva. In 1970 Czechoslovakia followed suit, signing an arrangement on steel, and others did likewise. In 1974, the EEC Council of Ministers offered the individual central European states formal trade agreements. COMECON, under Soviet control, insisted on a bloc-to-bloc umbrella agreement as a precondition. This was rejected by the EEC, which did not want to legitimise COMECON or reinforce its control over its members. There the matter rested after several abortive rounds of discussion though the 1970s.

By the mid-1980s the Soviet line was in danger of unravelling, as several central European states tried to chart a more independent course for themselves. As early as 1983, Hungary had sounded out the possibility of a trade agreement, but its demands were excessive. In 1985 Mr Gorbachev reversed the long-standing Soviet veto and sought normalisation of relations with the EC. Between 1985 and 1988, parallel tracks were pursued. On the one hand, a very general umbrella agreement was signed between the EC and COMECON on 25 June 1988. On the other hand, agreements were negotiated between the individual COMECON states and the EC. The first was signed with Hungary on 3 June 1988. A similar though much more limited agreement was reached with Czechoslovakia in late 1988 and an identical agreement was signed with Poland in November 1989 after the collapse of communism.

After the fall of the communist regimes, the EC and the west more generally needed to define a strategy towards the region. It had to offer aid and hope, but as we have seen, stopping short of an early offer of full membership of either EU or NATO membership. Thus, at the meeting at the Arche de la Defense in Paris in July 1989, 24 nations, including all EU members, agreed to establish the G-24 Group and conferred the role of coordination of the overall western effort on the Commission. Immediate food aid, the PHARE technical assistance programme for Poland and Hungary (extended to other countries in December 1989) and market-opening measures taken by the EC were the main elements of the package agreed.

The European Councils of Strasbourg in December 1989 and in Dublin in January 1990 and a subsequent Commission communication opened the way for the so-called 'second generation' of Europe Agreements, which were to be association agreements based on article 238 of the Treaty, covering more areas of cooperation than merely trade and involving forms of structured political dialogue. These negotiations were difficult, due to the extreme reluctance of some member states to make meaningful market-opening concessions, especially in relation to agricultural products. The three agreements were signed together on 16 December 1991. The split-up of Czechoslovakia in January 1993 meant that new separate agreements with the Czech and Slovakia Republics were then required and these were signed in late 1993.

Difficulties with the ratification of the Maastricht Treaty in Britain and in Denmark, the most pro-enlargement member states, and the need to maintain stability in this sensitive region between Russia and the EU led to a rapid evolution in EU thinking on the enlargement issue during 1992. The Copenhagen European Council in June 1993 in effect for the first time made a formal offer of willingness to open negotiations for enlargement with the associated central European states that met certain additional economic and political criteria. The 1994 European Council in Essen went a step further and established a pre-accession strategy involving measures to prepare the ECE states for integration into the internal market and intensify the political dialogue. The associated states now meet the European Council and the other Councils on a regular and structured basis. They are now in the margins of the EU institutions. Poland and Hungary formally applied for membership in early 1994 and the Czech Republic and Slovakia in January 1996. In all cases, there was broad domestic political support for the application.

The Madrid European Council in December 1995 took the decisive step of setting a timetable. It effectively set a date for the opening of negotiations. It called on the Commission to accelerate the drawing up of opinions on each application, as required under the treaty, and to draw up position papers on the financial and policy implications of enlargement.

Immediately after the conclusion of the Intergovernmental Conference at the Amsterdam European Council in June 1997, the Commission tabled its Opinions on the ten applicant countries in central and eastern Europe, including Poland, Hungary, the Czech Republic and Slovakia, together with the Agenda-2000 package that also included financing proposals and policy reforms related to enlargement. Poland, Hungary and the Czech Republic all received favourable opinions in regard to both the political and economic criteria for accession laid down by the Copenhagen European Council. Slovakia, on the other hand, though receiving a fairly favourable opinion on its economic progress, received a critical opinion on its compliance with the political conditions. As a result, only Poland, Hungary and the Czech Republic were, together with Estonia and Slovenia, proposed by the Commission and then by the Luxembourg European Council for inclusion in the first wave of accession negotiations. In a complex, multi-layered inclusive approach, the enlargement process was opened with all ten central European applicants and direct negotiations with the five countries of the first wave in March 1998. The negotiations were to last at least two years and the ratification process about the same length of time, giving an earliest possible entry date of 1 January 2002 for countries of the first wave.

In the meantime, the pre-accession strategy will continue. It is a joint endeavour, with the candidate states and the Union moving towards each other. The process of aligning the legislation and the administrative practices of central Europe with those of the EU, their gradual integration into the work of the Council and the necessary reform of the EU's CAP, structural funds and financial mechanisms, will continue. No doubt the lengthy process of adaptation that has, as with the EFTA countries, been 'front-loaded' by the pre-accession strategy and PHARE will continue after accession by way of long transition periods and various forms of differentiation and temporary 'opt-outs' for the central Europeans. In particular, this approach will be needed to reconcile the political imperative of ensuring the inclusion of Poland in the first group of new members – an absolute German requirement – and its greater economic weakness, compared to the Czech Republic.

PROBLEMS IN BILATERAL RELATIONS

Czech Republic/Slovakia

The break-up of the Czechoslovak Federation in 1993 has often been described as a 'Velvet Divorce' and it certainly was when compared with events in the CIS or former Yugoslavia. Certainly, the break-up was peaceful, consensual and relatively good-humoured. But of course there were some loose ends to tie up. The two countries operate a customs union. It was not possible to maintain a monetary union, and Slovak monetary policy, leading to the depreciation of the Slovak Crown against the Czech Crown, has led to a Czech trade deficit with Slovakia and some occasional recriminations. Border issues were very minor and have been resolved. There have also been some limited problems relating to Slovak citizens, mostly gypsies, in the Czech Republic. Relations have become reasonable. Both countries were able to enter the Council of Europe at the same time and signed their new Europe Agreements simultaneously. Clearly in future the Czech Republic would not wish its progress towards full EU and NATO membership to be impeded by any sort of *junktim* with Slovakia. Indeed, avoiding that was an important motive on the Czech side in the break-up of the old Federation.

Hungary/Slovakia

As we have seen, Slovakia was part of the Hungarian Kingdom until 1918 and during that period was subjected to a much resented repressive policy of Magyarisation. The reverse of the medal came during the First Republic, when the Hungarian minority of some 700,000 (4 per cent of the total population) remained marooned inside the Czechoslovak state. It felt itself victimised and became with the Sudeten Germans a revisionist minority in the later 1930s. The area inhabited by the Hungarian minority was awarded to Hungary by the Axis powers after the complete dismemberment of Czechoslovakia in 1939, but reverted to Czechoslovakia in 1945. During the communist period nationalist conflicts between communist states over minority issues were taboo.

It was precisely the revival of Hungarian nationalist concerns for Hungarians living in the neighbouring states in the late 1980s that was a sure sign of the implosion of the communist system. Indeed, the regime was powerless to prevent such expressions of nationalist feeling, and, as elsewhere, opportunistically sought to swim with the tide and tried to derive some legitimacy from its belated support for this popular cause.

Hence, demonstrations in favour of the Hungarian minorities increasingly were not only allowed, but enjoyed the tacit support of the authorities in Budapest.

An interlinked issue which led to severe conflict between Hungary and Czechoslovakia in the late 1980s and early 1990s was the Gabčikovo/ Nagymaros hydro-electric dam project on the stretch of the Danube between Bratislava and Budapest. This massive scheme was to consist of two major dams, one at Gabčikovo and another at Nagymaros, with related weirs and canals. It was intended to regulate floods, improve navigation and above all generate cheap hydro-electric electricity. It had long been planned. The basic treaty was signed in 1977 and construction proceeded, at times in fits and starts, with alternate acceleration and delay in line with shifting political desiderata, mostly in Hungary. Austrian financing was brought in as the recession bit. Increasingly, from the mid-1980s, vocal opposition and the strategic calculation of political reformers in the ruling party came to dominate the debate in Hungary. In Slovakia, on the other hand, the project remained both politically and economically popular.

Thus, the project became a symbol in both countries, but the opposite kind of symbol. In Hungary, the dam came to be seen as an unpopular symbol of the communist regime – of its methods, style and priorities. The battle against the dam, organised by a loose coalition of environmentalists and dissidents in the Danube Circle, used the issue as a broader battering ram against the regime. The reformist communist government was obliged to react. It temporised by setting up a Commission of experts that reported very critically on the project. The new government after 1990 sought to renegotiate or even preferably to cancel the project by agreement with Czechoslovakia, hoping that the Civic Forum leaders by now in power in Prague would be equally opposed to the scheme, which indeed they were in principle. However, their hands were tied.

For Slovakia, the project was a symbol of resurgent national pride and modernisation. It was 'their' dam. The Czechs could not afford to antagonise Slovakia further by adding a new area of dispute, as they struggled, in vain as it proved, to preserve the unity of the state. Increasingly, the Czechs opted out of the issue and left the Slovaks to make the running both in terms of negotiations with Budapest and in terms of preparing and implementing the so-called Variant C, which involved a unilateral diversion of the Danube north through Slovak territory to the Gabčikovo dam via an artificial channel and then back into the old bed further down stream, leaving only a fraction of the river's water in the old channel that constitutes the border between the two states. Variant C became a threat in the poker game played between Prague, Bratislava and Budapest. When the Hungarian side dangerously miscalculated by calling the Slovaks' bluff and unilaterally denounced the 1977 treaty in May 1992, Slovakia moved to implement Variant C in October of that year. The Czechs made no effort to prevent this, as by then the split was almost operative. Thereafter, under international and EC mediation , the matter was sent to the International Court of Justice in the Hague for resolution.

The dam's environmental impact has been felt most keenly in northern Hungary and in the Danube valley where the 600,000-strong Hungarian minority in Slovakia live. Hungary has postured as the guardian of the interests of this and other Hungarian minorities in the 'near abroad' such as Romania and the Voivodina. Nationalist populists in Hungary have made this a key demand. Governments – both the MDF-led coalition and the present MSZP/SDS coalition – have adopted a far more moderate tone. They have reassured neighbours that they are not looking for border changes, but only seek to defend the individual and collective rights of the minority. It is precisely the issue of collective rights of the minority, especially in local administration, that has proved controversial and was long unacceptable to Slovakia. In 1995, under western pressure, a Basic Treaty was signed between the new and less nationalist Horn government and Slovakia, which represented a compromise on these issues. The Slovak language laws still remain a cause of friction, but, in general, relations have improved.

Poland and her Neighbours

Poland had poor relations with almost all her neighbours in the inter-war period. In addition to the obvious border conflicts with Germany over Silesia and the Polish corridor and Gdansk, and with the USSR over the areas to the east of the Curzon line, she had more localised conflicts with Czechoslovakia over Teschen and with Lithuania over Vilnius (Vilna in Polish) which was illegally annexed by Poland in 1920. Like all other nationalities' conflicts, this was put on hold during the communist period, though the Polish communists often used anti-German rhetoric as a means of legitimising both the regime and its alliance with the USSR, especially given that West Germany refused to recognise the Oder–Neisse frontier as the eastern border of all Germany.

Time, exchanges of population and emigration and the need to avoid western criticism after 1990 meant that here, as elsewhere except in

Yugoslavia, the conflicts did not re-emerge after 1989 with anything like the old virulence and became localised and politically much more manageable than in the inter-war period. Though there remains a significant Polish minority around Vilnius, Poland gave assurances to the new Lithuanian state after 1991 that Poland entertained no claims to the area.

The only significant minority remaining in Poland today is the German minority in Silesia. Lower Silesia had become almost completely German in character. Upper Silesia was much more mixed. This area was the source of severe conflict in the inter-war period. Following a plebiscite and various localised uprisings aimed at securing or preventing Polish control, the great powers partitioned the area, awarding only 40 per cent of the population to Poland, but leaving large towns that had voted to join Germany, such as Katowice, to Poland. In the communist period, Poland denied the existence of the minority at all, expelled many of its members and adopted a policy of forced assimilation. Later after the 1970 Treaty, some 550,000 were allowed to leave voluntarily and legally in return for financial assistance to Poland from Germany.

The fall of communism in Poland and the reunification of Germany led to a radically new situation. The Solidarnosc government of Tadeusz Mazowiecki was supportive of the efforts of the minority to find a legitimate and accepted place in the new democratic Poland. In the course of the Two Plus Four talks that led to the treaty finalising German reunification, Germany committed itself to conclude a treaty with Poland on the vexed question of the Oder–Neisse frontier. In that treaty, finally signed on 14 November 1990, Germany at last recognised the Oder–Neisse line as the border of the new united German state. Poland for its part agreed, in a second treaty signed on 17 June 1991, to grant official recognition to the German minority in Poland. Figures for the size of this remaining minority vary greatly and are a matter of some contention. German minority leaders and organisations in the west claim up to 800,000. The German government claims 650,000. German academic experts suggest about 500,000 and Polish sources the lowest figure of about 400,000. German friendship circles with a total membership of about 300,000 have been formed in 22 Voivodships (Counties). In Silesia, the Verein der Socio-Kulturelle Gemeinshaften in Polen (VdSKGP) has been formed as an umbrella organisation to represent the minority politically. It is a broad church, with one traditional, conservative catholic wing and a more liberal wing that has cooperated closely with Solidarnosc and its liberal splinter parties such as the UW. The VdSKGP has won representation in the Sejm, where it currently holds four seats and in numerous local authorities in rural Silesia, including 26 where they form the local administration.

German Polish relations are now as good as they have ever been and Germany is now the main champion of Polish EU membership.

Czechoslovakia/Czech Republic and Germany

At present relations between Germany and the Czech Republic are actually worse than those with Poland. The several million expellees from the Sudetenland and their descendants represent a formidable pressure group in Germany, especially in the Bavarian CSU. At times, their most radical representatives have raised demands going beyond compensation for the expellees and calling for border rectifications including parts of the former Sudetenland going obviously beyond Germany's 1937 borders. As early as 1967, the CDU/CSU + SPD Grand Coalition indicated its readiness to negotiate a solution with Czechoslovakia for the vexed question of the validity and legal consequences of the Munich Agreement of 1938, under which the Sudetenland areas were ceded to Germany under extreme pressure not only from Germany but also from the allies of Czechoslovakia, Britain and France. The Czech view was that the Munich Agreement should be considered null and void *ab initio*, as it were. The German view was much more nuanced. It took until 1973 for agreement to be reached on a treaty, as part of the mosaic of Ostpolitik treaties of the SPD/FDP coalition that took office in 1969 and initiated the process of Ostpolitik. Under this treaty, Germany accepted that the Munich Agreement was indeed void, but shrouded this new position with obscure and threatening legal restrictions that seemed a negation of the principle of nullity. As with Poland, there were of course domestic political difficulties in the way of any German government simply accepting the nullity of the Munich agreement, as to do so would deprive it of any leverage over Czechoslovakia in relation to the claims of the Sudeten Germans.

After the fall of communism, President Havel apologised for the treatment of the Sudeten Germans in 1945, which he placed in the broader context of the mutual brutalities which had occurred between 1938 and 1946. This view was not easily accepted by everyone in Czechoslovakia or later in the Czech Republic, and several parties, including the Communist Party, campaigned against any concessions to Germany on the issue. Czech courts up to and including the Constitutional Court have validated the general expulsion decrees, the so-called 'Benes Decrees', though awarding compensation in some individual cases. The negotiations for a new treaty between Germany and Czechoslovakia in 1991 and then with the Czech Republic after 1993 turned on this issue. There was dispute over when the Munich agreement was void: *ex tunc* (that is, in 1938) or *ex nunc*, in the legal jargon. Though Germany is the largest investor in the Czech Republic and a supporter of her EU membership, relations between Germany and the Czech Republic remain difficult.

FOREIGN POLICY MAKING

As elsewhere, foreign policy has been very much an executive prerogative throughout the region. In Poland, Hungary and Czechoslovakia (later the Czech Republic), the President has played an important role in foreign policy making and in the foreign representation of their respective countries. This has been due more to their moral and international stature than to their constitutional powers, which are limited, except in Poland. Havel, the playwright and dissident, Göncz, the writer, and Walesa, the Nobel prize winner and historic leader of Solidarnosc with close relations with the Polish Pope John-Paul II, were 'assets' to their countries in the battle for western recognition and support. The Polish President has a larger constitutionally mandated role in foreign policy than his counterparts. The Polish Foreign Minister is one of the so-called 'presidential' ministers. There are annual meetings of the central European Presidents, including the Austrian and Slovenian Presidents, which is a useful forum for exchanges of views.

Heads of government are also key players in foreign policy where they are strong personalities and or have an experience in that field. In Hungary, the current Prime Minister Horn was Foreign Minister at the time of the fall of the iron curtain and was indeed himself instrumental in opening the borders to the west and allowing GDR citizens to pass through Hungary and on into Austria. Between 1990 and 1994, he chaired the Foreign Affairs Committee in Parliament. He takes a strong lead in foreign policy. In Slovakia, at least under Mečiar, foreign policy making is highly centralised, with the Prime Minister playing a key role. The Foreign Ministry is small, new and relatively inexperienced. Czech Prime Minister Vaclav Klaus, too, plays an important role in foreign policy making. In the present MSZP/SDS coalition in Hungary, the junior coalition partner, the SDS, has a State Secretary in the MSZP-controlled Foreign Ministry, which is the eyes and ears of the party in this key field.

The Parliaments of the region have all established active and lively Foreign Affairs Committees and separate committees on European

Affairs. These committees are charged with oversight and control functions. In Hungary and Poland, though not in the Czech Republic or Slovakia, there is a certain tradition of according the Chair of at least one of these committees to an opposition MP. In Hungary, in the 1990–4 legislature, the Chair of the Foreign Affairs Committee was held by Mr Horn (MSZP) and later by Mr Kovacs (MSZP), now Foreign Minister, and the European Affairs Committee was chaired by the FIDESZ Chairman, Viktor Orban. In the 1994–8 legislature, the Chair of the Foreign Affairs Committee is held by the SDS, the junior coalition party, and the European Affairs Committee still chaired by Viktor Orban. In Poland, Mr Geremek, leader of the UW, was Chair of the Foreign Affairs Committee, and the European Integration Committee is chaired by Mr Borkowski of the PSL. In the Czech Republic, the Committee is chaired by Mr Payne (ODS).

The role of the Foreign Affairs Committees and the European Committees is to receive information and promote debate on foreign and European policy issues and thereby to build and maintain the broad consensus that exists between the mainstream parties on these issues. These committees also serve to exert parliamentary control over the executive in relation to foreign affairs. There is a very broad consensus on almost all foreign policy issues across the main parties in each country and across the countries in the region, though divergences are greater in Slovakia on the priority of rapid integration in western security organisations and on relations with Hungary. Elsewhere, differences are more matters of nuance and presentation. The Polish Foreign Affairs Committee sees itself as a forum for continuity and consensus building between the government and the parties in the Sejm, especially between the ex-Solidarnosc parties and the present SDL/PSL coalition. The Polish and Hungarian committees hold informal but important hearings with ambassadors-designate.

The European Committees have a triple role: controlling government policy; monitoring national European conformity programmes designed to ensure that national legislation is aligned with the EU legislation; and providing the Polish, Hungarian, Czech and Slovak side of the Joint Committee established with the European Parliament under the European Agreements.

Sources and Bibliography

SOURCES

The core sources used by the author for each chapter are those indicated below, as well as interviews with political leaders and experts in each of the four countries in the course of at least three research visits to each country. He also used secondary sources in German and French and primary sources such as texts of constitutions, laws and parliamentary standing orders in translation.

BIBLIOGRAPHY

Chapter 1   A Modern History of the Region

T. Garton Ash, *We, the People: The Revolutions of 1989, Witnessed in Warsaw, Budapest, Berlin and Prague*, Granta, London, 1991.

J. Held (ed.), *The Colombia History of Eastern Europe in the Twentieth Century*, Colombia University Press, New York, 1992.

K. Henderson, 'Czechoslovakia: The Failure of Consensus Politics and the Break-up of the Federation', *Regional and Federal Studies*, vol. 5, no. 2, 1995.

R.A. Kann, *A History of the Habsburg Empire 1525–1918*, University of California Press, Berkeley, 1974.

J. Rupnik, *The Other Europe*, Weidenfeld, London, 1988.

G. Schöpflin, *Politics in Eastern Europe*, Blackwell, Oxford, 1993.

Chapter 2   The Collapse of Communism

T. Garton Ash, *In Europe's Name*, Jonathan Cape, London, 1993.

T. Garton Ash, *We, the People: The Revolutions of 1989, Witnessed in Warsaw, Budapest, Berlin and Prague*, Granta, London, 1991.

N. Davies, *God's Playground*, Oxford University Press, Oxford, 1982.

J.K.A. Hoensch, *A History of Modern Hungary 1867–1986*, Longman, Harlow, 1998.

J. Lettrich, *A History of Modern Slovakia*, Slovak Research and Studies Centre, Toronto, 1987.

V. Masny, *The Helsinki Process and the Reintegration of Europe 1986–1991*, Pinter, London, 1991.

G. Schöpflin, *Politics in Eastern Europe*, Blackwell, Oxford, 1993.

Chapter 3   Economy and Society

I.P. Czekely and D.M.G Newbery (eds), *Hungary's Economy in Transition*, Cambridge University Press, Cambridge, 1992.

Economist Intelligence Unit (EIU) Country Reports for Poland, Hungary, Czech Republic, Slovakia.

J. Fitzmaurice, *Damming the Danube*, Westview, Boulder, Col., 1996 (chapter 4 on minorities).

M. Myant, *The Czechoslovak Economy*, Cambridge University Press, Cambridge, 1989.

A. Reszler, 'Une longue souffrance improductive, essai sur l'identité des minorités hongroises', in A. Lebich and A. Reszler (eds), *L'Europe centrale et ses minorités: vers un solution européenne*, Presses Universitaires de France, Paris, 1993.

J. Sachs, *Poland's Jump to the Market Economy*, MIT Press, 1993.

Chapter 4   Theories of Transition

J. Batt, *East Central Europe from Reform to Transformation*, RIIA/Pinter, London, 1992.

G. Pridham and P. Lewis (eds), *Stabilising Fragile Democracies: Comparing New Party Systems in Southern and Eastern Europe*, Routledge, London, 1996.

G. Pridham and T. Vanhanen, *Democratisation in Eastern Europe*, Routledge, London, 1994.

Chapter 5   Constitution Building

A. Bazacki, 'Political Change and Constitutional Change in Hungary', in A. Bazacki *et al.*, *Post-Communist Transition: Emerging Pluralism in Hungary*, Pinter, London, 1992.

J. Elster, 'Constitution Making in Central and Eastern Europe: Rebuilding the Boat in the Open Sea', in J.J. Hesse (ed.), *Administrative Transformation in Central and Eastern Europe*, Blackwell, Oxford, 1993.

W. Osiatynski, 'Poland's Constitutional Ordeal', *East European Constitutional Review*, vol. 3, no. 2, 1995.

The Rebirth of Democracy: 12 Constitutions of Central and Eastern Europe, Council of Europe Press, Strasbourg, 1995.

Chapter 6   The Presidency

L. Garlicki, 'The Development of the Presidency in Poland', in K.W. Thompson (ed.), *Constitutions, Presidents and Politics*, University Press of America, Lanham, 1992.

V. Havel, 'The Power of the Powerless', in Keane (ed.), *The Power of the Powerless: Citizens Against the State in Central-Eastern Europe*, Hutchinson, London, 1985.

V. Havel, 'Living in Truth', in J. Vladislav (ed.), *Living in Truth*, Faber & Faber, London and Boston, 1986.

'Interim Constitution Adopted in Poland', *East European Constitutional Review*, vol. 1, no. 2, 1992.

J. Kurski, *Lech Walesa: Democrat or Dictator?*, Westview, Boulder, Col., 1993.

S. Zifcak, 'The Battle over Presidential Powers in Slovakia', *East European Constitutional Review*, Summer 1995.

Chapter 7   The Governments

J.J. Hesse (ed.), *Administrative Transformation in Central and Eastern Europe*, Blackwell, Oxford, 1993.

J.J. Hesse, 'From Transformation to Modernisation: Administrative Change in Central and Eastern Europe', in J.J. Hesse and F.A.J. Toonen (eds), *European Yearbook of Comparative Government and Public Administration*, vol. 1, 1994.

Chapter 8   Local Government

Structure and Operation of Local and Regional Government in Poland (1993).

... *Hungary* (1994)

... *Czech Republic* (1994)

... *Slovakia* (1994)

(Council of Europe Studies series, Council of Europe, Strasbourg)

Chapter 9   The Judiciary

J. Kroupa, 'The Constitutional Court of the Czech and Slovak Federal Republic', *Bulletin of Czechoslovak Law*, vol. 30, no. 1/2, 1991.

H. Schwarz, 'The New East European Constitutional Courts', *Michigan Journal of International Law*, no. 13, pp. 741–85.

Chapter 10   Parliaments

D. Butler and B. Särlvik (eds), 'Elections in Eastern Europe', *Electoral Studies*, special number, vol. 9, no. 4, 1990 (the chapters on each country give details of the electoral systems).

M. Calda, 'Parliamentary Rules and Legislative Dominance: Slovakia', *East European Constitutional Review*, Spring 1995.

M. Calda and M. Gillis, 'The Czech Republic: Is Legislative Illegitimacy the Price of Political Effectiveness?', *East European Constitutional Review*, Spring 1995.

D.M. Olson and P. Norton, 'The New Parliaments in Central and Eastern Europe', *Journal of Legislative Studies*, special issue, vol. 2, no. 1, Spring 1996.

Chapter 11   The Party Systems

A. Agh, 'The Case of the Hungarian Socialist Party', *Party Politics*, vol. 1, no. 4, 1995.

D. Butler and B.Särlvik, 'Elections in Eastern Europe', *Electoral Studies*, special number, vol. 9, no. 4, 1990.

K. Codell, 'Upper Silesia and the Politics of Accommodation', *Regional and Federal Studies*, vol. 5, no. 3, 1995.

J. Fitzmaurice, 'The Hungarian Elections 1994', *Electoral Studies*, vol. 14, no. 1, 1995.

J. Fitzmaurice, 'The Slovak Election of September 1994', *Electoral Studies*, vol. 14, no. 2, 1995.

J. Fitzmaurice, 'The Czech Elections 1996', *Electoral Studies*, no. 4, 1996.

J. Kopecky, 'Developing Party Organisations in Eastern and Central European Parties', *Party Politics*, vol. 1, no. 4, 1995.

W.L. Webb, 'The Polish Election of 1991', *Electoral Studies*, vol. 11, no. 2, 1992.

W. Wesolowski, 'The Formation of Parties in Post-Communist Poland', in G. Pridham and P. Lewis (eds), *Stabilising Fragile Democracies: Comparing New Party Systems in Southern and Eastern Europe*, Routledge, London, 1996.

G. Wightman, 'The Czechoslovak Parliamentary Elections of 1992', *Electoral Studies*, vol. 12, no. 1, 1993.

K. Williams, 'The Magyar Minority in Slovakia', *Regional and Federal Studies*, vol. 6, no. 1, 1996.

Chapter 12   Other Political Actors

M. Walker and M. Myant, *Parties, Trade Unions and Society in East-Central Europe*, Frank Cass, London, 1994.

Chapter 13   Foreign Policy

J. Fitzmaurice, 'Regional Cooperation in Central Europe', *West European Politics*, vol. 16, no. 3, 1993.

J. Fitzmaurice, *Damming the Danube*, Westview, Boulder, Col., 1996.

P. Lotowski, 'The Security Road to Europe: The Visegrad Four', Royal United Services Institute for Defence Studies, Whitehall Papers, London, 1994.

P. Ludlow, *The European Union ,and the Future of Europe*, CEPS, Brussels, 1992.

H. Neuhold (ed.), *The Pentagonale/Hexagonale Experiment: New Forms of Co-operation in a Changing World*, Braunmüller, Vienna, 1991.

J. Saryuz-Wolski, 'Integrating the Old Continent: Avoiding the Costs of Half Europe', in S. Blumler and A.Scott (eds), *Economic and Political Integration in Europe*, Blackwell, Oxford, 1994.

J. Zielonka, 'Security in Central Europe', *IISS/Adelphi Papers*, no. 722.

Index

Bold entries are the main entry for the subject.